TARGETING THE TOP

TARGETING THE TOP

EVERYTHING A WOMAN NEEDS TO KNOW TO DEVELOP A SUCCESSFUL CAREER IN BUSINESS, YEAR AFTER YEAR

Nancy Lee

Doubleday & Company, Inc., Garden City, New York
1980

ISBN: 0-385-13244-1
Library of Congress Catalog Card Number 78-22736
Copyright © 1980 by Nancy Lee

For my mother and father, who gave me the basics
For Katherine Vincent, who taught me how
For Sir Arthur Bryan, who gave me my chance
For John, Gregory, and Paul, who make it all worthwhile

ACKNOWLEDGMENTS

My thanks:

to all the women and men who gave their time and shared their experiences so that this book could be researched and written.

to my editor, Kate Medina, and my agent, Rhoda Weyr, for their confidence in me and their continuing encouragement.

to Francine Pennino for asking such perceptive questions and to Channa Eberhart for being an integral part of the process of producing this book.

CONTENTS

INTRODUCTION *xvii*

PART I: THE PROFESSIONAL YOU

1   WHO ARE YOU PROFESSIONALLY? *3*

*What Can You Do and What Are You Willing
   to Learn?* *4*
*What Skills are Necessary for Business
   Success?* *5*
Talking About Yourself *8*
*Know Your Weaknesses—But Keep Them to
   Yourself!* *10*
Women's Intuition *10*
Your Ethical Values *10*
What Is "Management"? *11*
How to Get That Vital Thing—Experience *12*
Sometimes You'll Be Wrong *12*
Expand Your Knowledge Through Education *13*
What Are Your Priorities? *14*

**2   A CLOSER LOOK AT VALUES AND
       PRIORITIES** *17*

Duty and Nurturing *18*
Friends and Companions *20*
Independence and Expertness *25*

3   DO YOU TRULY WANT TO BE BOSS?   **29**

Are You a Manager?   *30*
Power Games   *35*
How Do You Feel About Money and
Security?   *37*
The Energy Factor   *38*
What Do You Want Out of Life?   *39*

4   FACING THE OUTSIDE FORCES   **41**

Focusing on Family and Friends   *42*
Money, Money, Money   *47*
Moving Around   *49*

5   THE DUAL-CAREER COUPLE   **51**

Avoiding the Penalties   *53*
The New Commuters' Marriage   *54*
All Work and No Play   *56*
Family Pressures   *59*
Role Conflicts at Home   *60*
Competition   *66*
Who's Involved in a Two-Professional
Marriage?   *69*
Overloading   *69*
Rewards and Satisfactions   *70*

6   THE PROFESSIONAL MOTHER   **73**

Should You Become Parents?   *74*
Planned Parenthood   *76*
Parenting: Learning to Live with the
Unexpected   *78*
The Interrupted Career   *82*
What Do Children Need?   *85*
Help!   *89*

7   **WHAT DO YOU WANT TO MAKE OF
    YOURSELF?** 95

> *Setting Your Sights* 95
> *Write It Down* 98
> *Your Goals and Their Timing* 99
> *Change "Until" to "When"* 100
> *What Next?* 100

PART II: MANAGING YOUR CAREER

8   **FINDING YOUR ORGANIZATIONAL FIT** 105

> *Where to Work—When* 106
> *The Formal and the Informal System* 107
> *Corporate Enterprise and Corporate Values* 109
> *Changing Companies* 111
> *Analyzing Organizations* 112
> *Examine Your Career Stage* 118
> *Your Career and Your Organizational Fit* 121

9   **MENTORS, MODELS, AND SPONSORS** 125

> *Mentors* 126
> *Sponsors* 131
> *Role Models* 133
> *The Ideal and the Pitfalls* 134

10 **YOUR EDUCATIONAL PASSPORT** 137

> *Go Get That Degree* 138
> *Math Anxiety* 139
> *Getting Your Advanced Degree* 141
> *Other Sources of Education* 144
> *Read, Read, Read* 145

11 **YOUR PROFESSIONAL STYLE: FIND IT,
    FLEX IT** 149

> *Identifying Your Professional Style* 150

Are You a Doer?   150
Are You an Innovator?   151
What If You're a Relator?   152
What If You're an Analyzer?   153
Flexing Your Style   155
Multiple Styles   157

PART III: EXECUTIVE RESOURCES

**12   MANAGING TIME: THE FINITE
       RESOURCE**   161

Choosing Your Priorities   162
Effectiveness and Efficiency   163
The Pareto Principle   164
*Evaluating: Looking Back for Better Planning
   Ahead*   174

13   DECISION MAKING IN ACTION   177

Accepting the Risk   178
Two-Stage Decision Making   178
Decision Making in Action   181
Thinking Positively About Risk   184
Planning Dynamic Risk   187

14   HANDLING CONFLICT AND CHANGE   189

A Change in Attitude   189
Conflict: Personalities and Resources   194
A Winning Solution   198
Ambivalence About Conflict and Change   199
Creative Conflict   202

15   LEADING AND INFLUENCING OTHERS   203

*Conceptual Skills: Learning to Let Others
   Do It*   205
*Technical Skills: Overcoming the "Clean-Up"
   Syndrome*   207

Human Skills   208
Improving Your Skills   210
Motivations: The Five-Level Pyramid   210

16   THE PLACE OF POWER   215

Women and Power   215
The Power of Position   217
*Personal Power: Getting to Know and Like
    People*   221
*Expert Power: From Courses, Reading,
    People, Questions, Experience*   223
Risking Power to Get More   224
Maintaining It   224
Using It   227

17   EXCHANGING INFORMATION   229

Sending Messages   229
"Women's Intuition"   234

18   MAKING MEETINGS WORK   237

What's Going On   238
What's Your Role?   239
What Meetings Can Do   245

19   LESS STRESS, MORE ENERGY   247

What Is Stress?   247
Managing Stress   248
Energy   253
Using Stress and Energy   257

PART IV: MAKING YOUR MOVES

20   MOVING OUT AND AROUND   261

Routes to the Top   261
*Viewing Your Career from Two
    Perspectives*   262

Give Yourself Time to Move   263
Move Around Productively   264
Coping With Prejudice   265
Relocation   266

21   FINDING THE OPPORTUNITIES   271

Keeping Your Options Open   271
Look While You Are Working   272
How to Find the Opportunities   275
Advertisements, and How to Respond   278
Direct-Mail Campaigns   280
Placement Firms   282
Executive-Search Consultants   283

22   PRESENTING YOURSELF IN PRINT AND
     IN PERSON   287

Professionalizing Your Résumé   287
At the Interview   292

23   ASSESSING THE SITUATION   303

Noting the Negatives   304
Reviewing a Possible Position   306
Assessing the Fit   309
The Bottom Line   314

24   MONEY: OR THINGS YOUR FATHER
     NEVER TAUGHT YOU   315

Compensation Programs   317
Setting Your Sights   325
Moving for Money   326
Bonuses   329
Commissions   330
Risk Taking   331

25   PERKING UP YOUR NET INCOME   333

Benefits   333
Perquisites   335

26 GET SET TO JET 351

Tips on Keeping a Happy Family 353
Keeping Your Social Life Going 354
Pamper Yourself and Those Who Help You 355
For Your Health 358
On the Road, Solo 360
Explore the World 361
Travel Safety 361
When in Tokyo 363
Travel Light 365
A Travel Wardrobe 367
What Else to Take 369
A Summary for the Professional Traveler 372

27 THE JOURNEY AND THE ARRIVAL 373

Your Goals 373
Rewards and Responsibilities 374
The Central Task 376
New Questions Needing New Answers 381
Some Global Issues 383

INTRODUCTION

The progress of women up the corporate ladder has been extremely slow, despite the fact that more women are working outside their homes today than ever before. To secure their share of power positions in management, more women must acquire a variety of vital skills, resources, experience, and education. Do you know what it is you need to know and do if you truly want to go for a top position in business?

This book will tell you how to target the top. Since there are not yet enough female advisors, mentors, or role models to assist able and ambitious women on a one-to-one basis, I interviewed more than four hundred successful women, and the men who have helped them, and I have also gathered information from the hundreds of women executives who have attended seminars I have given on management and career planning.

I discussed with these middle and senior managers the problems they encountered on their way up the corporate ladder and asked them how they resolved their difficulties. The suggestions that they shared will help you benefit from their experience, so you won't have to "reinvent the wheel" as you move along your own career pathway. By anticipating common problems, you can be halfway to solving them for yourself—and you can use the energy you save to increase the momentum of your career.

The information in this book will be useful to you whether you are just beginning your career, are well on your way, or are returning to the world of business.

Part I will provide you with the means to take a look at your professional self and be guided through a self-assessment session that will help you determine what it is you really want and what you are willing to give up in order to get it. Part II will help you plan and manage your career. Part III will tell you what resources you must have and how to go about getting them. The final chapters suggest when and how to make strategic moves in your career.

You'll be given background that has been generally available to men, but difficult for women to acquire and evaluate—such as whether to be a company person or a mobile executive; what perquisites to bargain for; whether to take a staff or a line position; and how best to work with an executive search consultant.

Specific suggestions are included on how to balance the personal and professional demands on your time and energy; how to make executive decisions more easily; why you must be comfortable with power and able to take risks. The emphasis will be on how to become a generalist instead of a specialist because you must be a generalist if you want to make it to the top.

My background and experience as a professional woman provide me with a realistic perspective about the corporate world. I began my career in the late fifties and worked for such major corporations as General Electric and Macy's. I became a marketing executive with the international firm of Josiah Wedgwood in the early sixties and eventually founded my own marketing and management consulting firm, Lee Associates.

Since the mid-seventies, I have traveled throughout the United States giving seminars and workshops to business managers. I have taught business policy, planning, and strategy at Simmons College in Boston, and management development at the University of Washington in Seattle for the Pacific Coast Banking School. I have studied carefully the corporate system throughout the United States and the managers who run that system, and I have learned what it is that women need to know in order to succeed.

Throughout the past two decades I have found that women, contrary to the popular myth, are both willing and eager to share their experiences and to help one another. Then, as now, they formed friendship networks to assist each other on the way up. Every woman I approached for this book gave willingly of her time and her knowledge. Men, too, have been generous with advice and support, for the best men know that everyone benefits from filling positions with the *most able people*.

The vigorous development of a career is difficult and can be disillusioning. It is even more so for those who don't have a readily available group of peers and superiors on the job to help, encourage, and share information. And you'll find that the farther up you move, the more likely you are to be the only woman. This book is an attempt—by all those who have contributed—to give you some of the support you need as you move up in what has been largely a "man's world."

Until the sixties, men had virtually the whole power structure to themselves. No real challenge from women existed. Equal opportunity laws have changed this and created the potential for doubling competition for every position now held by a man. The changes that may eventually result in the work force have not even begun to be realized.

Women must be aware that men stand to lose both their traditional right to positions of authority and their helpmates at the same time. The potential loss of nurturers, supporters, and helpers, as well as the threat of being replaced at work, can cause many men in command to throw up conscious and unconscious barriers against the advancement of women. Mere equality of achievement for women may seem to many men like defeat.

Add to this reality the slowdown of growth in the economy, and you can expect the competition to increase, for scarce rewards and scarce positions at the top. The result of this intense competition is that women—and men—will have to be smarter, work harder, and more thoroughly understand the system and the dynamics of career advancement in order to keep moving up. You will be much more knowledgeable about both when you finish this book. And I hope you'll refer to it again and again, for it is designed so that you can reread and review relevant sections as changes occur in your personal and professional life. Career planning and strategizing is a dynamic, never-ending process. This book is designed to help you carry on this process on a continuing and informed basis, as you target the top.

TARGETING THE TOP

PART I

THE PROFESSIONAL YOU

1

WHO ARE YOU PROFESSIONALLY?

Dedication to a career is a demanding way of life for both men and women. If you are caught up in the career struggle, you may feel there is little time available for analyzing your personal and professional priorities and their relationship to each other. Yet a clear understanding of who you are professionally, what you want to accomplish, what sacrifices you are willing to make, and what is required to reach the top is fundamental to success.

In this first chapter, I'd like to try and help you analyze your abilities and your values to see how they affect your professional life and to see whether they appear to fit the requirements for upward mobility.

First we'll take a look at your abilities; both those you are using in your life and work, and those that have perhaps been lying fallow. Are you aware of your talents? And are you able to describe them clearly to others? Do you know what skills you lack? Are you willing to go after that training in an aggressive way?

One woman executive with a long and successful career behind her had specialized in certain areas of advertising and promotion and had handled them very well. A management consultant hired by her firm decided to computerize all the budgeting and financial accounting for the company—not an unusual occurrence these days. Since this woman had been educated before computers came into use and she had no background in this area, she felt very threatened. Not only would it be more difficult for her to do her job, but also it now seemed almost impossible for her to move up. If she were to move into any other department or even effectively administer people at the level where she now was, she would have to have a command of management information systems and of computers.

With the help of a friend, she stepped back and looked at the situation objectively. "In high school I had demonstrated a great deal of mathematical ability, even though it was not totally acceptable in those days for women to be so inclined," she recalled. "I realized there was no reason why I couldn't take a couple of university courses in computers at night and get my teeth into the field. So I did, and I've found I really enjoy it. I've substantially increased my chances of moving up in my company, and I'm thinking about some more courses to broaden my background."

WHAT CAN YOU DO AND WHAT ARE YOU WILLING TO LEARN?

As you were growing up, you discovered your talents and interests. What were they? Take some time to recall them. Write them down. You developed the set of skills that you are now using, but you've also left some behind. Start developing those forgotten skills now. A knowledge of—and some experience in using—the full range of your abilities will be necessary if you plan to compete with other highly talented and well qualified people in the ever-changing world of modern business.

You must know your own strengths—the whole range of them. You must be aware of those you are now using and those that you need to revitalize. Think back, and think ahead. Then try gradually to develop *all* your skills. Be aware of the ones you lack and work particularly hard on these shortcomings. Fortunately, management skills can be *learned*.

WHAT SKILLS ARE NECESSARY FOR BUSINESS SUCCESS?

The key traits that are necessary for success in business can be divided into three areas: (1) judgment, (2) personal attributes, and (3) human skills.

A discussion of each area follows. Read through the descriptions and figure out which ones you already have developed. Put a check mark after each word that describes an ability you *already* have. If you feel you are *particularly* talented with regard to any of the traits, give yourself two or even three check marks after that word. If you feel you are weak in certain attributes, place an "X" after the word.

Use a pencil for marking these lists so that you can change your ratings after you have done further thinking, and even later, after you have developed your management skills more fully. Don't hesitate to write in this book—*it is meant to be a workbook for your management career*. In fact, I believe it's all right to write in *any* book that you own and that you use to work with. It will save you time both now and later, when you want to refer to something important. You may, however, prefer to start a notebook to use while you are reading. If you do, now is a good time to begin using it. Use a looseleaf book for ease in updating the information you are gathering, information you'll use in planning and managing your career for years.

Whether you make your marks in the book or put your lists on a separate piece of paper, you'll have a clearer idea of how you rate in terms of management potential when you've scored yourself on the three lists that follow.

1. Judgment

The ability to view situations objectively—to make effective decisions and to act upon them—is essential for managers. The effects of judgment become increasingly critical the higher up you move, because the effects of each decision have a greater impact on the success of the organization. How do you rate yourself as a problem solver?

Problem-Solving Abilities

Accurate	Deliberate	Objective
Analytical	Efficient	Organized
Concise	Fast	Original
Confident	Imaginative	Practical
Consistent	Incisive	Realistic
Constructive	Innovative	Systematic
Creative	Intuitive	Other:
Critical	Logical	_____
Decisive	Methodical	_____

Add as many other descriptive words as you can think of that characterize what you think of as your judgmental ability.

As you move higher and higher in your career path, situations become more and more ambiguous. You will need all the faith in your own ability that you can muster to make the right decisions.

You may have noticed that some of the words on the judgment list are not ones that have generally been used to describe women. Dr. Virginia Schein, a professor of organizational behavior, has found that "successful middle managers are perceived to possess those characteristics, attitudes, and temperaments more commonly ascribed to men in general than to women in general." She has further asserted that to "think like a man may be vital for a woman if she is to be accepted and successful in predominantly male organizations." Most organizations are predominantly male.

It is not only all right for professional women to be analytical and logical, to possess strong quantitative skills and to be objective: it is absolutely essential that they do so.

2. Personal Attributes

Maturity and a stable approach to life are vital ingredients in leading others and in focusing clearly on desirable goals. How do you rate in this area? Make check marks to indicate your strengths and "X's" for your weak areas and see how you stand.

Emotional Stability and Maturity

Assertive	Predictable
Accepting of Criticism	Purposeful
Able to Admit Mistakes	Responsible
Calm	Secure
Committed	Self-Confident
Controlled	Self-Reliant
Cooperative	Sensitive
Dependable	Sincere
Ethical	Steady
Flexible	Other:
Forthright	_____
Integrated	_____
Open	

Don't hesitate to add any other personal attributes you possess.

3. Human Relations Skills

One of the most integrated and successful women interviewed for this book stated clearly that she was very "assertive, committed, and purposeful" in going about the performance of her job, but that when she was with her social partner after business hours, she was much "more emotional, less controlled, and less assertive." She was quite happy about being able to change to suit different situations.

Not only are different responses frequently more suitable in personal as opposed to professional situations, but they are also often required in different types of businesses and at different levels within an organization. In order to change your type of emotional responsiveness, you must be fully aware of how you normally respond. You need a clear perception of what your strengths are in dealing with other people. Put a check after those personal qualities you possess, two or three checks after a particularly strong point. Place an "X" where you tend to go wrong.

Human Relations Skills

Agreeable	Good Listener	Relaxed
Considerate	Helpful	Respected
Diplomatic	Intuitive	Sense of Humor
Direct	Loyal	Serene
Dynamic	Natural	Tactful
Eager	Outgoing	Thoughtful
Energetic	Patient	Understanding
Enthusiastic	Persistent	Other:
Fair	Persuasive	_____
Frank	Popular	_____
Friendly		

To rate yourself on these lists, go back and count the total number of check marks on all three lists. Where you have two check marks after a word, count this as two; if you have three checks, give yourself three points. Score 1/2 point for each weakness where you have marked an "X." Knowing your weaknesses is the first step toward correcting them or compensating for them.

Add up your score. If you find your total number of checks is under 50, you are probably very hard on yourself or find it difficult or uncomfortable to give yourself credit for things you can do really well. Or, you may have much to learn before you become a top professional!

The point of this test is to become increasingly comfortable with the vital process of continuing self-assessment. Give these lists to someone who knows you well and have him or her do the same scoring. Were you rated higher by someone else than you rated yourself? Probably—most people are. But you must be able to appraise yourself realistically and to give yourself credit for all of your skills and talents. Score yourself again on these points in a few months and see if your self-confidence has improved.

TALKING ABOUT YOURSELF

Many women are at a disadvantage professionally because they have been taught to be self-effacing and to take second place.

They have been discouraged from recognizing their talents fully, from being comfortable talking about them and from making full use of them. For many women, it has been taboo to call attention to their capabilities.

Doris, the most senior woman executive in her large organization and one who is obviously in line for still more responsibility, readily admits she is not able to discuss her talents easily. When asked why, she said, "When I was growing up, girls didn't push themselves forward. It wasn't nice. I was taught to be modest. But, I also think there is another reason, one that came along later. If I didn't talk about what I could do, but just went ahead and did it, I didn't threaten the men I worked with as much. I guess it was part of how I handled being a woman among many men. I just quietly went about my work. I'm finding my hesitancy to promote myself is now working to my disadvantage, though. I've got to verbalize my capabilities clearly if I'm to move up. And if I ever had to interview outside this company, I'd really have problems. At least here they've all *seen* what I can do."

Even an experienced senior woman executive can be uncomfortable discussing her talents. But when you interview for a job, you are expected to identify your abilities and to show how they fit the needs of the position for which you are interviewing. Furthermore, you must show that you're better than anyone else who is being considered!

The Five-Minute Brag

Are you able to tell people where your strengths lie? To do this, you must first know them yourself. Can you list right now your five or ten strongest professional attributes? What are they? If you can't discuss them quickly and confidently, go back over the lists and circle your greatest strengths. Practice being able to conduct a "five-minute brag." You won't really be bragging, of course—just stating your abilities in a concise and confident manner. But until you become comfortable doing this, it *feels* like bragging! You are working toward being able to describe yourself accurately when you are called upon to do so.

Modesty may have been a maidenly virtue, but it is counterproductive in business life. Self-confidence and self-knowledge are vital, as well as the ability to communicate a positive self-assessment.

KNOW YOUR WEAKNESSES—BUT KEEP THEM TO YOURSELF!

While it is important to recognize your weaknesses and work to correct them, women are often prone to dwell on their deficiencies. There's an old proverb that says that you should never draw attention to your faults; other people will probably not notice them! Remember that and *don't* draw attention to your weaknesses. Instead, set about correcting them, making up for them, or showing up your strengths.

WOMEN'S INTUITION

Of the three areas we examined—judgmental, personal, and human skills—women usually rate high in the latter two. Cultural conditioning of women has required that they develop techniques of working with and through other people. Women have generally trained themselves to pay close attention to others in order to understand their motivations and predict what is apt to happen. This is what men have called "women's intuition." It's a valuable asset in leading and managing people in organizations. Intuition, or accurately reading verbal and nonverbal signals, coupled with a genuine concern for other people, are great strengths that women are bringing with them into organizations.

YOUR ETHICAL VALUES

"An organization ultimately reflects the kind of person that leads it," states a successful businessman. "All the Machiavellian personal tricks advocated by so many business people will not cover up the essential character of the people in charge." Know what your ethical and personal values are and where you are willing and unwilling to make compromises. In the next section of this chapter and the two chapters that follow, you will have a chance to look closely at your personal values and how they affect your professional choices.

WHAT IS "MANAGEMENT"?

Although necessary, people and human skills are not sufficient for success in middle and senior management positions. *The art of management has been described as the ability to achieve the goals of the organization through others.*

Implicit in this description is the question: "How?" The answer is usually up to the manager. Furthermore, the higher up you move in a company the more responsible you become for determining what those goals are to be, as well as deciding on the means for reaching them.

The whole area of the exercise of judgment and the ability to make and implement decisions must be well developed. Managers must be able to set policies, determine objectives, and do long-range planning. They must establish priorities, defend and promote their decisions, and see that they are carried out. Then they must judge these decisions after they have been implemented and choose another path if the results are not as anticipated. The higher up you move in an organization, the more exercise of this judgmental, or conceptual, ability is required.

Women have been generally disadvantaged in this area. They have not occupied positions that enabled them to gain practice in making this kind of decision and defending it. They have not been encouraged to take the kind of risks that are involved in making forward projections in ambiguous situations. Lack of self-confidence and lack of opportunity have worked together to keep women from gaining background and experience in the conceptual area, but this must change.

HOW TO GET THAT VITAL THING—EXPERIENCE

Anita, a marketing executive, found she had trouble getting the responsibility for making the budget decisions in her product area. Her boss had been promoted to a group product manager over several different people, each of whom had charge of an individual item. These product managers had the responsibility for making a profit on their product, but Anita's boss wouldn't relinquish the authority to her for making the financial projections and then living with them and making them work. "I'm inclined to think that his wife isn't too good with figures—or maybe his mother wasn't. His reluctance to let me handle the full scope of my job is really handicapping me."

Sometimes it isn't the woman's inability to make decisions and projections—as in Anita's case, it can be a man's perception of women as being less than fully capable in these areas. It takes confidence and perseverance to get the experiences that enable you to become confident and to get the opportunities that allow you to gain this conceptual knowledge and good judgment. Anita will have to keep after her boss until he gives her all the same latitude for success or failure that he has given to the other—male—product managers.

SOMETIMES YOU'LL BE WRONG

It has been said that all management decisions are made on the basis of inadequate information. It takes confidence to make a decision when you don't know all that you need to know in order to make a fully informed decision. It takes even more confidence to admit to a mistake and set about rectifying it.

Managers are deemed successful, in many cases, if only 51 per cent of their decisions are good ones. Nonetheless, even with this modest goal in mind, it is often hard for women to accept the fact that perfection is not required; decisiveness followed by action is.

A willingness to accept the responsibility for your actions is essential as well.

EXPAND YOUR KNOWLEDGE THROUGH EDUCATION

One excellent way of gaining confidence in your judgments, and learning to make better management decisions, is to acquire more knowledge of business through continuing education. Attend seminars on various aspects of management, such as decision making; managing information systems; business policy, planning, and strategy; and other advanced topics. Technology and theory are changing so rapidly that no one can hope to move ahead without expanding his or her horizons or even just trying to keep abreast of the changes.

It is also useful to attend seminars and courses on the more psychological aspects of management, such as leadership, motivation, handling change and conflict, negotiation, communication, and other important elements of the executive's job. Concentrate on those areas where you believe you are weak. And even where you feel your human and personal skills are well developed you will find you still have a lot to learn about applying those talents in the most effective way in business situations.

Education in business administration, particularly at the graduate level, is a rapid, though demanding, way to acquire both the conceptual skills and some of the technical background vital for business success. In fact, in the near future, a Master of Business Administration degree may become almost a requirement for entering the management track.

The M.B.A.

In the mid-sixties, only about 6,000 M.B.A. degrees were granted, very few to women. In 1978, 35,000 M.B.A. degrees were given, and by 1982, it is estimated that 60,000 will be awarded—about 12,000 to be granted to women, or double the number awarded to anyone, male or female, less than twenty years ago. (Actually, the estimated number of women who will receive an M.B.A. degree in

1982 is probably on the low side, judging from the many graduate schools of business administration that have seen their female enrollment rapidly rise to 50 per cent and more in the past few years.)

"Getting my M.B.A. from one of the leading schools meant a salary increase from the high teens into the low $30,000 range," reported a hard-working young woman still in her twenties. "It was really worth the effort, and I'm now rapidly on my way up in a direction of my choosing."

"I've been told that I can't progress further until I hone my business skills at the Master's level," commented another woman in middle management level at her financial institution.

Another ambitious executive emphatically stated, "I wouldn't even want to *try* to compete with the other women and the men out there, without starting from the base level of a good business education. It's only from that starting line that we're all trying to run the race."

In Chapter 10 we'll take a deeper look at the need for education and the particular academic strengths helpful for targeting the top.

WHAT ARE YOUR PRIORITIES?

Once you begin to think about what you may need to learn and what abilities you now possess, it's time to turn your attention to what you *want* to do. Most people don't have a clear idea of their personal value system in relation to their professional aspirations. This may be even more true for women than for men. Most men have grown up knowing they would have to work and that a career might well be the driving force in their lives. Examples of men committed to career progress were all around them. They expected their identity and their personal satisfactions to be tied to their work. Women have had much more mixed messages of what they should do and what should be the most important values in their lives. Most women grew up with the expectation that they should get married, and that they should find their satisfactions through other people—especially their husbands and their children.

Some of this is changing, but perhaps not so much as many people theorize or hope for. For centuries women have put the values of others ahead of their own, or at least gone along with the value systems set up by society in general and their spouses in particular, because there was little economic option. It is only very recently that women have been free to look at their personal value systems in terms of their own wants, needs, and abilities. It's hard to get past all the "shoulds" to determine what you really want to do.

Here is a list of values considered to be motivators for the striving professional. Rank these items from 1 to 13 in order of their importance to you. If several of them seem to have equal importance, give them an equal ranking.

_____ INDEPENDENCE—the opportunity to do things on your own; to have freedom to do as you believe best

_____ POWER—controlling the situation around you

_____ LEADERSHIP—being able to influence others; having followers

_____ EXPERTNESS—being the best in some area

_____ SELF-FULFILLMENT—having the opportunity to develop your capacities, to realize your potential

_____ DUTY—doing what is expected of you

_____ NURTURING—contributing to the welfare of others

_____ FRIENDSHIP—being liked by others; having companionship

_____ FAMILY—meeting the needs of family members

_____ HEALTH—taking care of yourself

_____ SECURITY—not having the worry about present or future income or welfare

_____ PLEASURE—being happy and having fun

_____ WEALTH—earning a great deal of money

After you have ranked these items, reread your list. Your childhood and school years laid the foundation for the values that now play a major part in many of your decisions. On reviewing your list, you may find that your rankings significantly reflect ideas that you gained from your parents or other influential people in your early life.

Think how you really feel about each of these values. Are there any changes you want to make in the rankings? Make them. The resulting list will begin to give you an idea of your priorities in how you spend your time and energy. It will help you make well-thought-out career choices that will nourish the values most important to you.

You might have two or three friends or associates do this exercise, too, and then talk about the differences in each person's list. This discussion should help you understand some of the reasons behind your rankings and see your own priorities a little more clearly. You'll be surprised at how different other persons' lists often are.

The process of analyzing your own values and giving them a priority ranking is not a one-time undertaking. They may change. You will find that you will want to re-evaluate this list at regular intervals. Values and priorities change with age, with your stage of career development, with changes in your personal life. Your first list is not engraved in bronze; it is written in pencil and can be erased at will! In the next few chapters, *each of these values* will be examined more closely, both in themselves, and in how they affect a successful professional career. When you have finished reading these next chapters, you may want to make some changes on your list.

Women are only beginning to realize that they can develop a value system of their own and work toward clearly identified career goals on a planned basis. You can take control of your own life, and you must, *if professional achievement is one of your goals*. Professional success is something that must be sought actively. Being reactive will not help you achieve it; *action is what will count*. The reward for developing and using your abilities in the working world to their maximum, within your value system, is self-fulfillment, and can lead to economic independence. Not all women will choose to compete in the business community, nor should they. But for those who do, success comes only to those who have a clear understanding of themselves, of what they want to do, and how and why they want to do it.

2

A CLOSER LOOK AT VALUES AND PRIORITIES

In the preceding chapter we focused on the skills, values, and abilities you have. You took a look at what motivates you to work hard and to achieve. There are no right or wrong answers to where you derive your personal satisfactions. For example, whether you value doing your duty as you see it, or taking care of others, or having many friends on and off the job—what you value most is all up to you. Perhaps you need independence and enjoy working alone. Or you are really striving to be the best in your field and to do a perfect job at everything you tackle. All of these values are important, but some of them are more effective, some less, if what you are really after is to reach a position of leadership and power.

Let me emphasize that you are the only one who can decide what is required for you to develop fully, to be happy and fulfilled in a career or without one. You decide what interpersonal and physical penalties you are willing to pay to be successful in a career. One purpose of this book is to help you see which values are most likely to play a role in career success if you choose to target the top.

If you truly want to be boss, there are certain values you cannot do without, and which you will probably have to emphasize—

values held by people who have made it to the top. These important values will be discussed in the next chapter. In this chapter
we will take an in-depth look at some of the values often held by
women that prove to be *less* conducive to making it to the top as a
manager. These values are to perform your duty; to take care of
or nurture others; to have friends and companions and be part of
the group; and, finally, to have independence and achieve expertness and perfection.

DUTY AND NURTURING

One of the most successful woman entrepreneurs interviewed for
this book was asked what changed most in her attitude toward life
when she went from being a wife and mother of three children to
heading a multi-faceted corporation. She replied, "I learned that
men aren't always right."

The socialization of women in our culture has often made them
pay more attention to the opinions of other people—particularly
those of men—than to their own. Women are also taught that what
other people think of them is vitally important. Cynthia Epstein
points out in her landmark book, *Woman's Place,* that for girls,
"compliance and willingness to please are clearly valued traits."
This is part of the explanation of why so many women choose to
enter the nurturing professions of nursing, social work, and
teaching.

Two women who rank duty first on their list of values, and nurturing second, are working successfully in the health-care area:
one as a professor of physical therapy, and the other as a nursing
administrator in a prestigious hospital. When they analyzed their
reasons for working hard and succeeding in the area of health
care, both realized that they had been taught from early childhood
that they must do their duty and that their duty was to do what
others wanted and needed. They were surprised in comparing their
lists with others that not everyone put duty first in the rankings.
Both find their careers in the nurturing professions rewarding, but
they both want more.

If you are in the nurturing profession as a nurse or other

health-care worker, or as a teacher or social worker, there are some important facts that you should know if you want to move up. More women are in these fields than in others. *Women at Work,* a 1976 report of The Conference Board, points out that "the economic return on greater educational attainment is typically low in occupations employing large numbers of women." Even if income is not one of your important values, most of the senior administrative positions in the helping professions are filled by men, despite the fact that the vast percentage of workers in the area are women. Men have sought and attained these administrative positions since these jobs are the ones that have power and responsibility and that pay the best wages. It takes careful planning to move up even in the predominantly female fields.

This planning has been done well by the two health-care professionals mentioned before. Both have clearly identified their career objectives and have set about getting more education to help them obtain these goals. The professor is getting an M.B.A. degree because she would like to become the dean of a college in her area, and she needs the generalized administrative background. The nursing administrator is getting a business education because she plans to systematize hospital nursing administration, using the most advanced management techniques.

Can You Fire Someone?

For women whose backgrounds have not emphasized duty and nurturing, the socialization of women, which makes them sensitive to other people and their problems, exacts its price. Can you fire someone? Can you fire a whole department if company reorganization requires it? Would the psychological cost to you be too great?

As her company grew, Grace expanded her abilities and knowledge along with her job, but her secretary was not able to. The president suggested that the secretary be replaced, despite the fact that there was no other job for her in the organization. Grace resisted, because her secretary was in her late fifties, supported her aged mother, and would surely have a very difficult time finding another job. The president directed Grace to replace the secretary with an administrative assistant. Grace still resisted, even though everyone knew that what Grace was doing was not best for the business. Finally another job opened up in the company, and the secretary was placed there. The whole episode did not enhance Grace's standing as a corporate administrator in the eyes of senior management, but Grace could not have lived with herself if she had acquiesced to the needs of the company in this situation.

Grace realized from this experience that she truly did not want to be a top executive. She was happy to stay at a level where the stakes weren't too high, and where she could consider other people's needs, even if they were occasionally to the detriment of the company.

Another rising young manager in a larger corporation says that she pays a high personal price when she has to fire people, but she has learned to do it because it is a requirement of her position and of those above her. "No matter how many articles I read that tell you that firing someone who is not performing is really helping that person, I don't believe it. And you don't always fire people because they are not doing their jobs; sometimes it's just a cutback. In either case, you are removing their income and doing serious damage to their egos. I don't like firing someone, and it's tough to do."

FRIENDS AND COMPANIONS

For people who are employed full-time, the company for which they work usually becomes their second most important social unit, next to their immediate families. Affiliation with groups at work can be a continuing source of pleasure. But, for many women, moving up often means leaving their friends behind. The new peer group generally contains fewer women than the last group—if indeed it contains any women at all. It isn't easy to move ahead of your friends, it's hard to make new friends, and it's often more difficult if your new peer group is mostly male. But it can and must be done. You may also have to do with fewer friends at work or find professional friends among women in other organizations.

Mary Lou, a scientific Ph.D., joined a large multinational company as a technical research scientist and was assigned to her own office and given several male research assistants. Try as she might, she could not find any other women in technical positions anywhere near her level in the corporation. "I went searching around the plant and through the company literature. I was lonely. Finally I just set up an informal organization of women who were above the secretarial level so I would have someone to talk to. There were very few people I could include who were doing anything other than secretarial work, and, frankly, I have to admit that with all the technical education I have, I just don't have much in common with secretaries. I'm thinking of looking for another job where I'll have some women associates."

When Jean took a position as marketing manager, for which she was well qualified, she found that she was the only woman in the company at management level. It had never occurred to her that she might have problems because of this. "I didn't know if I really ought to go to lunch with the men—and, not only that, I didn't even know where the men went to lunch," Jean lamented. "I don't have problems working my way into male groups usually, but these men were lots older than I, and they weren't used to including a woman or even taking women seriously as professionals. I believe it was a mistake on my part not to have recognized that there was too much ground to break in this situation before I took the job. I did my best to be accepted—because you can't succeed in a company unless you are part of the grapevine, the informal network of give-and-take that exists in every company. And I just couldn't break in. I was cold-shouldered on every attempt." As you may imagine, Jean's job did not work out for her. Her isolation at lunch was symptomatic of her lack of acceptance as a peer and a member of an informal organization within the formal setting.

Sexuality and Male Friendships

Are you comfortable in largely male situations? How do you feel in male-female business situations that contain sexual overtones? Not many people have directly confronted their own feelings on this issue, nor do they have a clear understanding of the attitudes of others. It's an area that contains a lot of surprises. It is also an area where it is well not to be caught unaware.

Gerry knew from various spoken and unspoken signals that her boss's boss found her very attractive. He never made any overt moves in her direction on home base, but he came very close to doing so when they traveled together. "Since I was only too aware that any promotion I would get was dependent not only on a good recommendation from this man, but on his actively championing me, I felt it was imperative to avoid a direct confrontation. I didn't want to be put in the position of rejecting him—which was what would result if his attraction to me ever came out in the open. I took every precaution possible to make sure that he never had an opportunity actually to get to the point of making a pass. I always socialized as far away from him as possible when on the road, and I made sure never to answer the phone when I was in my room. It was a difficult spot to be in, but I made it up and out of his area eventually.

"I don't really think there is any point in getting upset about this sort of problem. It is an occupational hazard for women as long as men and women find each other attractive. The secret is to handle the situation analytically, like any other business problem."

It has often been said that women, too, send out signals about whether they are sexually available. Do you know what signals people get from you? Apparently Gerry's superior got a clear non-verbal message that she was not interested.

To take an opposite example, a woman spoke up in a seminar and said how difficult and annoying it was for her at work when men made advances. She asked what she could do about it. Virtually every woman in the room knew immediately what the outward manifestation of her problem was. She dressed in a provocatively tight skirt and blouse. Furthermore, the blouse was low-cut and unsuitable for work. She seemed to be sending out ambivalent messages. She liked to dress as a sex object, but then she was annoyed when she was treated like one.

Although not all sexual advances are invited, consciously or unconsciously, it is still useful to examine your own feeling on the subject of sex and sexuality in the work place. It's often useful to get the perspective of trusted friends, because sometimes you are sending out messages of which you are unaware. Sharing experiences in this complex area often can help you to identify your own feelings and values as well.

Two women worked in the same office as middle managers: one with years of experience and the other new to the situation of being an available and interested woman among many available and interesting men. The younger woman's work required a great deal of travel with male peers. The two women spent many after-work hours discussing the problems and possibility of blurring the line between professional life and personal life. The older woman recounted various people's experiences, which she had witnessed over the years in this area, and their consequences.

· A very able and attractive young woman took one of the top jobs in her field, had an affair with someone at work, then had to leave the company when her relationship broke up. She wasn't forced out, it was just too uncomfortable for her to face him day after day. She's still building her way back professionally in another city.

· One of the women accepted in a formerly all-male company had various exploits, which were discussed far and wide both within the company and with all its suppliers. She's not making it easier for other women to be added to that company's roster, nor is she smoothing her own pathway up.

· A large company moved from a big city to a small town and, with the move, it became increasingly obvious who was involved with whom and when. This company gossip is probably not helping anyone's career—men or women.

· Yet, another able and upwardly mobile woman had a fairly short-term relationship with a man to whom she reported. It ended amicably, and she doesn't feel it affected her career one way or the other.

More often than not, it seems that a personal involvement with a professional associate ultimately works to the detriment of the careers of both people—but most particularly to the woman.

With the benefit of this counsel, the younger woman worked out a set of standards for herself. She decided to keep her personal life entirely separate from her business life. She became a vice-president of the firm in just a few years.

Do You Like to Win?

Problems involved in office friendships are not limited to male-female problems. Although it might be pleasant to think that people succeed by cooperating, there is actually a great deal of competition. Striving for a senior position means moving up in a pyramid-shaped hierarchy. Each time you move up a level, you leave others behind you at a lower level, and there are fewer persons at your new rank. You make it apparent that you are more able, that you successfully competed for the next higher position.

Do you like to compete? Do you like to win? Much research has been done concerning the theory first advanced by Dr. Matina Horner of Radcliffe College that women unconsciously throw up barriers to success.

Often starting in grammar school, women were discouraged from outshining their male peers. Sometimes, being a good student worked against success in the social sphere, depending upon the values of your group. So, hiding or making light of one's abilities, or doing less well than you might was a frequent result. Happily, this is perhaps less common in schools today than even ten or certainly twenty years ago, but the women out in the world of work today sometimes have difficulty overcoming the old training that caused them to value friendships over ability. Have you done this, either consciously or unconsciously? How do you feel about a promotion that puts you way ahead in both status and salary of men and women in your social group?

Fast-track executives often do not have time to build a real group of friends in the office. They have neither the time nor the desire to socialize with subordinates. Upwardly mobile managers look upon their peers as competitors for the next higher position. Obviously, this is not conducive to developing close friendships. Instead, their attention is upward, toward making acquaintances in the organization who can be helpful to them in their careers: those who can help them get their work done more efficiently, or who can act as mentors or sponsors.

How important are office friendships to you? How does this affect your ability to make and carry out unpopular decisions?

In her study of a major Fortune 500 company published in her book, *Men and Women in the Corporation,* Rosabeth Moss Kanter found that "the less advantaged in opportunity, regardless of organizational level . . . may develop a counter system built around peer relations instead of ladder climbing." She observed that people who find their upward mobility blocked seek protection and status from their peer group. It appears that these people, whom she referred to as "powerless," often had to spend more time protecting and defending themselves than they did working toward the goals of the organization.

Since women have almost always been among the less advantaged in organizations, peer-group loyalties have been especially strong among women at work, quite possibly for the self-protection that Kanter writes about. But people on the move establish alliances up the ladder. They are necessarily more concerned with effective working relationships with their peers and subordinates than personal friendships. Take a close look at your friendships at work and see if they are helping you or hindering you in your attempt to target the top.

INDEPENDENCE AND EXPERTNESS

In *The Managerial Woman,* Drs. Hennig and Jardim state that a woman's commitment is often to "current performance and to on-the-job competence," and that this helps her develop "a sense of legitimacy, of having a right to do the job she does, both in her own mind and, as she sees their reaction, in the minds of others."

Women have been rewarded for doing their jobs perfectly and becoming highly skilled technical specialists. Unfortunately, this has tended to keep women at lower level, repetitive jobs, which are also at low salary levels. The reward for being virtually infallible as an executive secretary has most often been years of service in that particular job. In the past it has been safer, easier, and more socially acceptable for a woman to be a specialist than to seek out aggressively the variety of experiences that would enable her to become a generalist, to learn how to manage others, and to be fitted for the more powerful positions in organizations.

To move up in an organization, you must move from viewing your job in isolation to being concerned with the total organization, and how each task and each area fits into the end goals of the company. Since women have often been encouraged to be specialists and to operate independently on the job, they have lacked the opportunity to develop skills in motivating others and confidence in delegating responsibility and being dependent on the performance of others.

Even where women are moving up, too often they do so as specialists and are moved into higher-level staff positions, rather than being encouraged to prepare themselves for the more powerful positions that bear profit responsibility and are called line jobs.

The Velvet Ghetto

Frances Lear, an executive search consultant, calls jobs that are isolated from the corporate thrust "velvet ghettos." No matter how much status these jobs may appear to entail, they do not carry any real decision-making responsibility. Women are permitted to excel in these functions. People who do their jobs well in their velvet ghettos do not threaten or compete with those who are on their way up or who are already at the top. Examples of areas that can prove to be velvet ghettos are accounting, economics, financial analysis, affirmative action, personnel, and public relations. While it may be useful to spend some time in any of these functions, remaining there overlong may put an end to your upward aspirations. In an article in the New York *Times,* Frances Lear made the point: "Virtually all jobs held by women and minorities are in ghettos." Are you in a velvet ghetto?

There are several tests to determine which are ghettos in your organization and if you are in one. Historically, ghettos have been areas with very carefully defined boundaries, in which people have been enclosed to keep them from threatening those in power. *Power in business is synonymous with making decisions*—particularly decisions that concern money and that affect the profit picture or the ability of the company to achieve its goals. Do you make decisions for your organization? Do these decisions directly affect the profit of the company or have a direct bearing on the expenditure of company funds?

Line Jobs Versus Staff Jobs

Line positions are those that directly affect profits. Staff jobs are advisory positions that help line managers do their jobs. There are no line jobs in velvet ghettos. How many women have line positions in your company? With the advent of equal employment opportunity laws, it has been necessary to promote women, but in many instances they have been placed in areas that are comfortable, probably given impressive titles, and possibly are even being well paid. But these are positions that are staff functions and from which it is virtually impossible to move up—except to another staff function. A position in a velvet ghetto may be a very pleasant one to have, day in and day out, year in and year out, but it will not be a stepping-stone. Watch for these comfortable spots and sidestep them if you are truly interested in working your way up to the top.

Here are some other indicators of your movement potential in your company. Is the job you hold usually filled by a woman? How many of your close associates are men or women you consider powerful in the corporate structure? Are there any powerful women in your company, or are they all relegated to the ghettos? Where have others moved up to from your job? How long has it taken them to do this? How long have you been in your present job? Where and when can you expect to move? Men frequently take positions not to see how well they perform them, but to see what they can learn that will prepare them for the next higher position.

To move up, get out and stay out of velvet ghettos, get staff experience when appropriate, but get yourself into line positions where you can make decisions that directly affect the success of the company. You will find you will become more dependent on other people, since you will only be able to do your job with their help, but you will become less concerned with nurturing them. At the same time you will have to become more discriminating about when to be a perfectionist and a super expert. You'll have to become more concerned with the larger picture: where the organization is going and how it's going to get there.

In the next chapter, we will look further at the values that are more consistent with upward career mobility: managerial ability, the seeking of power, and the desire for self-fulfillment and personal development.

3

DO YOU TRULY WANT
TO BE BOSS?

Stephanie, a successful woman in public relations, made a lunch date to renew her acquaintanceship with Annette, an old friend from high school who was now an executive in a major corporation. When she went to pick up Annette at her office, Stephanie was impressed to find that Annette oversaw six supervisors, who in turn administered two hundred people. In the brief period that Stephanie was waiting in Annette's office, several minor and major crises arose, all of which required Annette's attention. This scene caused Stephanie to think seriously about whether she would really like to do what Annette was doing—motivating so many different individuals into a smoothly functioning unit—and, further, whether she *could* do it even if she decided she *wanted* to do it. Later, discussing her thoughts with Annette, Stephanie found out that Annette not only found her job challenging and exciting, but that she thrived on her responsibilities and the opportunity to interact with so many people. Stephanie realized this would not be true for her—she was much happier working on her own, thinking up ideas for feature articles and dealing with media people and clients on a one-to-one basis. Stephanie will probably stay at the professional level where she now finds herself. Annette, on the other hand, is gaining experience in the dual arts of management and motivation—areas that will enable her to move up.

ARE YOU A MANAGER?

Do you prefer working alone, being part of a group, or leading a group? Do you consider yourself an effective leader?

A great deal has been written about being a successful leader and manager of other people. As I pointed out in Chapter 1, a manager achieves the goals of the organization through others; thus, one of the requirements of a good manager is an ability to get others to do the necessary tasks. This is leadership ability. As yet, no one has been able to define just exactly what makes a good leader, but we can pinpoint some of the key elements: (1) the ability to analyze situations well, decide what has to be done, when to do it, and how; (2) the ability to communicate this information effectively to others; and (3) the ability to influence and motivate people to work toward identified goals and to achieve them.

Leaders Are Made, Not Born

Many people believe that leaders have a particular set of innate characteristics that enable them to influence other people. Although hundreds of studies have been made to determine leadership traits, specific traits were not found consistently in people who held leadership positions. There does not seem to be a consistent personality pattern that distinguishes leaders from followers. It seems to be more a matter of developing certain traits more fully than other people have. Many of these leadership abilities are in the areas in which you examined yourself in Chapter 1. They are human skills and personal traits that help you to deal with people effectively and influence them to work toward the goals of the organization; and the judgmental skills that help you analyze what needs to be done and how to go about doing it.

It is encouraging that the skills of an effective leader can be learned. But it also means that since we are not born with these traits, they *must* be learned if we are to become successful managers. We develop them as we gain experience and maturity.

Your Equipment: Human Skills

A vital function of a leader is the ability to motivate people, to blend divergent personalities into an effective team working toward common goals. A great deal of skill in handling people is needed at every level, whether you are a first-line supervisor or the chief executive. This is true to an even greater extent for women managers, who are reaching positions that have never before been held by women and where they will undoubtedly be supervising men. Men have a deep-seated cultural resistance to working for women. If you don't believe it, wait until you find yourself in this situation for the first time!

Janet was promoted to area head in competition with Bert, who then had to work for her. He made it very plain that he would not do what she wanted and would resist her at every turn. In fact, on occasion, she had reason to believe she was being sabotaged. Bert also seemed to be trying to turn their peer group against her and her leadership. Fortunately, Janet was very confident and knowledgeable in the abilities required to perform the job. She decided to confront Bert directly, and she asked him into her office. "I know that you are disappointed because you didn't get this job, and that I did," she said. "But if you want this job or another equivalent one, you'll have to work with me to make this whole area look good, and the quicker we do it the better it will be for all of us."

She then told him what she looked for as her next move and when she hoped to make it. "But I can't do it without your support. If you don't feel you can give me that, I'll help you find someplace else to go in this organization or outside it. I plan to succeed and I hope you'll help me. You and I both know that you can do this job when I leave, so the sooner I move up, the sooner you move into this office."

Janet was self-confident enough to address the problem openly with Bert. She was objective and direct. Bert realized that she was well aware of what he was doing and that she intended to deal with the problem. He began to perform better, and the working relationship between them improved sufficiently that she was able eventually to recommend him for a promotion elsewhere in the company. Both people came out winners in this situation because of Janet's skillful handling of a male subordinate.

Good skills in working with others are complex, and they are even more difficult in some of the new professional relationships. You might want to take time to look back at how you rated yourself in your human skill and personal attributes in Chapter 1 to see where you feel you might want to strengthen your abilities or change your approach. Sometimes, growing up as women, we've been encouraged to manage situations involving other people by indirect methods, rather than dealing with the matter at hand openly and objectively. Would you be a better manager if you could deal more directly with difficult people? Can you start doing this whenever possible to gain experience and increase your ability in this regard?

Teams and Coaches

There is a theory that men are better equipped for managerial positions than women because most men were involved in a good deal of team interaction during their formative years. This enables them to be not only better members of the team, but better coaches and owners as well. Most women, on the other hand, spent much of their developmental years alone or with one or two friends—or cheering the boys' teams on—rather than gaining team skills.

Have you ever watched a group of young boys playing basketball, football, or baseball? The coaches are often yelling directions and corrections. Frequently the young men respond just as directly if they feel the order is unfair or incorrect. There's little subterfuge in these interchanges, and the team members learn to take it. They learn that the directions or corrections are not necessarily aimed at them personally, but rather aimed at the proper performance of that particular function. You'll also see certain of the team members assume the role of managing the other members of the team; they get the others to do what has to be done to win the game.

In many respects, this behavior is carried over into organizations that have heretofore been largely male-managed. It's necessary to be able to take strong direction, open criticism without feeling it too much emotionally. It's also necessary to be able to give correction frankly and objectively. Fortunately, more and more girls are being encouraged to participate in team sports—sometimes even on teams with boys. However, bodily development and skeletal development appear to preclude as much of this as might otherwise be desirable.

"I remember how surprised I was when I first came across this idea," remarked Evelyn, an upper-management executive clearly marked for more responsibility. "I wasn't surprised that a lot of competitive sports helped give people the experience of winning, losing, and getting the group to work together no matter what. I was surprised that most girls didn't have team experiences while growing up. No one ever told me that I could not play baseball and football with the boys, though I think my mother did try to encourage touch football rather than tackle when I was somewhere in my teens. This was the way we grew up in my neighborhood—both boys and girls."

Probably one of the reasons that Evelyn was successful before it became usual for a woman to succeed in a large hierarchical organization was that she had grown up in a less sexually structured environment. As she grew up, she had been "one of the boys."

While the analogy of team participation and leadership development skills in school-age sports can easily be carried too far, there remains important food for thought in the whole area. Hennig and Jardim deal with the problem of women's lack of team skills extensively in *The Managerial Woman*. In addition, they point out, "the guys with the imagination to plan and anticipate possible outcomes achieve a value of their own." This may be part of the beginning of the training in judgment of what has to be done and how it should be done, which we call conceptual skill.

Your Equipment: Seeing the Big Picture

As you move up the career ladder, your ability to exercise good judgment becomes more and more important. You'll be deciding what others should do and how they should go about it. You'll be committing your group to action and, at higher levels, you'll be committing the entire organization to action.

As president of a manufacturing company, Peter managed a profitable operation with three production facilities: one on the West Coast, one on the East Coast, and one in the Midwest. Because of soaring manufacturing costs, after careful study, Peter decided to consolidate operations and close the East Coast plant. He successfully negotiated the sale of this plant, conducted the very painful process of laying off three hundred employees. Everything seemed to be moving along as planned.

Suddenly he was roused by a phone call in the middle of the night with the news that one of the two remaining plants had just burned to the ground. How would he manage to meet orders from the one remaining plant? How fast should he have the burned-out facility rebuilt, and where? What should be done about the employees in the interim? These and myriad other problems and decisions had to be handled by Peter and handled quickly. His firm's competitors would be looking eagerly to provide products to any customers whom he could not supply. Several hundred people depended upon his ability to make the decisions that would enable his company to remain in business. The responsibility and the accountability for the decisions rested squarely on his shoulders. How do you develop the skill to make these kinds of decisions? Do you want this type of responsibility?

Robert L. Katz, a professor of business administration, states: "At the lower levels, the major need is for technical and human skills. At higher levels, the administrator's effectiveness depends largely on human and conceptual skills. At the top, conceptual skill becomes the most important of all for successful administration."

Historically, women have neither been allowed nor encouraged to become involved in the making of decisions such as those Peter had to make, which affect resource allocation and ultimately the profits of a company. Nor have women been involved in long-range planning. Women have excelled in the areas of technical skills and human skills. Because women have been so thoroughly rewarded for expertness, it has been hard for them to decide what has to be done and to *let others do it*. Yet, if you are to move into more and more responsible positions, the need for conceptual skills increases in almost direct proportion to the decreased need for specific technical knowledge. An effective manager—of either sex—must decide what has to be done, and then motivate others to perform the tasks.

Peter moved his production manager and family from the corporate headquarters to the town where the remaining plant was located. He made the manager responsible for seeing that maximum production was achieved. Peter stayed in close touch with him as well as with the people who were rebuilding the burned-out facility, giving them constant encouragement, backup, and support. With hard work on everyone's part, not one order was missed, and the year-end profit exceeded projection. Peter's philosophy is, "You've got to have good people working for you, then depend on them and give them lots of support."

We'll take a further look at the relation between your human skills, your technical talents, and your need to develop more conceptual and decision-making abilities in Chapters 14 and 16.

POWER GAMES

Helen is a senior vice-president of a major company. She has been with her corporation for more than a decade and is recognized as one of the most innovative people in her field. Vying with her for the presidency of the company is a man who recently joined the organization. Both contenders have management styles as different as their backgrounds. One or the other must lead the company in his or her own style, and each is struggling with the other for the total leadership position. One will win; the other will lose and probably move to another company. "My competitor really doesn't seem to get the work done effectively," Helen explains. "In fact, he even holds up my work quite often, due to his indecisiveness. Many of the decisions he makes are unrealistic and just plain don't work. But he has a long business history and lots of varied experience.

"Another thing that concerns me when I think about who will succeed in this contest is that the owner of the company always uses a different tone of voice when talking to me than when he is talking to men—which says to me that he never stops thinking of me as a woman. I'm never just an able *executive* who works for him. In the final analysis, I think this may work to my disadvantage.

"I know I can do a better job running this company than anyone else can, and I hope I get the chance to do it. I'll fight for the top position to the bitter end." The outcome is not yet known. Would you be able to participate in this type of toe-to-toe power struggle?

In his book, *The Gamesman,* psychiatrist Michael Maccoby asserts that the new type of successful leader sees business life in general and his career in particular in terms of options and possibilities, as if he were playing a game. Maccoby says that the Gamesman competes for "the exhilaration of victory." The man who is trying for the presidency of Helen's company has no strong company loyalty and seems to be out for his own success. He may well be motivated by Gamesman-like goals.

Helen's motivations appear more likely to be a desire for power, in the sense that this word is used by Dr. David McClelland, a professor of psychology at Harvard. In his book, *Power,* McClelland identifies a desire for power as the key motivating force for individuals who strive for the top. He points out that assertive actions are indicators of a power motivation. A manager decides what should be done and sets about getting other people to do it by a variety of means. McClelland describes professional power as the ability to get things done by having "an impact on people," and by being "strong and influential." This kind of power is distinct from dictatorial power.

In studying individual managers of large United States corporations, McClelland reported in the *Harvard Business Review* that a manager's need for power "must be disciplined and controlled so that it is directed toward the benefit of the institution as a whole [and it] ought to be greater than his need for being liked by people." McClelland suggests that a manager must have power as a goal, and that the power motivation—the desire to get things done—must be stronger than the need for affection and friendship.

What is your attitude toward this kind of power? Do you want it? Do you know how to acquire it and then how to use it effectively? Professional power and its exercise is such an important attribute of successful managers that we'll look at it in greater depth in Chapter 18.

HOW DO YOU FEEL ABOUT MONEY AND SECURITY?

Women over sixty-five who are living alone are the least powerful and poorest segment of the United States population. Although money has not been considered much of a motivator for educated women workers, it may be time for women to begin to think of income in the broader perspective of security, and even power, and have it rank higher in their value system.

There are many aspects to financial security. The most important of these is to be engaged in a stable career in a growing field. Further, financial security consists of earning a regular income with increments that at least cover the cost of inflation. It also enables you to provide for persons who are dependent upon you until they can work. Finally, financial security gives you benefits that will enable you to live adequately if you become ill or disabled, and to retire at an appropriate time with sufficient guaranteed income.

When a woman interviewing for a middle-level position with a financial institution was asking questions about fringe benefits, the president commented, "I hope you are not going to delve into our retirement system, too." He implied that since she was a woman, she probably would be supported by someone else and really shouldn't worry about such practical matters as how she was going to live when she was no longer able to work.

Do you know what your pension rights are? Do you know when you become vested and can take your equity in the pension program with you to a job in another company? Will your health insurance remain in force if you become disabled or retire? What salary do you expect to be making in one year? In five years? Ultimately? What is your definition of being wealthy? Is it one of your goals?

There is no question that money brings with it increased power to get things done and increased freedom of choice. *Money matters*—especially to the working woman. It not only buys present and future security, but it also buys services that give you more time and energy to earn more money and take better care of yourself and your family. We'll take a close look at specifics of remuneration in Chapters 23 and 24.

THE ENERGY FACTOR

A strong constitution is a great asset in professional striving. It is the rare top executive who has not worked ten- and twelve-hour days, plus transportation time, for months and years on end, at some point in his or her career. Many have reached senior levels only to find the demands on them require that they keep up this pace. Since professional women are still having to prove themselves, they are having to work as hard or harder than the men with whom they are competing.

In considering a position, Carol asked the senior vice-president what hours he worked. He said he was at his desk each morning at 7:30 and he left the office at 6:30. He further volunteered that the two women who worked for him as technical specialists were there when he arrived and often worked weekends as well. Carol knew from much experience that she could not work these hours without paying a physical penalty, and she decided against this position.

Carol said, "In my first job—the one that really gave me the training and experience that has enabled me to move upward rapidly—twice a year I had to work ten or twelve hours a day for thirty days in a row. I always lost about fifteen pounds, and I didn't have them to spare. But I got the training I needed, and then became a corporate manager elsewhere. Later, I worked as a consultant for a man who regularly logged a work week of about one hundred hours. Can you imagine how much work a person generates who works two and a half times a normal schedule? So, again, I found myself working both Saturday and Sunday to keep up. At least on that job, I limited myself to an eight- or nine-hour day. I'm not prepared to do this again. I need some fun, and I need some exercise to do my best work."

What balances do you need between work and other activities

in order to stay in top form? What penalties do you pay if you don't get enough rest or enough exercise? How does this affect your work? How much sleep do you need? How much time with friends? Family? How much time for yourself?

Most successful women have thought through their mental and physical requirements. And most of them have a regular exercise program of some type. Anne takes her jogging shoes with her wherever she goes. Linda takes ballet lessons regularly. Donna teaches yoga two nights a week. Activities like these not only help to maintain physical condition, they also relieve stress.

Men in top positions have long suffered the consequences of continuous stress in the form of high blood pressure, heart attacks, and ulcers. As women are getting increased responsibilities in business, so, too, is the incidence of these diseases increasing in females. How do you react to continued stress? How does this manifest itself? Is there anything you can do about it? Meditation and biofeedback seem to be useful for executives when they do not have a chance to exercise, or as an addition to exercise. Claudine says that after a tough day she always meditates, and then finds herself quite refreshed and relaxed and able to enjoy an evening out.

WHAT DO YOU WANT OUT OF LIFE?

All work and no play not only make Jill dull, but badly balanced as well. An enjoyable life is finding the right balance between vocation, leisure, family, and friends. Only you can decide what is the right mix for you to thrive on. Only you know what makes your existence meaningful.

However, professional success can be a great source of pleasure. Marshall McLuhan has said, "Today, work is becoming involvement or leisure. No one who is totally involved in his activities or interests ever really *works.*" Men have long pursued professional interests that are fulfilling. Now women are beginning to look for self-realization in their work.

The late Dr. Abraham Maslow of Brandeis University identified achievement and self-actualization as important motivating forces.

Achievement can be thought of as getting a chance to do things that you are capable of doing and enjoy doing. Self-actualization carries this concept still further and implies the opportunity to develop yourself to the fullest extent. Realizing your potential creates an upward spiral of success breeding more success. According to Maslow, people who are self-actualized have a good perception of reality, a greater tolerance for ambiguity, and are accepting of themselves and of others. They tend to be natural, spontaneous, and creative. Women have not always had the opportunity to know the pleasures of achievement, particularly at the level that could be considered self-actualization. There still exist many barriers to the full use of female talent and resources. The old myths and stereotypes about women and work may be holding you back without your realizing it. You may never have considered setting your sights as high as you are capable of doing.

When asked how she had been able to achieve so much so rapidly and what enabled her to continue to work with such intensity, a woman executive replied, "I really enjoy doing a difficult job well, and I like the power. It's a lot easier and infinitely more rewarding to work when you really enjoy it."

What do you really enjoy doing? What gives you a sense of fulfillment and accomplishment? Go back to the page where you ranked your values and motivations. Do you still agree with that ranking? If not, change it. Only with a clear understanding of what you enjoy doing and why you enjoy doing it can you make maximum use of your potential. You are now aware that certain values seem more related to professional achievement than others. These are a desire to lead and motivate others, pleasure in having power, and an interest in developing yourself fully. If you really want to exercise leadership and power, you probably have already answered the question of whether you truly want to be boss—in the affirmative.

But your chances for professional success are not totally controlled by your own values, goals, and abilities. You must also take into consideration outside factors that will have an impact on your professional life. In Chapter 4 we'll take a closer look at outside forces that may affect your professional life and your chances of making it to the top.

4

FACING THE OUTSIDE FORCES

To assess your own career potential realistically, you must be fully aware not only of your business values and your professional strengths and weaknesses, but also of the outside forces that affect you. You must know what these forces are and be able to estimate how long they will have an impact on your life. The most important of the forces that can cause you to alter your plans and hold you back from seeking the maximum development of your career center around (1) the people in your life; (2) a need for a substantial or secure income to handle responsibilities; and (3) geographical constraints.

In this chapter you'll have a chance to consider these very real obstacles on your road to the top. You'll also be able to see whether these obstacles are beyond your control, or if you can still do something about them, and when you can do it. Many of the career conflicts that seem to be caused by outside forces are actually the result of people's attitudes toward domestic roles. You may find you are living a certain way and encountering certain obstacles to career progress because of society's expectations. Fortunately, professional people are discovering the advantages of breaking out of molds. Perhaps some new solutions will occur to

you as you read this chapter and analyze some of the outside
forces that affect you.

FOCUSING ON FAMILY AND FRIENDS

Undoubtedly, the pressures brought about by family members are
the most difficult for professional women to handle. Pursuing your
career and simultaneously fulfilling the roles of daughter, wife,
mother, sister, niece, or whichever of these roles and other relationships you have, requires an enormous amount of energy and
maturity—energy to do what you must and maturity to know what
you can avoid doing.

"First-Phase" Professionals

Formerly, successful professional women avoided such conflicts
by not marrying or by marrying later in life. In the late sixties,
Margaret Hennig studied twenty-five career women who held positions of corporate vice-president and above for her doctoral dis-
sertation. Only half of the women had married, none of them until
they were in their thirties. None of these women had children of
their own. The women in Hennig's study might be considered
"First-Phase" women professionals, people who were willing to
suppress most of their personal life in order to succeed in business.

"Second-Phase" Professional Women

The trend among women toward finding fulfillment outside the
home, which began in earnest in the sixties, and the enactment of
equal-opportunity legislation, provided for the emergence of the
"Second-Phase" professional women. This second-phase career
woman was unwilling to forgo being a wife and often chose to be
a mother as well. The second generation of career women attempted to handle multiple and conflicting roles by trying to do it
all, and doing it perfectly, too. She attempted to be a superwoman
—super housekeeper, super chef, super wife, super mom, and
super professional—all at once. It is no wonder that the medical

community has noted a sharp increase in stress-related illnesses in working women in recent years. Some women have nerves of steel and limitless energy. But for most women, as for most men, it is unrealistic to strive for perfection in all areas.

"Phase Three"

The emerging professional woman has begun to move into "Phase Three," where she realizes she can't be all things to all people all the time. Women are maturing; they are accepting their limitations and developing a more realistic outlook on the demands of career success. They are also beginning to look at all their roles and to establish more realistic priorities in handling their own needs, the needs of others, and the requirements of their careers.

This can be very difficult to do. Patrick, who is the head of a trade association, needs a wife who can accompany him to his conferences and act as his hostess. His wife Margie has a career that doesn't allow frequent absences from her office—she's expected to be on the job fifty weeks out of fifty-two.

A better position opened up for Christine. However, her small children are frequently sick, and she can't find good household help on whom she can rely. If she takes on more responsibility, it will be even more difficult for her to stay home with a sick child.

In the case of Christine, there is perhaps nothing she can do until they outgrow this phase, which so many young children go through. She may just have to slow her career progress unless she can find a suitable surrogate mother. In Patrick's case, a change in employer could be made by one or the other of the couple. Patrick could take a position that doesn't require the help of a wife to do his work, or his wife might choose a job where she could get more time off. At least they might consider these alternatives and weigh what's most important to them as individuals and as a couple. It's easier to live with decisions that you have made together after studying possible options.

You Can't Have Everything All the Time

A few months into a new marriage, Louise realized that she was being pulled in too many directions and trying to do too many things. She traveled at least three days a week and she could see that her husband wanted and needed some undivided attention when she was home. Louise wanted to spend time with him, but on weekends she found herself trying to maintain her home instead of enjoying her husband's company, and renewing herself for the strenuous week ahead. She decided to change. She made it a policy to stop bringing work home. She determined to work more efficiently when at work and only carry it over into her personal life on very rare occasions. She hired a housekeeper to free her on the weekends from routine chores that someone else could do.

As an unexpected benefit from her new resolutions, Louise now has the energy to participate in sports with her husband. This new activity enables her to keep trim and fit, which is another important priority for her and one for which she formerly could not find time. By analyzing the needs of her husband and their relationship, looking at her own needs and habits, and by realizing that she doesn't have to do it all herself, Louise has chosen the things that are most important to her, eliminated some pressures, and delegated some domestic tasks. Five or ten years ago, Louise, who is a perfectionist, would have felt that she must prove herself by doing it all and doing it meticulously into the bargain.

How Much of an Obstacle Are You?

Not every woman has been able to move into Phase Three successfully. Also, as pointed out earlier, it is not always uncontrollable outside forces that get in the way of professional advancement. It is often your own perception of others' needs and your own internalization of what is expected of you. Most working women today were raised by mothers who stayed at home—they had little choice in the matter. If your mother spent the majority of her time keeping the house clean, having the laundry washed, sorted, and put away, and had regular meals on the table, you tend to think this is what you must do when you become a wife and perhaps a mother. These beliefs are reinforced if your husband's mother spent her time in a similar way.

But do these repetitive chores have to be the wife's responsibility? Do they have to be done and do they have to be done to the degree and in the way your mother did them? It is not easy to eliminate the programming and patterning of what a woman should and must do, which you have been exposed to over your lifetime, but it is possible to make some adjustments, eliminate some tasks, and share some of the responsibility.

Loretta is an excellent example of this problem. She was a doctoral candidate nearing completion of her degree requirements and is considered one of the outstanding people in her field. Her future was clearly mapped out ahead of her until her husband took a job in a town three hundred miles away. They moved their home to this new location, and Loretta commuted to the university to complete her course work. Her husband's new job required that he do a great deal of entertaining and he preferred to do it at home. In addition to the stress of frequent commuting, Loretta had to cope with cleaning and cooking meals for the business guests. She felt that her husband needed these services and expected them of her.

When she explored her situation in depth, Loretta would often mention what an excellent housekeeper and superb cook her mother had been. In trying to do it all in the same way her mother had, Loretta overtaxed herself and jeopardized her promising career. She had failed to examine the conflicting demands of her own aspirations and the expectations of her husband. If she wants to succeed professionally, she must discuss her situation thoroughly with her husband, and they must sort out their priorities. Why don't they hire a cleaning woman or a caterer, or both? Why doesn't her husband do more of the cleaning and learn to cook? Why don't they do some of the entertaining in restaurants? Does Loretta have to do all the commuting? What roles are her husband requiring of her and what performance is she demanding of herself because of her image of a perfect wife? How is this inability or unwillingness to assess her time and energy limitations going to affect her career?

Loretta is twenty-nine years old, extremely able, and working hard in a field of study dominated by men. Even with a degree from one of the most prestigious institutions in the country, what do you think the chances are at present for her to compete successfully for a professorship with the men in her field? What might happen to Loretta if she and her husband decide to have a child?

Children compound an already complex situation for working women, since most primary child-care still falls to the mother. How does one make the daily, even hourly choices of what must be done first, when *both* your child and your career constantly need to be first?

Problems and pressures in a marriage where both partners are career oriented will be looked at in greater detail in Chapter 5. The further complications of being a mother and a careerist will be examined in depth in Chapter 6.

Who Needs You and Whom Do You Need?

It isn't only wives and mothers who must find a viable balance between the conflicting pressures of professional achievement and personal responsibilities. Parents, siblings, aunts, uncles, nieces, nephews, and other relatives often have legitimate claims to our time and attention. Friends and companions do as well.

"I must have my group of friends to rely on for relaxation and companionship," comments Anne, a management consultant working a fast-paced fifty-hour week. "I've even jeopardized my chances at promotions by occasionally refusing long-term travel assignments. I find I lose contact with my friends and it takes too much time to get back into a comfortable rhythm of sharing if I've been away too long. It's just not worth it for me. I've got to have lots of outside things to do and people to do them with in order to enjoy life and to be able to do my best work."

Judy took another route for a while, when she thought about how time consuming it is to be a friend. She has a job in a highly competitive environment, where people have to have reached a certain level before they are thirty years old or else look for a job with another organization. She explained, "Before taking this job, I decided that I would commit myself totally to work until I could see that I was going to make it here. For three years I worked nights and weekends and had little contact with anyone outside of work. Fortunately, I have succeeded as well as anyone my age, and I reached the required level before turning thirty. I'm starting to develop some friends now and have more of a life outside of work. You know, I really didn't mind dropping out for a few years. It seemed to be easier than the kind of constant juggling that some of my coworkers were involved in."

Both of these women considered their options and made decisions that suited their own needs and career goals. The only outside forces affecting Judy were her friendships, and she chose to do without them, at least for a limited period of time. Anne, on the other hand, regarded her friendships as more important than anything else, and so she cut back on her professional commitment.

Only you can decide whom you need and who needs you. Think about who are the significant people in your life and analyze how they affect your career planning in a specific time frame.

MONEY, MONEY, MONEY

Review your financial situation thoroughly. Financial security or the lack of it has a great bearing on your willingness and ability to take risks along your career path. Your age and the years you have left to work until your retirement are fairly fixed factors that will influence your career decisions. Who is dependent upon you for support and how much money this takes is often a firm outside force, although one that will change with the passage of time.

What sources of income do you have? How stable are these sources? What income will you need in two years, in five years, in ten years? Begin to develop specific financial goals for these time periods.

When do you expect increased or reduced financial pressures and from what causes? When might someone become dependent on you for part or all of their support? When might someone cease to be dependent on you? The need for additional education by you or by members of your family often causes large fluctuations in financial need. Is this likely to occur? When? How can you plan for it?

Alice needs maximum income now since her second child is about to start college. She feels she is unable to consider a change of occupation that would otherwise make sense for her, because it will mean a substantial cut in salary—at least temporarily.

If Alice had spaced her children further apart, she wouldn't find herself with two in college at the same time. That kind of post facto planning won't help Alice now, but may be useful to those who have not yet started their families. Alice has recently discovered that what she really wants to do is to teach at the university level. If she had planned her career more thoroughly a few years ago, she might have been able to reach this goal before her children started college and to offset her lower earnings by getting the perquisite often offered to faculty members: free tuition for family members.

With only nine years until retirement, Maria is hesitant about taking a job she has been offered by another company. Although she feels it is a good career move, she is concerned about taking the risk because she is afraid she might have difficulty finding another position at her age if this new opportunity should prove unsatisfactory. Maria's age is a factor in her decision beyond her control, and she is wise to think about it seriously in making her decision. She must look at the options she'll have if she takes the new job and it doesn't work out. She would not want to find herself without an income for the next nine years until she is eligible for Social Security. And she also needs to consider the source and the amount of income she can depend upon to supplement the modest payments from Social Security.

Laura's superiors all have M.B.A. degrees; it appears to be an essential for moving up in her company, but Laura doesn't have the money. It often takes $8,000 to $10,000 just for tuition and books. Laura could have chosen to work for a company that pays for advanced education or she can now plan to go to work for a company that does so. She might, instead of changing jobs, attend school part-time and spread the tuition costs over a number of years. She'll need to take a look at her budget and her career plans from a long-range viewpoint and see what seems most advantageous to her.

Careful planning is vital for Alice, Maria, and Laura, as well as precise budgeting.

MOVING AROUND

One of the most disruptive outside forces that can have an impact on you and on your family and friends is the need to relocate. Your physical location and your ability to change it by choice or at the request of your employer is an important factor that can substantially affect your chances of advancement. The possibility of relocation often depends on the situation of the people who are important to you. If you are married, you also have the complex issue of what happens to your career if your husband has to relocate, or vice versa.

Virtually all career positions in Joanne's field are found on the East or West coasts. Joanne's husband has his own business in Dallas. Can their marriage survive a separation of temporary duration or a permanent commuting relationship? Joanne and her husband may find their marriage strengthened by her professional fulfillment, even if they live apart some of the time. Weekdays spent working and weekends spent together may prove to be a happy situation for them.

Is anything or anyone preventing you from wanting or being able to relocate? When might you be able to consider relocation? What effect will it have on your career if you cannot or will not relocate? Relocation is frequently necessary if you want to get ahead. Think about when it might be a necessity for you and plan ahead for it.

Your chances for professional success can be greatly enhanced if you analyze thoroughly what you expect to happen in the future, and if you anticipate the events and forces you're likely to encounter. Then you can decide how best to deal with them and fit them into your career plans.

5

THE DUAL-
CAREER COUPLE

Clearly defined roles in society can be very efficient. There is a strong resistance to changing these patterns even when the pattern doesn't fit new requirements. And, whether you share them or not, society's values *do* exist. Acting contrary to traditional roles and values exacts its price—often a very high one.

Most professional women who hold middle and senior professional positions are married or sharing their lives with a companion partner. Usually these partners are fully embarked on their own career paths. Here lies a whole new generation of problems that are only now beginning to be looked at.

Until recently, both partners in a marriage combined their efforts to assist the career of the husband. The wife remained at home providing a smoothly functioning base for her husband: doing the cooking, cleaning, shopping, laundry, entertaining, and taking care of the children. She participated in community activities, yet was home to listen and support her husband when needed. She often spent eighty or more hours a week on these efforts; in many marriages, she still does.

But as the number of educated and employed women continues to increase, the number of couples involved in dual careers will also increase. It has often been said that "every professional needs a good wife." Where's that support to come from in a dual-career situation? How is the running of the household to be accomplished? What other problems will arise?

Lillian has a highly satisfying position and is the senior woman in her field. Her husband just received an extremely good job offer from a firm on the other coast of the United States. If he accepts it, how will this affect their marriage?

Alicia's mother-in-law is an invalid and will have to come to live with them. This will require their moving to a larger apartment. How will it be possible to make time to look for a new place to live and do all the work involved in moving? Who will be able to look after the patient, who requires a great deal of help?

Jeannette always wanted to own a home of her own. Her husband is opposed to this because of the work involved, and preferred a small apartment in the city. She has just seen her dream house in the country. Her salary is more than adequate to purchase this house, and it would also provide tax savings. Should she buy it on her own?

Just two months away from being awarded her M.B.A., Rosemarie is appalled to discover that all the positions for which she is really suited are located away from her husband. "I'm not sure our relationship will survive a weekend marriage," she laments.

"Jessica is never home when I need to talk to her," Harry complains. "I really wonder why I got married at all. When she's home, she's too tired to talk—let alone make love."

Marion has just bought a home with her partner in Denver, where he works and where she expected to be transferred. Instead, she is transferred to San Diego. How much time do they need together to keep a mutually rewarding relationship and how will they arrange this time? How can they both find rewarding careers in the same city, preferably Denver, where they now own a house?

Entirely new forces are at work in these situations. As recently as twenty years ago, in the fifties, there was little difficulty about what would happen in each case. The woman in the partnership would forgo her career interests and aspirations in favor of her partner, or defer to his opinion in major decisions.

Times are changing very rapidly, but perhaps not as quickly as it may seem. Studies conducted in the late seventies show that many women still subordinate their career aspirations to the needs of their husbands and families. For example, women professors have frequently been shown to work fewer hours, publish less, and have fewer people working for them than their husbands. A study appearing in the May 1977 issue of the *Journal of Marriage and the Family* showed that in 200 marriages between professional psychologists the "women were willing to place their careers secondary to (a) the needs of their families and (b) the needs of their husbands' careers."

But are they *willing*—or is it because of society's underlying expectations? An earlier study, appearing in the *American Psychologist* in January 1976, concluded that "wives are more willing to make sacrifices for their husbands' careers than they *expect* their husbands to make for them."

An article in the book, *Women in the Organization,* edited by Harold Frank, reveals that the number of professional couples requesting counseling or individual psychotherapy has increased fifteenfold between 1970 and 1975. This article (prepared by Ellen Berman, Sylvia Sacks, and Harold Lief of the Marriage Council of Philadelphia) further states that "women professionals have a higher divorce rate than the general population." They state that the "two professional marriage is one at risk."

AVOIDING THE PENALTIES

In order to minimize the stresses and strains of a dual-career marriage, it is essential for both members of the couple to face directly the disruptive issues at work in the relationship. These issues arise from many sources: too many roles to be played simultaneously, too many demands on time and energy, too many new problems to be resolved.

There are so many new problems and situations facing the dual-career couple that not only are viable answers not known, but also most people in dual-career marriages haven't even yet begun to realize what questions must be asked.

An excellent illustration of this is the effect on a marriage of the partners living in different cities; they each pursue their careers during the week, and they meet only on weekends, or perhaps even less frequently. What effect will this have on their relationship? How much time is necessary—as a minimum—for people to continue a mutually satisfying relationship? How will this life-style affect them?

Since corporate upward mobility often requires relocation, marital dislocation is one of the newest problems arising from a dual-career relationship. Unless one partner is willing to have his or her career aspirations take second place to the other's, a commuting marriage is apt to result.

THE NEW COMMUTERS' MARRIAGE

Edward, who lives in Chicago, has just been offered a job in Boston. His eyes sparkle whenever he discusses it, despite the problems he knows it will create for his wife's successful career in finance and their situation as a couple. The fact that his career takes him in one direction while hers takes her in another will probably begin to be more the rule than the exception in any marriage of two professionals.

No one really knows what is the minimum time necessary to continue a relationship of intimacy that is satisfactory to both partners. Different couples involved in such a relationship have different answers to the dilemma of separation.

Betsy's husband of a few years lives several thousand miles from where she has established a vital, expanding consulting business. Her life-style choice is to be with him three or four days a week and work twelve hours a day on the other days. This means she has to take an all-night flight once a week. "It may shorten my life," she admits, "but I'm enjoying such a complete existence that it's worth it. I have the best of both worlds."

Bernie must live near his work because his engineering job requires irregular shifts. His wife can't stand daily commuting to her job, so she has a small apartment in the nearby large city. She commutes home on weekends, and he commutes to the city if his weekend is scheduled to be other than Saturday and Sunday. Bernie's wife says this life-style requires them to make certain adjustments. "We've learned to allow each other re-entry time. We don't

discuss controversial or even important issues until we've been together for twenty-four hours. We talk on the phone every day to
keep up on trivia. After all, real relationships are made up of lots
of mundane incidents in between the few very precious moments
of real sharing and real togetherness."

Wilma has a full-time position traveling throughout the United
States. Fortunately for both of them, her husband is located in a
major city. She bargained with her employer for four days off
every other week in the city where her husband is located, plus the
plane fare. "We've got to be together at least four days in a row to
maintain a satisfying relationship. As long as we have four days
together at a time, it doesn't matter so much how much time has
elapsed between our getting together—though we'd like to keep
those intervals as short as possible."

Many single-career marriages survive on weekend relationships.
The husband departs on Monday not to return (physically or psychologically) until the following Friday. Two-career marriages
may be even better suited to this pattern since both partners are
deeply involved in their work and often prefer no diversion. Fifty-
two honeymoon periods a year is not so bad! The crucial factor
may be the ability of both partners to leave the cares, stress, and
depressive factors of their work week behind and just enjoy companionship, renewal, and refreshment.

Diane and Winifred have a thriving, nationwide business. Winifred says, "I never take a briefcase with me when I return home
for the weekend. It stays at my office, which is about an hour's
commute by air. Diane and I share an apartment in Chicago near
our office so that we can work long and effective hours when we
work, and also eliminate the need for packing and unpacking,
which we both regard as an unnecessary use of time. This way I'm
completely free to enjoy my husband and children on weekends.
Fortunately, I have an ideal housekeeper, and my children are old
enough to take a great deal of responsibility. Frankly, I think they
enjoy not having a 'smother' mother."

Not everyone is able to handle the fatigue and stress of constant
travel and of living in two places at once. Are you? What do you
and your partner need for a comfortable, happy, supportive, and
satisfactory relationship?

ALL WORK AND NO PLAY

For the dual-career couple, there is never enough time. Your time is a very precious resource. It has to be used wisely, and that requires understanding how you are now using it—and how you would prefer to use it.

"I like my husband and I enjoy being with him. I'm careful to plan time together as often as possible," explains the wife of a busy civic official. She herself works five long days each week, plus about half a day on Saturday and Sunday.

As strange as it seems for two people living together, if they are fully involved in their careers, it is often necessary to schedule *pleasurable* time together. Too often, togetherness of dual-career couples is dictated solely by their having to face and solve mutual problems.

One busy couple schedules one lunch together each week to face difficult issues. This may not be good for the digestion, but it eases tension on weekends.

Managing Your Time

Time for yourself must not be left out of your scheduling. Too often this critical element in leading a balanced life is the first to go when life is overloaded with commitments. It is essential for the busy career person to have personal time for exercise, for thinking, and for just doing nothing.

Effective use of time requires understanding where time is now being spent and planning ahead to spend it where you would prefer to, and also where you must. Every possible timesaving device must be used, such as employing all the outside help you can find, handling each piece of paper only once, listing special tasks and who is responsible for them, and eliminating unnecessary chores. All this is done in the interest of freeing up maximum time for yourself and your spouse. It will also allow you to fit in some time with friends.

Finding Time for Friends

If a dual-career couple seeks out friends as a couple, it is most often with other couples who are also involved in a two-professional marriage. More and more often, groups are being formed where couples can spontaneously share mutual problems and solutions to these problems. Sometimes these groups even organize themselves with leaders or facilitators.

One of the major difficulties of friendships between two or more dual-career couples is that of scheduling. Since all parties are so busy, social engagements often have to be scheduled weeks or even months in advance, removing the pleasure of the get-together and adding pressure to everyone's life.

One happy solution occurs in a neighborhood where almost all husbands and wives are careerists. There is a neighborhood club that gives informal parties about six times a year. It's not necessary to decide until almost the last moment whether you are going. This sort of gathering allows everyone to see friends and acquaintances in a relaxed setting, with a minimum of planning ahead.

Embodied in a few studies of career couples is the idea or expressed opinion that for them their neighborhood does not matter as much as for couples in which the wives stay home. With the rapid increase in number of dual-career marriages, this is probably no longer true. A neighborhood populated by many dual-career couples will contain people who are understanding, cooperative, and supportive of each other. In that type of area, various civic and other volunteer functions that were formerly handled by the nonworking wife will now have to go to paid professionals or be split with a greater degree of equality between the husbands and wives.

"I don't want to have any additional pressure on my wife, who is both working and going to school for a graduate degree," Stan declares. "I've taken on the local chairmanships in her place, and our social life is very informal. On weekends, when we both have energy left and feel like doing something, we call one or two couples whom we like . . . on the spur of the moment. If we have any takers, we all go out to a restaurant. This doesn't require any work or any planning. If no one else wants to go, we happily end up with a spontaneous and romantic evening for two."

Undoubtedly, as the dual-career marriage becomes more widespread, this sort of sharing will increase. In the meantime, the wife in this situation needs all the help she can get, and she can often get it from other women who are facing the same problems.

One convenient way to have friendships you are able to maintain is to look for friends where you work. This usually happens naturally, since you share so many experiences with those you work with and it's easier to find time to be together without taking time away from your spouse. But not all these friendships are between women. They are often between men and women who share common interests.

And often the factor of sex does enter into the dual-career couple's understanding and handling of these outside heterosexual friendships. It is often quite threatening to the husband for his wife to have men friends. She well may have her husband's "permission" to pursue a career, but this does not always cover friendships with men, even though they may help her in her career. This is one of the many areas where mixed values and feelings complicate an already ambiguous situation. Here, as elsewhere, it is wise to discuss the situation straightforwardly and to set up the guidelines, which obviously apply to the husband as well as to the wife.

Frequently, the problem encountered is not one of a potential sexual relationship—an implicit possibility in any heterosexual relationship—it is really a practical matter of time away that causes the unhappiness. "I really don't understand why you have to have dinner with Jim (or Jill) tonight when we haven't had a chance to talk to each other for a week," is very stressful to hear when you have a knotty business problem that requires immediate attention, and the only time available to you and Jim (or Jill) is tonight over a quick business dinner. Here is a typical example of conflicting roles between the needs of your business life and the needs of your spouse. This situation is equally as likely to occur for either party; the major difference is that the husband has rarely been expected to put his wife's needs for attention and companionship ahead of the demands of his work. What happens when the situation is reversed? Is the wife free to put her professional needs first?

Both partners may already be under pressure because of commuting demands, too much work and career striving, and just not enough time to relax and enjoy each other's company. Business demands are constantly pulling them away from one another. It is vitally important that dual-career couples find time to be with each other in a relaxed and enjoyable setting.

"Each year we vacation at the same place and I go into complete neutral," explains a senior manager. "I hardly talk to anyone other than my husband. The other people we see there don't even know I work, let alone what I do."

"We spend several four- or five-day weekends a year at a small house we own in the Caribbean," says another woman who has her own business. "We just want to be together away from all of the pressures and get reacquainted; a tropical setting is perfect for us."

"Weekends are for the kids, and we try to do family activities like skiing, but every so often my husband and I go off for a weekend together at a nearby resort that we are very fond of." This is the way of life chosen by another much-traveled woman executive.

If you are a woman professional, demands on your time and energy are made not only by your job and your spouse. Most working women have families to contend with as well.

FAMILY PRESSURES

The whole topic of combining motherhood and career will be dealt with in the next chapter of being a professional woman and mother. But most people also have immediate and extended families who need them, not taking into consideration any children of their own.

Pressures from family responsibility and relationships create conflicts because it is hard for your family to adjust to your role and time demands, especially if the mothers and mothers-in-law involved have never worked outside the home.

Helen's family is very close, and the family members all live within blocks of each other. Since Helen has taken a full-time position, her mother complains that she never sees her. Helen's sister, who had been very dependent on her for companionship and intellectual stimulation, is constantly voicing the same complaint. They are both right. Helen no longer has the time and energy to be as supportive of her family as she formerly was.

It is hard for family members to understand the time pressures, particularly on a career wife. Alienation from the family because of lack of leisure time can cause added pain and guilt to an already taxed professional. Some of these problems can be eased with explanation, some just have to be lived with, and some can be resolved by new types of solutions.

Louise lived hundreds of miles from her parents. She was accustomed to spending her vacation with them once a year. After she married, neither she nor her husband wanted to spend their extremely short two-week annual vacation visiting her relatives, but neither did Louise want to miss seeing her aging parents. Together Louise and her husband decided that two long weekends a year would be devoted to Louise's parents. Her husband would go along on one trip; Louise would go alone on the second. Their relatively comfortable financial situation as a two-wage-earning family makes several expensive plane trips a reasonable expense for them.

What about the demands on time and energy in running a home? How does the dual-career couple handle the day-to-day needs of their household, without suffering role conflicts?

ROLE CONFLICTS AT HOME

There seems to be little dispute that the burdens of the household fall more heavily on the dual-career wife. What to do about it is another matter.

Dr. Ellen Berman, psychiatrist and professor at the University of Pennsylvania Medical School, has developed a helpful way of analyzing each dual-career marriage (originally identified by Rhona and Robert Rapoport) in order to see what patterns are being followed. The relationships of two-career couples are divided into the following categories: Traditional, Neo-traditional, Matriarchal, and Egalitarian.

1. Traditional

In the traditional type of dual-career marriage, the wife handles her career and takes virtually full care of the home as well. Harold Frank, in his book *Women in the Organization,* characterizes this as a woman with "one full-time job—her career—and another more-than-full-time job, managing the household." The wife's career takes second place to that of her husband. If relocation is required, she pulls up roots and follows him. If family demands create a need for someone at home, full- or part-time, it is she who gives up her career aspirations.

In the late sixties, Margaret Poloma studied fifty-three married couples where the wife was a professional in law, medicine, or college teaching. Virtually all of these women handled the strain of conflicting roles by reducing their aspirations and by compromise.

The dual-career wife in a "traditional" relationship typically either takes care of the cleaning herself, or, if she is willing and able to hire cleaning help, she sees to their hiring and supervision. She organizes the couple's social life, and it is often extremely active. A recent article in the New York *Times* described such a superwife creating a dinner for sixty-five guests. Another one reupholsters and refinishes her furniture, at the same time she is providing candlelit, gourmet dinners each evening for her husband.

Admittedly, such superachievers do exist, but this kind of pressure on mere mortals can and frequently does cause severe stress symptoms. For this reason, many dual-career marriages are evolving into a "neo-traditional" relationship.

2. Neo-traditional

In the neo-traditional relationship, perhaps the most significant factor is that both partners explicitly agree that the wife's career is important, possibly equally as important as the husband's. The husband is supportive and proud of his wife's accomplishments.

It has been shown that, based on a 112-hour week, the traditional dual-career wife spends 105 hours working on the job and in her home. This is obviously not possible for most women involved in ongoing relationships and demanding careers.

Many—but far from all—husbands have been gradually assuming tasks in dual-career marriages to the extent that these chores can be identified, the wife is willing and able to relinquish them, and the husband is willing to take them on. Usually the neo-traditional couple is trying to figure out how to restructure their roles in order to find a more equitable division of labor. Often the husband takes on some chores and feels quite good about it—even noble—as he does the weekly shopping or prepares the Monday-night dinner. He feels that he is shouldering a good portion of the work in the home. Ask the wife about his degree of participation in the home, however, and she'll say, "He's very good about helping with the grocery shopping and he'll cook several times during the week, but I've usually got to prepare the shopping list and clean up the kitchen."

The underlying factor at work here is that the husband is magnanimously taking on some of his wife's socially prescribed duties in order to *let* her work. Embodied deeply is the idea of permission to work—the husband is allowing his wife to work and is helping her do this by taking on a few of her duties in the home. He frequently receives sympathy from well-wishing friends for being tolerant of having a professional wife and for taking on some of her burden. Still, it's better for her than trying to do it all herself, and the issues are addressed fairly realistically, although the husband usually takes more credit than the wife would—in fact —give him.

3. Matriarchal

In some couples, a complete role-switch takes place. In this situation, especially among older married couples, the woman either has outdistanced her husband, or the husband's career has burned out entirely.

Matriarchal marriage was quite common in the fifties for the somewhat deviant woman who was an outstanding professional success and who often married late in life. It was the rare male who could tolerate even a neo-traditional type of relationship, and it was and still is practically impossible to reach the top of the heap if you are involved in a traditional type of marriage.

In the matriarchal marriage, it is clearly spelled out—both between the couple themselves and to the outside society—that the wife's career takes precedence. The wife's personal and professional needs come first in an effort to give her something like the support a man receives in the stereotypical one-career marriage, where the husband is the breadwinner.

The "matriarchal" life-style is sometimes consciously chosen by younger couples, and the relatively new role of "house-husband" has come about. Most often the husband is a creative person, perhaps a writer or a painter, and he is freer to pursue his talents with a steady income provided by his wife. In exchange, he takes charge of the home. Formerly the wife in such a marriage might have taken merely a job from time to time to supplement their income; now she is actively pursuing a career.

4. Egalitarian

Theoretically, the optimum solution to a dual-career marriage is an equal partnership where gender-related task division is reduced to an absolute minimum.

An enterprising pair of university professors listed every single task they could conceive of with regard to their home and life together. First, they discussed all the chores and crossed off tasks that neither of them cared about. For example, they discovered that making the bed in the morning didn't matter at all to either of them. Next, they delegated everything to someone else where they would be able to find and pay an outsider to do the work. Then, they bargained with each other to take the tasks that they personally abhorred. (Washing the dishes usually falls into this category, as does emptying the trash and cleaning the cat's box, or walking the dog.) Once the emotionally charged duties were disposed of, they equitably divided the remaining work. This method of attack on household chores and other unproductive, recurring duties has proven very effective for them, although they did mention that a semiannual review and renegotiation kept the egalitarian pathway operating without resentment building up.

One couple, both lawyers, decided each would only work part-time so that they could be home together more of the time. This way, necessary and leisure activities were enjoyable for both of them. Together they decided to lower their career aspirations in favor of other values.

Not every couple is able to—nor wishes to—strive for an egalitarian marriage. Furthermore, it is difficult, if not impossible, to cast off all the cultural conditioning to which each partner has been subjected.

Research for the Berman article on "The Two-Professional Marriage" indicated that "underlying the overt illusion of an equal relationship is a covert traditional stance, that is, a superior, strong male, and a more helpless, dependent female." As the wife acquires her professional status, she "still demands unconsciously that her husband be her superior (her old conditioning) while consciously she expects him to be an equal (her new ideal)." She places her husband and herself in a double bind that often requires counseling to identify and resolve.

Add to this the fact that even the most egalitarian of husbands usually finds that, as he moves up the ladder, his needs and expectations change. Frequently he begins to see the usefulness of a wife who is at home most of the time looking after his needs. Because the egalitarian marriage is quite a change in societal patterns, frequent renegotiation of roles is usually needed. Otherwise the changing situations and changing expectations can become the basis for feelings of resentment and competition.

Resentment and Responsibility

Whenever the wife feels she is bearing an unfair amount of the household responsibility, or the husband is asked to do things that he believes his wife should be taking care of, feelings of resentment begin to build up. One very effective way of looking at the problems of the recurring chores that must be performed in every marriage is to analyze the social and household tasks in terms of the underlying responsibility and the chore itself. Every job has two components: the work itself and the responsibility for seeing that the work gets done.

It is not unlike being a manager or a worker in an organization. The manager decides what has to be done, and administers the task. Sometimes the managers must do the job themselves; sometimes they delegate the chore to a worker. But, even in the latter case, the manager sees to it that the job is satisfactorily completed.

In a two-professional marriage, the grounds for potential conflict are obvious. In the first place, you have two managers involved, both of whom are probably used to delegating. In the second place, most of the management responsibility for the couple's family, social, and home life falls on the woman's shoulders.

While the husband may actually be the one who mows the lawn and puts out the garbage, if the wife feels compelled to check to see if these jobs are done and reminds her husband to do them, she is taking the responsibility, even though he is doing the chores.

Tasks are relatively easy to accomplish, especially when someone else takes the responsibility for seeing that they are carried out. Tasks take little emotional energy and cause little stress. They can be set aside or forgotten. People who take or are given the responsibility for something will rarely forget it. They will make time to do it or see that someone else does it.

As a joint owner of a piece of income property, Claudine looked over the house twice annually to see what had to be done to maintain it properly. She then asked her husband to do the required painting and repairs, or hired someone when her husband couldn't spare the time. She considered this joint undertaking a very onerous burden but didn't understand why, since her husband was both willing and able to do a very large share of the work. It wasn't until she understood the concept of responsibility as distinct from the actual chores that she realized why she so resented her share in the work on the house. It was she who worried if the plumbing repairs were not completed, if the roof leaked, or if the rent checks were late. It was she who balanced the books on the property and had to face the I.R.S. audits.

No matter who handles the chores, *responsibility* is still most often divided along fairly stereotyped sex-role lines. Even in a neo-traditional or a matriarchal type of relationship, a disproportionate amount falls to the wife.

Marital arguments frequently center on the chore itself, without the couple's looking at who shoulders the responsibility. Once this distinction is understood, these confrontations can prove more productive. One of the great advantages of marriage is that there are two people working at it. Theoretically, each can take half the responsibility and do half of the chores. Dividing up the business of life with an eye toward R&C (responsibility and chore) can be a giant step toward more equitable distribution of both the work and the stress involved.

A word of advice to dual-career wives is in order here. Once you give up the responsibility for a chore, don't keep checking on it. This is a natural tendency among executives, and it is a sure way to get the responsibility right back again. It is not easy for two people who are used to controlling situations to give up some measure of control. This is especially true of those responsibilities which have traditionally been the wife's. Competition for control, as well as competition to avoid responsibility, will continue to exist, and renegotiation of both chores and the responsibility for carrying them out will have to be done from time to time.

COMPETITION

Competition in dual-career marriages exists not only for control of various family duties, decisions, and responsibilities, but also usually (overtly or covertly) in the striving for professional success.

Two practicing lawyers were asked how their marriage might be affected if the wife became nationally known. The husband answered, "I don't think it would affect our relationship, and I know that it's likely to happen." Later in the same discussion group, he was asked the same question, but it was phrased more specifically: "It looks like your wife is going to appear regularly on television and the lecture platform. Does that bother you at all?"

"You know," he replied, "it might attack my ego somewhat."

His second answer is probably closer to the truth than the first one. It is sad but true that when the husband's position as chief breadwinner is threatened by his wife's accomplishment, most men's self-images suffer. It is especially true if her income exceeds his. Since professional women tend to marry professional men, there is a good chance for her to equal or outdistance his accomplishments—particularly where she is not willing to take the secondary role professionally.

A study done in 1977 by the Population Reference Bureau of 22,335 families showed that 7 per cent of the wives earned perceptibly more than their husbands, 3.5 per cent earned slightly more, and 9.5 per cent earned about the same—making a total of more than 20 per cent of the women who earned the same as or more than their husbands. This situation will probably become more common.

It is greatly to be hoped that men and women alike learn that when one member of the pair gains, the other does not necessarily lose. But money and the ability to earn it have long been inextricably intertwined with self-esteem. The men involved may be concerned that their marriage relationship is headed toward a matriarchal one, with or without their consent. According to Rhona and Robert Rapoport, pioneer researchers in the area of dual-career marriage, it takes "a husband who is either very strong or very identified with the efforts of his wife to allow her to equal or exceed his own accomplishment without major disruption in the relationship."

Dual-Career Paths

Whether or not the marriage of two professionals results in problems directly related to their work depends largely on how their two careers relate. They may have careers that are parallel, competitive, disparate, or joint.

A parallel relationship is one in which two people are involved in similar fields, but are going down separate and divergent tracks. This is often a very synergistic setup if each person respects the other's professional opinions. Competitive relationships exist when both are in medical school or residencies together or pursuing careers in the same field.

Disparate dual careers occur when the professional interests of the couple have no common ground whatsoever. This makes it a little difficult to discuss the intricacies of the job, but that may sometimes be a blessing in disguise—especially when you consider the strains of a joint dual career, where the husband and wife are working together, perhaps as owners of the same business or as coauthors or coresearchers.

Gregory and Elizabeth had a fairly smooth marriage while they were engaged in parallel careers. They both respected—and were greatly helped by—the opinions of the other. Eventually Gregory started his own business with Elizabeth as partner. They found nothing but unending disagreement and stress right from the start. Their styles of management, of administration, and of problem solving were so very different. Fortunately for their marriage, they returned to parallel careers and are once again mutually supportive.

More than one medical school graduate found she was Mrs./Dr. Jonas upon entering a residency with her husband. "Under no circumstances would I consider a residency where my husband is, and I will choose a field of specialization other than his choice. We've been competitive enough in school," states a third-year student. "I want my own separate identity as a doctor. I don't think I could do this if I work at the same hospital with my husband."

Stuart couldn't bring his engineering problems home to his wife, who was a stockbroker, because she didn't understand them. This often frustrated him because the problems he encountered could have benefited from discussing them with her, but it was a situation he had learned to live with. Although it seemed somewhat easier for his wife to discuss her problems with him, since they were most often problems involving people; in reality, Stuart wasn't interested in the finer points of interpersonal relations. He'd rather concentrate on technical matters. Not much sharing of professional problems and day-to-day experiences on the job took place in this marriage.

Nicole and her husband both had Ph.D.s in the same field and decided to combine their research efforts in order to make some real breakthrough efforts in the field of microbiology. The strain of working and living together, and her resentment at his being given the larger share of credit for their work, eventually led to discomfort in their marriage and, ultimately, a divorce. He ended up with a professorship in his field, and she ended up unemployed.

Many universities still have written or unwritten antinepotism clauses that can work undue hardship on one spouse or the other, since college towns are frequently located off the beaten track. But, working and living together is an extraordinarily difficult thing to do while still remaining friends and lovers. Yet, where it works, it is invariably characterized by the couple as the ideal way to live.

WHO'S INVOLVED IN A TWO-PROFESSIONAL MARRIAGE?

Successful and striving career people have certain similarities. They are usually highly intelligent, possess a lot of energy, and tend to be perfectionists. They have drive and determination and demand a lot of themselves and of others. They are highly motivated and seek self-realization and power.

What happens when two such people meet and decide to make a deep emotional commitment to each other? Sometimes a great deal of conflict. Professional people are used to being assertive and controlling. When they can't control a situation, their first reaction is to become even more assertive, which can produce a very noisy relationship. If this doesn't work, or if people do not like to become controlling, or to be controlled, much anxiety is produced.

This anxiety produces symptoms not unlike those caused by overloading: fatigue, irritability, unsatisfactory sexual relations, and constant battles about issues other than those which are probably the real problems. It is necessary for dual-career couples to carry out continual reassessment of family roles and individual identities, as well as to define clearly who should hold the emotional responsibility for various power situations in the family.

OVERLOADING

Reassessment is essential not only for avoiding conflict, but to prevent undue strain caused by too many roles and too many responsibilities. More often than not, overloading affects the wife.

Overloading can cause severe stress symptoms in addition to those listed for anxiety, such as asthma, difficulty in sleeping, eczema, appetite change, excessive drinking and smoking, and decreased libido and loss of sexual interest. Often the symptoms are self-treated or are handled by a physician with tranquilizers or a prescription for a vacation; but the underlying causes remain, and the symptoms will reappear until the career couple examines the foundations of the stress and takes steps to alleviate it.

Rapoport and Rapoport have helpful suggestions to avoid overload. They recommend that dual-career professionals:

1. Plan leisure so that they have holidays and breaks in their routine on a regular basis.

2. Delegate as many routine household tasks as possible to others. Rearrange other domestic duties more equitably.

3. Work somewhat less. Almost everyone shows fewer hours on his ideal work schedule than on his actual schedule. It is usually constructive to the marriage to make an effort in this direction.

REWARDS AND SATISFACTIONS

This chapter has dealt at great length with the pitfalls and problems of a two-professional relationship. Fortunately, that is only part of the story.

There are great rewards and a very satisfactory life-style to be enjoyed when two adults have worked through their personal and professional conflicts. Perhaps the very best partner is someone who has a healthy sense of who he or she is, someone who has ample opportunity for creativity and self-expression.

Another great advantage of a dual-career marriage which cannot be underestimated is adequate income. Usually two professional people working full-time can produce a comfortable income which relieves the economic strain felt by so many single-earner families in this period of rampant inflation.

While the two-career marriage may be at a somewhat greater risk than the single-career one, since it is still flying in the face of social norms, the rewards often prove to be greater as well. And a happy marriage is something that can develop between two people or deteriorate—whether or not the wife is a career professional.

Marital happiness has never been totally defined, but many characteristics have been identified. A good marriage usually embraces a mutuality of goals and should provide continuing satisfaction to each partner. Marriage is fundamentally a relationship between two people who like each other and enjoy each other's company. It is the continuing intimacy of shared experiences, punctuated by occasional golden moments of spiritual, intellectual, and sexual meetings. Perhaps these moments are even more precious and intense for the Dual-Career Couple.

6

THE PROFESSIONAL MOTHER

Until recently, one of the few socially acceptable occupations for women was that of full-time mother. Now that a significant number of women are pursuing a career outside their homes, and many professional women are also choosing to become mothers, many women are combining what are essentially two full-time occupations—in addition to being a partner and companion to their spouses.

Despite the difficulties involved in combining motherhood and a career, almost without exception, women interviewed for this book who chose to become mothers would not have lived their lives in any other way than to experience both the joys of parenthood and the rewards gained from professional achievement.

In this chapter we will look at some of the issues for those couples who do not already have children and who are considering the possibility. Then we'll look at some of the problems of people who are already parents and how this has affected their careers. At the same time we will present some suggestions of how successful women have been able to combine satisfactorily the roles of manager, mother, and wife.

SHOULD YOU BECOME PARENTS?

If you desire to combine the roles of wife, mother, and professional successfully, you and your husband will need to examine your situation thoughtfully and carefully. You will need to have a very clear understanding of both your personal and professional priorities, which will be put to some extreme tests once you become a parent. You will also need to be aware of and anticipate the problems of combining these often-conflicting roles. With a clear understanding of your priorities and an awareness of some of the problems, you will then be able to plan effectively for parenthood in an effort to lessen its negative impact on your career performance.

The question of whether to have a child confronts most women and most couples at one time or another. It is a difficult question for anyone to answer at any time. The decision is one that will profoundly affect the rest of your life: it will change your marriage, your way of viewing the world, and your whole orientation toward the future. The ramifications of this decision are particularly complex for a woman who has committed herself to a career. We will examine the effects of parenthood in this chapter largely from the point of view of its impact on career women who also *choose* to be mothers.

Until recently, most persons had children because it was the social prescribed thing to do and, until contraception became widespread, they had little choice. Even into the sixties, few couples questioned whether to have children. Often, since birth-control methods were less than fully effective, even the timing of parenthood was removed from their hands. *Becoming* a parent was perhaps easier in the unplanned past. *Being* a parent may be more rewarding now that it's a matter of choice.

No matter how cooperative your husband may be, it's your life that gets reordered to the greatest extent when a baby comes. Primary child-care still falls most heavily on the woman's shoulders. The belief that "children will suffer unless they are cared for by their mothers" is one of society's strongest fiats. The fact of the matter is that *someone* must take care of a child, and adequate—much less excellent—parent surrogates are hard to find.

A Conjugal Summit Conference

In her book, *A Baby . . . Maybe,* Dr. Elizabeth Whelan points out that "the constellation of motivations that may precipitate a pregnancy is extraordinarily complex, characterized by an intricate network of rational and non-rational components." In an attempt to get at as many rational components as possible, Dr. Whelan suggests a variety of issues to include in what she terms the "conjugal summit conference." These include:

1. Consider all the available options.
2. Anticipate the impact a child will have on your lives.
3. Think about your own particular needs and circumstances. It's your decision—not your parents', not society's.
4. Talk to as many couples as possible about their experiences of being parents or being child-free.
5. Think about children at all ages and the problems of each age: infancy, childhood, and adolescence.
6. Consider how you view parenthood and why. Do you see it as an enrichment or a burden?
7. Think about how you will accept the ambivalence of a decision—either way you make it. How will you handle these consequences?

There are some additional issues that must be explored in depth by the professional woman if she plans to continue her upward striving in her career. These issues are:

1. What impact do you expect pregnancy, birth, and parenthood to have on your career? On your husband's career?
2. When might a pregnancy be timed to cause the minimum personal and career stress?
3. Specifically, how do you and your husband plan to rearrange your lives to provide optimum care for your child while you continue your career plan, assuming an affirmative decision?

The end result of the summit conference should be to make a decision for or against parenthood for a period of time, leaving the issue free to be raised again by either partner. It is not easy to choose either to undertake the extraordinary demands of parenthood, nor is it easy to decide to miss one of life's major experiences.

PLANNED PARENTHOOD

With the inevitability of unexpected events brought about by becoming a parent, one of the most essential elements in attempting to combine successfully a career and motherhood is *planning*. Every aspect of the situation that can be controlled needs to be, since so much is likely to occur that is beyond your control. Timing your parenting years, relative to the demands of various stages of your career development, is part of this planning, as is the spacing of your children and the decision as to how many children you will have. Anticipating the fact that you will probably need help in your home if you choose to have a child and continue a career, and specifically looking for ways to obtain this help is another essential planning step toward achieving professional and parental objectives realistically.

Timing

Career mothers who seem to have the least difficult time are those women who had established their careers before adding the commitment of parenthood to their lives. By waiting until they had built a solid professional base, they also had the benefit of a larger income, a more established marital relationship, and the advantage of greater maturity. I'd advise a young woman to find herself both personally and professionally before becoming a mother. I've never felt the resentment I've seen in so many women who had children when they were very young. They seem to feel that their children have prevented them from doing so many things. I had a chance to gain a great deal of experience before becoming a mother.

The disadvantages of postponing childbearing is that, statistically, fertility rates decline with each passing year, so your chances of becoming pregnant decrease. Also, having a child is physically taxing both during pregnancy and for the years spent in infant and toddler care. Nature is easier on younger parents.

Compressing

Dedicated career women who also choose to be mothers frequently compress the childrearing years in addition to, or instead of, postponing them. Having children close together enables you to turn attention back to work sooner. It also avoids the problem of having children at different developmental stages at the same time. It's more efficient if they are doing about the same thing at the same time. You can find yourself very fragmented, as parents of mixed-developmental-age children are, between going to nursery-school meetings, Little League games, and taking a high-school-age child around to look at different colleges.

The disadvantages of compressing the child-producing years is that the workload of more than one infant is enormous. However, this disadvantage is somewhat reduced in proportion to the amount of help you are able to find.

An Only Child

Another means of combining motherhood and career aspirations more comfortably is the decision to have only one child. Until recently, when couples had only one child it was usually not by choice. With the serious entry of women into professions, having one child only is now sometimes becoming a consciously desired option.

Eleanor had waited until she was thirty to have her first child. Her education was completed, and her career was well established. When her daughter was a few years old, Eleanor's husband suggested that they have a second child. Eleanor weighed the impact that this would have on her career, based on her experience with her first child, and she made a proposal to her husband. She said she'd be glad to bear the second child if her husband would assume the major portion of the responsibility for the care of the child. *He* would have to plan to get up in the middle of the night, with the crying infant; he would have to see to the hiring and administration of the baby nurse and later the housekeeper; he would have to stay home if the help was ill and couldn't come.

Eleanor was not willing to divert her energy and attention to handle these details a second time. Her career was moving along at an exceptional pace after she had restarted it, and she didn't wish to get sidetracked again. In most families, this suggestion would be impossible to implement, although it is interesting to think about why and how a mother can be expected to do it and not the father. Eleanor's husband was a professional, with his own well-established business. He would have been able to make this commitment of time and energy. You won't be surprised to learn that he decided against it.

Ellen Peck, a founding member of the National Organization for Non-Parents, examines the advantages of having just one child in her book called *The Joy of the Only Child*. She points out that the reason most often given for having a second child is to "avoid having an only child." This does not seem to be a reason at all, in light of other information in her book, which shows that only children tend to be high achievers and that there is an inverse relationship between the number of children and family happiness. She points out that you "don't have to endure sibling rivalry," that "one child can be taken in stride and doesn't take over your life," and that "low fertility spells liberation for both spouses, bringing more control over their lives and futures."

Postponing children, compressing the childrearing years, and having an only child are some fairly new options that professional women are considering and successfully implementing. You may want to think about explicit timing.

PARENTING: LEARNING TO LIVE WITH THE UNEXPECTED

It is extremely difficult—if not impossible—to anticipate all the ways in which parenthood will affect you, your husband, your marriage, and your career. But a look at the experiences of other professional women may eliminate some of the unexpected consequences.

Probably the single most difficult aspect of pregnancy and early childhood parenting for career women is the lack of control that they are able to exert over their situations. Able women are skilled in controlling circumstances and expect to be able to do so. In pregnancy you are coping with many unknowns—things often do not work out the way you want and plan them to. Once you become pregnant, your body is no longer yours alone—there are other forces at work. There is no way to tell until you become pregnant just how much of an energy drain it will be for you or how your body will react. Most women are able to go more or less about their normal lives during pregnancy, but some find unexpected difficulties. When you become a parent, you and your husband take on the prime responsibility for another human being, whom you can only partially control.

Sally and her husband badly wanted a child. Time was running out on them—as Sally was in her mid-thirties—but after great difficulty in conceiving, she was overjoyed to find herself pregnant. She felt well and planned to continue her job as long as possible and to return to work shortly after the baby was born. Because she was extremely thorough and efficient, she had already found an excellent baby nurse. But the course of the pregnancy did not run smoothly, and, in her fourth month, Sally was told by her doctor that she was in danger of losing the baby unless she stayed off her feet. Even then it was not certain that she would be able to carry the baby to term. Between one day and the next, Sally turned from being a dynamic businesswoman, fully engrossed in her job, to being a bedridden patient. Can you imagine yourself in bed all day, every day, for months on end, while all the time feeling well? How would you occupy yourself? How would you feel about the necessity of being waited on by your husband and anyone else you could find to help?

It wasn't easy for Sally. She became an expert on the most intricate of jigsaw puzzles because she found she could read only for a certain number of hours each day. Her concerns alternated between whether she would indeed be able to have the baby and what was happening on her job, now that she had an enforced absence of six or seven months that hadn't been planned. The outcome for Sally was a happy one, personally—she had a healthy child. But her career never fully recovered its earlier momentum, partly due to her prolonged absence and partly due to another factor she had not anticipated: she found a change of attitude among the men who had formerly been championing her, now that she had become a working *mother*.

The Emotional Response to Motherhood

One of the most enlightening books about the impact on careers of having a baby is *The Balancing Act,* edited by Sydelle Kramer, in which five young women tell of their expectations of motherhood and the actual results after the arrival of the baby. Two of the women had twins, which really caused some unanticipated consequences.

In all five families, the preparenthood relationship was unusually egalitarian, with the chores and responsibilities of life equitably divided between husband and wife. No matter how hard the couples tried to maintain that balance after the arrival of the baby, in most cases, it just didn't appear to be realistic. It was clearly much more efficient for one parent to take the primary responsibility, and, for a variety of reasons, this naturally fell to the wife. One woman stated that her "emotional focus had begun to shift . . . toward motherhood." Another said that she had to "retreat from career into parenthood as a strategy for self-preservation." A third said that she became "completely immersed in baby care, the experience of pregnancy, birth, nursing, and adjusting to two babies."

None of these women had anticipated these results. Four of the five women settled for a reduced version of their career aspirations. The extent to which they were able to maintain careers at all was largely a result of their attitudes toward having help in caring for their children. Even in these five young women, who had very clear career goals, the tendency to believe they or their husbands had to do *all* the parenting appeared. They felt uncomfortable about having a parent substitute. One woman said she felt it was not quite "legitimate" to have live-in help. She felt she wasn't doing her duty as a mother. She was amazed at "how quickly traditional assumptions surfaced."

Another of the mothers stated that "family backgrounds convinced one to care for the child without help," and, for her now, "the role of mother predominates." A superwoman/supermom complex seemed to arise with the birth of the baby, despite the former egalitarian nature of these marriages. Even the woman who was able to turn the "major focus of mental attention" back to her career was uncomfortable when her husband's career needs forced them to have someone looking after their children more days than they themselves did.

The Course of Infant Care Never Runs Smooth

Almost all women attempting to combine motherhood and career find that, because of both the physical and psychological uncertainties and changes involved, motherhood demands a great deal more energy and attention than they had been able to anticipate—even in their wildest speculations.

Betty had planned to have her baby in January, during the slow time at work. The baby came early, and badly interfered with reports she had to complete in order to close the company's fiscal year, disrupting everyone's schedule. Betty had intended to return to work six weeks after the baby was born, enabling her to nurse the baby for the first few weeks, and then switch to bottle feeding. "After all, having a baby is a perfectly natural thing to do, and I'm very fit. The pregnancy has been not at all difficult," Betty stated prior to having the baby.

After the baby was born, Betty lamented as the six-week date for return to work drew near. "The last thing I'm ready to do right now is go back to work. I'm still tired from the birth of the baby—they don't call it labor for nothing. I'm worn out from never getting a decent night's sleep and from nursing. Even though the baby is sleeping pretty well, nobody ever told me that it takes an hour or so to feed the baby and then some more time to clean up. Just as I'm getting back to sleep, the baby is getting ready to wake up again. Even though it would be easier to have my husband give the baby a bottle in the middle of the night, letting me get one spell of sleep uninterrupted, I find I'm not ready to give up nursing yet. I seem to be full of all sorts of new ambivalences that I hadn't expected. Besides that, the house is in complete chaos. I don't have the energy to keep the kind of order we've been used to. Babies require a lot of equipment and make a lot of mess. All in all, I'm not ready to go back to work—but I have to if I want to keep up my professional momentum."

Victoria, another new mother and a corporate senior vice-president, experienced problems from an entirely different source. Her pregnancy and birth went off essentially as planned and hoped for. She had been at work the day before the baby was born, and she was eager to get back to work after six weeks at home. "I was used to the constant action and stimulation of events at work. Before the baby was born, I had hired someone both to care for the baby and do some light housework. I'd worked with her during the six weeks I was home, and I knew I had made a good choice. But just after I returned to work, she got a call from Germany to say her mother was very ill and she'd have to come home. She's leaving in a few days, and I'm frantically searching for someone. And I don't even know whether I'm looking for someone temporarily or permanently. I'd rather have my first woman back if she is able to return to the United States. Somehow I have this vision of myself, now that I've become a mother, spending the next fifteen years constantly searching for someone to replace me at home. I can't possibly do my work well when I'm worried about how my daughter is being cared for. It's so frustrating."

THE INTERRUPTED CAREER

The experience of many career mothers bears out the problems that Victoria was foreseeing: they were continuously concerned about some aspects of child care, particularly finding and keeping good helpers. For this reason, many women are forced to remain at home during the childrearing years. Many other women choose to stay home. Most people feel that no one else can take care of their child as well as they can, and others don't want to miss any of the pleasures of parenthood. In either event, it is often easier to do it yourself than to try to find an adequate replacement.

Even when the initial decision before having a child was that the mother and father would both continue to pursue their careers, this intention may have to be re-evaluated. What is the usual end result of this re-evaluation? In most cases, it is the mother who must adjust her career needs and expectations. Although there are cases where the father has chosen to remain at home, or where the couple is fortunate enough to be in a profession where they can share the child-raising responsibilities by sharing a career position or by each working part-time, these solutions are still relatively rare. It is generally the mother who must change her career plans.

Both economic and societal pressures exert force on the professional mother. Generally, the husband is out-earning his wife, and his long-term income expectation is higher than hers. While this may be less than fair, it still remains a fact. It makes better economic sense for the mother to be the one to work less or take a temporary leave of absence from her career. Furthermore, a woman can interrupt her career and re-establish it with fewer penalties than most men would suffer. It would be difficult to discover men in the business community today who interrupted their careers to care for their children for some years and then successfully returned to pursue a career to its fullest extent. Even where the father is the sole parent, he rarely can take time away from his career path if he is upwardly mobile. Until he retires, a man is expected to pursue his career uninterruptedly throughout his lifetime.

Women, on the other hand, are given approbation for accepting the responsibility of motherhood and staying home with their children. In fact, they feel a great deal of prejudice that they did not anticipate when they continued to work at a career after becoming a mother. Furthermore, it is assumed that you can't be so serious about your career once you become a mother because you now have other important obligations. Becoming a parent often enhances a man's image in the eyes of his employer as he becomes a "responsible family man"; the woman is more likely diminished when described as a "working mother." All these forces combine to discourage a woman from having a child, for her career will probably not reach its maximum potential.

There is apparently a professional penalty to be paid at present for taking more than a few weeks or at the most a few months off from the corporate environment. While legislation now requires companies to grant maternity leaves in most cases, this leave is of fairly short duration. And statistics show that women under forty who are moving up take only a minimum amount of time away from their careers when they have a child. A 1979 study of women corporate officers done by Heidrick and Struggles, a management consulting company, showed that even though 27.5 per cent of the women under forty were mothers, only 1.4 per cent of the total group had interrupted the continuity of their careers. By contrast, 17 per cent of the women over fifty had interrupted their careers for an extended time.

If you choose to interrupt your career to be a full-time parent for five or ten years, you probably will lessen your chances for obtaining a top-level job. The decision of whether and how long to interrupt a career is a very difficult one for many couples.

Carla had established herself professionally for fifteen years and then stopped working for two years and had two babies. "Six weeks after my second child was born, I started looking for the logical next career step, as I was blessed with lots of energy, healthy children, and first-rate help at home," Carla related. "Imagine my shock during the first few interviews when the prospective employers expressed concern over the fact that I had been out of the job market for two whole years. I couldn't decide whether that was their real reason, or whether they couldn't cope with the fact that I was returning to a career with two babies at home. You can be sure I didn't mention the children in the next interviews; I merely explained that I had left my last job and moved to a different area of the country because of my husband's job requirements. That's not an explanation guaranteed to get you the best job results, but at least it enabled me to get a job and get my career back on track.

"I do think that there was some genuine concern about my being away for two years as well. It really reinforced for me the fact that my husband and I had made the right decision about my returning to work. Imagine if I had stayed out for five or six years, until the children were in school, which we also seriously considered. I could never have made up the lost time."

It's difficult to get career momentum going again after a five-year break. Technological change takes place at an ever-accelerating rate in professions today. The knowledge gap is enormous and difficult to fill in. Even when that's been taken care of by part-time work or continuing education, there still is the loss of credibility as a dedicated professional that attends any amount of time out.

For the woman who takes ten or more years out of her career, another significant factor enters in. While she was gone, an entirely new generation of people entered the job market and moved up. She returns to work to find herself competing against able people who are succeeding, who are younger, and who don't have the handicap of some years away from work.

Two, five, or ten years is a long time in a highly competitive business environment. But at least it is still possible and acceptable for a woman to interrupt her career and resume it, particularly if she is willing to accept the fact that she may then not achieve her maximum professional potential. This is a penalty many women have to pay in exchange for the pleasures of parenthood. It is almost impossible not to have to take some time out of career striving after becoming a mother because of the difficulties of combining the conflicting roles and because of the many uncertainties that cannot be anticipated. Perhaps after more women achieve senior positions, some changes can be made that will enable both men and women to be full-time parents for a period of years and still achieve their career potential.

WHAT DO CHILDREN NEED?

The First Five Years

Kay's daughter seemed to respond well to the person who came to take care of her while Kay went to school for a professional degree. After she completed the degree, Kay took a full-time position, and within a few weeks her three-year-old began to display some serious personality problems. Apparently, at this stage of development, the child could not tolerate her mother's being gone all day every day. Kay had to take a leave of absence from her job and stay home for a while. Gradually, she was able to return to work part-time, starting with two days a week and then three. Kay's career was substantially affected by this.

The first five years of a child's life constitute a definite time during which it is especially difficult to find a parent substitute. Not only does the child require physical tending and protection, but he or she also needs a great deal of love and attention in order to mature normally and happily. Often child-care help provides the physical care, but is not willing or able to provide enough warmth and affection at the same time.

The needs for togetherness are not limited to the child's need for the parent. Most parents have children because they want them; they need and want to be with their children. Developmental strides during the first five years of life are continual and awe-inspiring. How would you feel if you were not at home when your child turned over by himself for the first time, or said her first really meaningful word, or took his first step? These moments are ones in which most parents hope to participate, not to hear about secondhand. It's difficult to make the decision to be working full-time on a career when the alternative exists to be home and with your child.

How do you feel about delegating life-and-death responsibility for your child to someone else? It's not unusual for a child to swallow some poisonous household substance or to run a dangerously high fever—often just an hour or two after appearing perfectly well. Getting the doctor often takes time, and it's hard to sort out symptoms and communicate them properly—even for an experienced parent. Doctors often don't take too kindly to the fact that the mother isn't there. One career mother changed pediatricians several times until she found one—not surprisingly a career mother herself—who found it acceptable that the housekeeper would call when the children were sick.

The Needs of School-Age Children

Five years is a relatively short time to spend home with your children. Children in the school-age years of five to ten also have a great need for easy accessibility to and availability of their parents. The needs that children have change somewhat from preschool years. School plays and school conferences are most often during the day, on the assumption that mother is free and able to attend. After-school hours seem to be taken up with endless chauffeuring tasks, as children's interests get more varied and far flung. It's the rare family that lives within walking distance of schools and after-school activities, although it's a very desirable condition and should be sought by a career mother. Another solution to the constant transportation need is a charge account with the local taxi service. But this will only help some of the time because the child's needs extend beyond the physical requirement of being brought to where his activity is taking place. Children must have their parents' interest and support.

"My son had just begun to get interested in basketball and joined the local league," contributed a career mother. "Fortunately, practices were at night and games on Saturday, so I could get him back and forth outside work hours. The round trip is so long that it is easier to stay for the hour and a half rather than making the trip twice. It made a very taxing evening, because the gym is noisy. It's hard to pick up and go out again after a tough day at the office, but the basketball games were played too far away for a taxi. Fortunately and unfortunately, my son's team did very well in the playoff competition, and then there was a game almost every night. I surely didn't do my best work in the office that week. But there's a special closeness and support a child needs and benefits from when a parent really participates in the child's activities."

Many women who choose not to work full-time during the first ten years attend school for further education or work part-time during this period. This is no doubt more productive from the point of view of career success than just remaining at home, but part-time involvement is not without problems. In a family where the mother chose to work part-time to maintain her career skills, the children never really liked the days when she was not at home, and they didn't hesitate to tell her so. Every day her son would ask her if she would be there when he got home from school. He was happy when the answer was yes, and disappointed when she said she would be at work. She, too, hated to miss that special sharing time that follows the greeting, "Hey, Mom, I'm home."

"The paradox to making the effort to be home at three-thirty in the afternoon is that, after our brief time together, the children are quickly off again, involved in their own activities, and I'm sitting there wondering why I'm not at work," volunteers a mother who is working part-time designing computer programs. "I feel that sometimes I'm a half-career person trying to be a whole mother, and other times I'm a half-mother trying to be a whole-career person . . . and not succeeding at either one very well."

Many studies have been carried out on the effect on children of having mothers who work. It's a fairly clear social commentary that virtually no studies have been done on the effects of the working *father* on a child. If we look beyond some of the bias against working mothers that exists in many of these research projects, the results show that the emotional problems of children that have a causal relationship to the mother are related not to her work status, but rather to her emotional health.

Parenting and Adolescence

At around ten to twelve years of age, children need less direct supervision from their parents and begin to reach an age of some responsibility. Career mothers find they are able to devote more of themselves to their career striving. It is frequently stated that children's need for their parents' time changes gradually from a need for quantity to a need for quality. That idea is somewhat misleading. Children need both quality and quantity. Although quantity needs may diminish somewhat as the child matures, there is a certain minimum required in terms of time and attention. The physical demands made on you tend to lessen, but the emotional demands and stresses may more than make up for the lessened labor requirements. This becomes most evident during the teen years. But by the time children have reached the end of elementary school, their mothers have probably damped down their career striving to some extent for more than a decade, whether they were working full-time at less than full capacity, working part-time, or getting further education. This ten-year time period seems to be the longest time that a career can be slowed down or interrupted if there is any intention of reaching a respectable middle level.

HELP!

Most women find that raising children is physically and psychologically demanding when this is their major and primary role. When you superimpose upon this strenuous task the demands of a difficult job, almost no one can manage both well—something and someone suffers. Women who have succeeded in combining marriage, career, and motherhood are women who seek and use all the help they can find.

Husbands

The child's father is the most readily available source of assistance. One of the women in the book, edited by Sydelle Kramer, *The Balancing Act,* divided up with her husband the time devoted to caring for their children. On certain days it was his responsibility after work to supervise dinner and get the children to bed, and on certain days it was hers. One parent or the other had duty in half-day stretches during the weekend so the other parent could have free time. This idea would be rather strange to many men who grew up in traditional families where the mother took care of the children. It's not easy to restructure a family relationship without giving a good deal of thought to what is happening and why it is happening. This analysis can use the same idea that we introduced in Chapter 5—looking at the specific tasks and then analyzing who does the chore and who takes the responsibility for seeing that it gets done. The why behind these facts most often is that "that's the way my mother did it." But that way doesn't work effectively, from a career mother's point of view, because too much of a burden falls on her.

Who, for example, keeps track of the dental and medical checkups—when they are due and what shots are necessary? Who watches to see that the children's shoes are still big enough and plans the trip to the store when new ones are necessary? There are few families where this sort of decision and follow-up is taken on by the father—even those men willing and able to devote a substantial amount of time to their children. These tasks, their administration, and the attitudes toward them have to be examined in detail. Only then can a more even distribution of parenting take place.

Professional Help

Reluctance to hire help, both for routine household chores and for child care, is exceeded in our society only by the difficulty of finding such help when you decide you want and need it. Possible solutions, which might have widespread application, have not even begun to be sought in realistic terms. Each career mother today has had to make do in an ad hoc way. Finding household help takes a great deal of creativity and frequently takes a good deal of money as well.

A recent article in *New York* magazine listed agencies in the New York City area that supply child-care professionals. Salaries ranged from $150 a week for someone to care for older children only to $200 a week for a trained baby nurse. Hiring help at this price, largely paid in after-tax dollars, is not a viable alternative for most women—even those who have waited to have children until they had fully established careers.

Student Help

"I've been lucky in living near several colleges," explains a career mother who has solved her problem with college students. "I look for a college freshman and provide room, board, and a modest salary in return for child care. I try to get the younger students, with the idea that they will stay with me throughout their college years. This way my children don't have to adjust to too many people. But this solution to the child-care problems has its drawback. It's rather like having another child; you tend to take on their troubles. Then there is the inevitable loss of privacy that you have when someone lives in your house who is not family. It takes some getting used to."

Foreign Help

A highly educated research scientist who had administered a large governmental program complains, "Can you believe that I couldn't get permission for a European baby nurse to work in this country so that I could continue to work on the project I'm heading up. The university got their grant only because I'm working on it. I absolutely could not find someone acceptable to care for my child, despite months spent in looking. Finally, I found the perfect woman in France but couldn't get a work permit. I resolved the problem by taking it up at a fairly high level in Washington and telling them that I'd have to leave the project unless I got the work permit. I did get it, but it's too bad to have to go to such extremes. And, unfortunately, most women don't have the connections that I do."

Work permits for foreign help are almost impossible to obtain, even though people to take child-care jobs are not generally available in the United States labor force. For a number of years, it was possible to get a mother's helper—usually a well-educated European girl who wanted the experience of living abroad. They were called "au pair" girls, which meant "on a par"—that is, the young woman lived as a family member while helping with the daily tasks, in exchange for room, board, and spending money. But in the past few years, the Immigration and Naturalization Service has virtually closed off this possibility for obtaining child care, which for some time had enabled many women to remain in the work force on a part-time or full-time basis.

Day-Care Centers

Because of the frequency of illness in children, many professional women do not consider day care a solution to child-care needs. One of the most difficult aspects of providing substitute care for your child surfaces when the child is sick. Day-care centers are rarely equipped to tend a sick child, nor do you want to take a sick child outside to get to the center. Children are sick frequently, and their illness causes serious conflicts between the child's needs and the demands of a job. The needs have to be resolved in favor of the sick child.

A mother who is also a manager for a large corporation recounted her problems with childhood illness. "I was really at my wit's end. My child got sick with regularity every three weeks, all winter long. Every time he finished his course of antibiotics, back would come the ear infection and fever. I finally had to take a leave of absence—I just couldn't send him to the day-care center, and I couldn't keep missing work. These illness problems seemed like they would never end, but my son finally outgrew them. Now I'm back at work full-time, but I have another problem. Although my son can now stay home alone with minor illnesses, he can't stay home alone during the school vacations. There is an after-school day-care center at his school, but it is closed during their holidays."

Day-care centers usually operate on fixed time schedules, but professional mothers are rarely able to adhere to normal business hours. Until the problems of timing, vacations, and illness can be solved by community child care, career mothers will have to continue to find individual solutions.

Other Solutions

"I've placed advertisements in papers in very small towns in the United States to find someone who has finished high school and who would like the experience of living and working in our large city. Their parents are more apt to let them go if they know they will be living with a family," volunteered a mother with two young children. "You've got to know what you are looking for when you do this. What I look for is a girl who is responsible and who is physically strong. I've had the most success with someone who is the older child in a large family because she's used to children and to helping in the house. I actually go and interview both the girl and her family. It takes a lot of effort, but this way I know my children are well cared for, and I can continue to work toward a partnership in my law firm. I'd never make partner if I had to interrupt my career."

Another creative solution to the child-care problem was worked out by Edna, a woman whose work takes her to Europe frequently. She explained, "Since it is not at all difficult for a foreigner to get a student visa, I look for a young woman who wants an American college education. I help her choose what college she wants to attend from among the several that are located near me. I help her to enroll and to apply for the visa. This method has worked well for me. My first girl stayed for five years while she went through college, and then her sister came to replace her. We've enjoyed having these additional family members and at the same time helping someone to get a college education. You really have to be very flexible, though. These students are going to school full-time and are very busy. Anytime that one of my children got sick, my husband, my student, and I had to hold a conference to see whose work demands could most easily be set aside that day. I hope to be able to afford a full-time professional someday, but in the meantime this has worked for us."

In Chapter 5 we examined how difficult it can be to combine the role of wife with that of career professional. In this chapter we have looked at some of the difficulties of adding a third demanding role, by becoming a mother as well. Nothing in society is organized to assist you in the arduous task of handling these multiple roles. On the contrary, most forces seem to be working against women who attempt to be professional, wife, and mother at once. In the final chapter of this book, we will look at some of the changes that career women working together may be able to bring about to reduce some of the pressures on triple-careerists.

7

WHAT DO YOU WANT
TO MAKE OF YOURSELF?

The world-famous psychoanalyst Erik Erikson posed an important life question in this way: "What do I want to make of myself —and what do I have to work with?" We dealt with aspects of this searching question in Chapters 1 through 6. In this chapter we'll look in greater detail at the first part of it: What do I want to make of myself? Then we'll go on to consider how you can pursue your chosen path despite obstacles and forces that seem to be in your way.

SETTING YOUR SIGHTS

What do you want to do? Where do you want to go, professionally? Be open and creative in thinking about these questions.

Start by asking yourself what it is that you *might* do. What is the range of things that are conceivably open to you? Allow yourself some fantasy, at this early stage of career planning.

Your ultimate goal can be called your "star." This term was suggested by Caroline Bosly (a woman who started her own highly successful international business) for what you are truly after, what you are truly working for. She recommends that each woman should ask herself: "If I could do anything I want to, what would I choose to do?" She also suggests that you don't stop asking yourself this question after you find an answer that satisfies you. Caroline Bosly went on to become a scuba diver, an expert horsewoman, and an artist of note, as well as a successful business-woman—while still only in her thirties.

Yale psychologist Dr. Daniel Levinson calls these deep-seated desires your "dream." Let yourself dare to admit what it is that you truly dream. Try to discover the star that marks the direction in which you want to go.

The reason for identifying your dream or your star is to help you stretch in setting your objectives. If you know what you really want, you'll be more likely to take risks to try to move in that di-rection. Admittedly, there is risk involved in disclosing to your-self what it is you really want. Women frequently avoid taking this sort of risk because they have so often been unable to achieve their objectives. They have become accustomed to setting very short-term and narrow goals that they are sure to be able to reach.

Nadine, a leader of seminars on career planning, found, in working with several hundred middle-management women, that most of the women set their sights far short of what they were able to attain. Frequently, participants in her seminars reached their five-year goals in less than two years' time. "There are several reasons for this," she suggests. "Women are unskilled in long-range career planning and can't accurately judge where they might go within a given time. Then, too, it's only recently been realistic for women to advance up the corporate ladder. It's taking them some time to adjust to their new opportunities. And I've found that most women feel very uneasy about setting goals they're not sure they can achieve."

Many of us have been set on courses that have largely been chosen by others. First, there were our parents, who had definite ideas about what girls and young women should, and should not, do. They passed these ideas on to us. Often parents were the first to suggest that a girl not try to do too much—it might make her unpopular and scare off boyfriends and eventually make it difficult to find a husband. Sometimes it was because it might demoralize a brother if a girl outshone him. For many of us, the first problem we have in setting our sights is to overcome the limitations imposed on us during childhood.

In a postdoctoral training program, one of the more talented members of the group kept doing less well than the others believed her capable of doing. When questioned about this by a close friend, she said it was because her parents always tried to keep her from shining because her brothers were not so smart as she was. Her parents were afraid it would discourage the boys. "I still have to fight that early training, even after all these years of scholastic achievement. Every time I have to disagree, or present a well-reasoned conclusion, I hesitate. I realize clearly what's going on," she admitted to her friend, "but it still slows me down and holds me back."

The major goal set for many women by their parents and other relatives was to marry and eventually to become a mother. These parental aims often dissuaded a woman from developing her intellectual skills to the fullest. This has made it difficult for many women to allow themselves to decide what it is they are really suited for and what they, at heart, really want to do. Are you striving for things that your parents wanted you to achieve or things that *you* truly want? It's hard to erase the ideas parents put into our heads. But, once you realize that you, and you alone, have the responsibility for making your decisions and then acting on them, it becomes easier.

When she approached her career plans from the point of view of what she truly wanted to do, one woman identified her star as the desire to live in Europe. She hadn't dared to admit this to herself before because she was afraid her family and friends wouldn't understand, wouldn't find it completely acceptable to strive to become an expatriate. Now that she has determined where she really wants to go, career planning has become much easier for her. It isn't only parents that may keep us from identifying our own needs and goals, as the internationally minded woman found out. It can be spouses, children, friends, and coworkers as well.

At the end of a long session on career planning, a woman came up to Nadine, the seminar leader mentioned earlier. She told Nadine that her company had chosen her for an important promotion and that she would now be on her way to bigger and better things in the corporation. "My husband and my children are all so proud

of me and have offered to do even more around the house than
they are now doing, so I'll be free to tackle this new assignment.
"But," she lamented, "I don't want the job. I don't want to have
to work that hard. I like what I'm doing now, and it leaves me lots
of time and energy for my family. I'd be happy to keep the job I
have now until I retire." What this woman needed and wanted was
someone to tell her it was all right not to do what everyone else
thought she should do; that it was *her* career and *her* life and *her*
choice. Her star was to continue life as it now was for her.

"Did it ever occur to you to ask yourself what it is that you really *like* doing?" asks Peter Aldrich, the president of a financial
company. "You'll be most successful working at something you
really enjoy doing." Have you asked youself what you enjoy
doing? It's *all right* to like your work. In fact, your career will
probably go much better if you do.

WRITE IT DOWN

Can you identify your dream? You may not yet be able to identify
exactly what it is, but if you can begin to describe it, write down
whatever thoughts you may have. As Alan Lakein says in his
book, *How to Get Control of Your Time and Your Life,* "aims
get narrowed down, because you can't write very many words,
compared to the millions you have thought in your lifetime. In
fact, your selection of what you write down indicates priorities
that might surprise you."

It is useful just to put down your ideas as "stream of con-
sciousness" without considering whether you can actually reach
your targets. It will help you stretch for goals if you don't concern
yourself yet about whether you can actually do what you want to
do. Concentrate first on stating what you want to do, along with
some idea of when you want to do it. You may find you develop
some new ideas in the process. This section represents your free,
early thinking in the process of planning your career. If specific
objectives or your timing seem unrealistic at this point, don't let
this prevent you from revealing to yourself what's really important
to you.

By stating your goals clearly in your notes to yourself, you'll gain a valuable perspective and begin consciously to take control of the management of your career. After you have done some of this free thinking, it's time to begin to look at some practical questions and to write out your thoughts on these issues as well.

YOUR GOALS AND THEIR TIMING

It is easier to establish concrete career objectives when you think in terms of three time periods: short, medium duration, and long-range. Long-range goals usually take about ten years; mid-range planning uses a five-year time frame; short-range goals may take anywhere from six months to two years. Many people have several short-term goals, often with different timing.

Try answering some specific questions like the following to help you begin to think in a variety of time periods:

1. My long-range career objective is:
2. I plan to achieve this within ten years or _____ years.
3. My mid-range goal is:
4. I plan to achieve this within five years or _____ years.
5. Another mid-range goal is:
6. The time period for this is _____ years.
7. My short-range plans are:
8. The time period for this is within two years or _____ months.
9. Additionally, my short-range plans include:
10. I plan to achieve this within one year or _____ months.
11. My other short-range goals are:
12. The time period for reaching these goals is _____.

If you have more objectives, write them out and try to identify whether they are short-, mid-, or long-range goals and attach a specific time to each if you can.

CHANGE "UNTIL" TO "WHEN"

When most businesswomen are asked how far ahead they have planned, the answer is usually, "one year" or "two years." Many women do not allow themselves to look further ahead than this because they have so many "until" constraints in their lives. They cannot change jobs "until" the children have completed grammar school. They cannot take a more demanding assignment "until" their husbands finish their education, or "until" their youngest children start first grade.

The only way to do long-term planning for women with these very real time boundaries is to use them as a positive point of action rather than as a limiting factor. Change the "untils" in your thinking to "when":

"When my second son has completed sixth grade, I will plan to relocate. In the meantime, I will get the education I need."

"When my husband completes his residency, I will move to another company, and we will hire a housekeeper to relieve me of the pressures of housework."

"When my younger child starts first grade, I will accept the vice-presidency. I will let it be known that I want that job in two years."

This is an important reason why you shouldn't limit the timing of your objectives to two years, five years, and ten years. The "when" in your life situation may suggest entirely different timing for your short-, mid-, and long-range objectives. Use the timing that suits you and your life.

WHAT NEXT?

Now that you have made a start at answering the first half of Erikson's question—What do I want to make of myself?—the next questions for your consideration are: (1) Are my objectives realistic? and (2) How can I plan to achieve these goals?

In order to help you answer these questions, in the next several chapters, we'll examine important factors that will affect your movement along your career path. We'll look at such things as the need to find sponsors and to get the appropriate education, at how to choose the right company at the right time. We'll help you analyze your professional style. Then we'll discuss essential resources that you'll need to acquire and perfect as you move up. Finally, we'll give you some suggestions on making your moves.

As you read the information contained in this book, you will find it useful to come back to some of the questions in this chapter and see what changes you might like to make in the answers you have written down. Not only should you have several alternative ideas that you are working on at one time in a variety of time frames, but also you should be aware of the fact that career planning is an ongoing process that is constantly subject to review and revision.

PART II

MANAGING YOUR CAREER

8

FINDING YOUR ORGANIZATIONAL FIT

One of the two most important professional decisions you will ever make is the choice of organization for which you work; the other is the field in which you choose to make your career. Neither the choice of occupation nor of organization is a once-and-for-all decision, and changes can be made. But the suitability of choices that you make at each opportunity can be an important determinant of career success. A lot of importance is attached to your choice of occupation, much less to your choice of organization. Yet, in order to do your best work you must be employed by a company whose needs fit your abilities.

Despite the publicity given to the fact that managers are more mobile these days than formerly, research shows that most senior managers, male or female, have spent at least twenty years with the company they are leading. So, when you select a corporation, be certain that it can contain your career aspirations, in addition to being the right place for you at your stage of career development. This chapter will give you some suggestions on how to choose the right company.

WHERE TO WORK—WHEN

Patty was still in her twenties when she completed graduate business school. She felt she had some time to experiment and determine where she could best perform in the business world. She joined a consulting company to see a wide range of businesses both in size and type. The travel was taxing, but the exposure helped her to plan her next move carefully.

After joining a small entrepreneurial business, Arlene found that the personality of the owner accounted for both the strengths and weaknesses of the organization as a whole. Decisions seemed to reflect his personality and values, rather than sound business judgment. The owner was unwilling to delegate responsibility, and Arlene felt that the chances of the company's growing were minimal. She realized this company was not going to allow her to grow, and so she decided to leave.

Beth had the opposite experience. She joined a young organization as the financial officer and watched it grow steadily and soundly in the three years she held the position. She believed that the company was just the right place for her, and she took advanced courses in information systems in order to be able to handle her job as it continues to grow.

After many years in a well-established company, Lorna Jean came to the conclusion that she was not going to move up any further. "It seems pretty hopeless to me," she reported. "All the line positions above me are filled by men, and they get and keep their clients through social occasions, which consist of either duck hunting or golfing. I'll never make a golfer, and women aren't welcome on the duck-hunting trips. I'm either going to have to accept the fact that I've gone as far as I can go, or else I'll have to plan to move to a large city, where the informal contacts take place in a different way."

Consider the organization where you now work. Is it the right place for you? Is it growing and will there be greater opportunities for you there? Can you work within the informal system as well as

have your name appear where you want it on the organization
chart?

THE FORMAL AND THE INFORMAL SYSTEM

Every organization has two structures: a formal system and the
way things *actually* work.

The formal arrangement is a hierarchy of reporting relationships that can usually be illustrated by a chart. Are you familiar with the chart for your company? Get one for yourself if you
don't have one. If the names of the persons holding the various
positions that are important to you and your job performance are
not included in the chart, fill them in. If you don't know who these
people are, find out. If your company is too small to have a formal chart, draw one for yourself.

In addition to the formal relationships illustrated on the chart,
there will be an informal network within your organization—within
any organization. This informal network usually represents the
way things really get done, and the way promotions are actually
accomplished.

Take a pencil and draw dotted lines between people who have a
close working or social relationship outside the formal scheme of
things. These informal relationships may exist between bosses and
subordinates, or between peers. They often jump several formal
levels on the chart. Next, with a ballpoint pen or colored marker,
draw dotted lines between yourself and other people with whom
you have close contacts. You must do this on paper because the
situation will become so much clearer when you actually chart
what is going on in an organization—rather than just think about
it. Once you have done this, you may find you will become considerably more astute, politically, within your organization, and more
effective in the job you are now doing. You truly recognize both
the formal and the informal organization if you know who fills
each slot and what their relationships are to each other and to
you.

Review the chart again and mark with an asterisk those persons
who might prove helpful in sponsoring you in the company; those

who can give you the training, experience, and exposure that you need. Draw a circle around those persons whom you've identified as potentially helpful to you, but whom you don't now know. Start thinking about how to let them become aware of you and your work.

An experienced woman banker decided she wanted to move from operations into commercial lending. When she went through the exercise of drawing the informal dotted lines onto the formal chart, she realized that she had direct contact with the senior vice-president who was in charge of lending. She marked his name with a dotted line, since they were working together once a month on a special community task force. Before using the chart, she had been concentrating her efforts on the vice-president of lending, since she thought he held the key to her being able to switch into a line position. With the help of the chart, she saw that she had a golden opportunity to get where she wanted to go by using her informal connection to a person in a still higher position. Since this man was a senior manager and three levels above her, she had not previously even considered him as a possible aid in achieving her objective. She hadn't even identified him with the lending department until she saw the chart.

Then, too, filling out the chart with actual names of employees helped her discover something else that she hadn't realized. Every loan officer—in the main office and every branch of the bank—was male. Without doubt, the bank was already looking, or might soon be, for a woman to take one of these positions. With her short-term goal of moving from operations into lending clearly identified, she stood a good chance of getting the position, particularly now that she had found someone who knew her and, very likely, would be able to help her do it.

Another experienced woman had clear knowledge of her organization's formal chart and also of who occupied each position that could have a bearing on her career. This astute woman manager always made the effort to attend company social functions with the idea of seeking out, in an informal manner, those senior managers who only knew her as a statistic on a computer printout. She arranged for someone to introduce her around. She met the men she needed to know, and, more importantly, who needed to know her. Then, when it came time to select someone for promotion, they could visualize her as a real person. The organization chart of her company holds no mysteries for her, either on a formal or an informal basis, and she makes maximum use of this information.

Formal relationships—the ones on the company's chart—indicate the theoretical structure of a company. However, this basic design is subject to the personalities, to the strengths and weaknesses of the various supervisors. Every time someone new takes a job, sooner or later, there will be a change in the informal structure. Be on the lookout for this and take advantage of changes when you can.

About every six months or so, examine your organization's chart and look closely at the dotted lines you have made in order to keep up with the changes. Since you have marked the informal organization in pencil, you can easily alter it when necessary. Be especially alert to any new persons with whom you need visibility or persons who have moved into positions where they can act as your sponsor or mentor. In the next chapter, we'll look more closely at what these persons can do for you and why you need them.

CORPORATE ENTERPRISE AND CORPORATE VALUES

Consider the business your company is in. Do you like the business, or would you rather be working in another kind of industry? Different businesses have different personalities, partly due to the service or product they offer, partly due to the values of the persons at the top. Consumer product companies can be very different from industrial corporations. Service industries are different from manufacturing businesses.

Sometimes a chosen profession may enable you to move about from industry to industry. If you are a financial person, you can work for a variety of companies: an advertising agency, a heavy industrial manufacturer, or a company that produces food products. You have a broad choice of industries, particularly when you are at the lower levels of your career. Think about what sort of people you enjoy working with. Do you like working with technical or research-oriented people—engineers and scientists? Do you enjoy creative people, like those in advertising? Are you happiest with highly verbal people, like lawyers and sales people? These are important questions. To a great extent, the kind of people a company employs will set the climate in which you work. Try to identify what climate best suits your personality, values, and talents.

One woman sales manager found an excellent position selling high-technology equipment. Even though she had no trouble selling in this industrial area, she was not happy spending her days talking to people who were mostly Ph.D. research scientists about extremely technical matters. She decided to take less money and sell a wide variety of products of both industrial and consumer types, which were purchased by ordinary business people. Through personal experience she discovered that the climate of the high technology industry was not for her.

Consider your industry as a whole. Is the industry growing? Will there be lots more opportunities? How does your company measure up against other firms in the same industry? Moving up is obviously going to be easier in a growing company, in a growth industry.

Perhaps the most important consideration of all is how your values fit with the needs and demands of the organization for which you work. What penalties do you pay for ignoring your own values? What problems do you have in going along with corporate requirements that are counter to your value system? This is a complex issue, and these questions are not easily answered. Perhaps now is a good time to go back and review the professional values you identified in Chapter 2. Do they fit comfortably with the kind of performance that is rewarded in your company? Some companies, whether knowingly or unwittingly, produce goods that are dangerous to people and to our environment. What about your company? How do you feel about it?

Although Peggy had once been a fairly heavy smoker, she stopped smoking when her boss and mentor became ill with lung cancer and died. This deeply affected her, and she did a great deal of thinking about her feelings about smoking. She decided that she would not go to work for any tobacco firm or even for a subsidiary that was engaged in some other form of business that contributed to the profits of the tobacco company. She decided instead to work for companies whose products she could personally endorse. In discussing her stand recently with someone who wanted her to take a position with a company whose parent organization was in the tobacco industry, Peggy's friend could not totally understand or endorse her decision. But for Peggy the decision was the right one.

Fortunately, there is room for individual judgment and for your personal value system, particularly if you figure out where you do not want to make compromises before you join a company.

CHANGING COMPANIES

Have you considered whether your career plan is best accomplished in the organization where you are currently working? The next section of this chapter will give you some new ways of looking at that question.

Whether to go or to stay is always a difficult problem. It is often useful to look at the reasons for *not* making a move.

When a person decides to change jobs, a great deal of time and energy can be lost in searching for another job. Many people who have had to change companies describe the process of finding potential positions and evaluating them as among the most difficult tasks they have ever undertaken.

There is always risk and uncertainty in moving from a known situation into an unknown one. It is very hard to assess accurately a job and a company from the outside. We'll give you some information on ways of doing this in Chapter 14, but the reality of an organization is often very different from the way it appears when you are on the outside.

"Once I took a new job and then left it at the end of the first week," a mobile woman manager stated. "I knew exactly what I was looking for in my job and in the company. I even wrote out the things we agreed upon in the interviews, and all seemed to be very suitable. We were in perfect accord. But, from the moment I started on the job, things were not as promised or as I'd anticipated. I decided to cut my losses quickly and left right away. The trouble was that now I had to start job hunting all over again. I've often thought of a boss, a job, or an organization as having an aggravation level, which is relative to my tolerance level. If there is too much aggravation, and it is about things that especially disturb me, it will rise above my tolerance level. It's very tricky to find a spot where all three factors—your boss, your job, and your company—have a tolerable aggravation level. Now that I'm in a position that I like reasonably well, every time I think of changing jobs I remind myself of the old adage, 'It's better to live with a devil you know.' That—and my one week's bad experience—keep me from getting too restive."

Besides the risk, it takes valuable time after you change jobs to learn your new job and how your new company really works—its informal structure and its politics. Yet, despite the problems that arise in making a job change, it's often necessary. One of the ways to help you decide if you will have to make a change is to view organizations from several perspectives.

ANALYZING ORGANIZATIONS

There are different ways to look at corporations and to discover what they need and reward in their employees.

One way is to consider the stage of growth of a company and the implications of this development phase. Another way is to look at how a company is managed, particularly with regard to the industry it is in and how these facts may contribute to the development of your career. Each method of analyzing your organization and others will have some important implications for your career management.

Stages of Organizational Growth

Business professor Lawrence Greiner has identified distinct phases of the growth of organizations.

I. The first phase of a company's growth is *birth and youth*. Usually such a company consists of the founder and a few trusted people who together do all the work. Infant companies struggle day-to-day and often seem to operate without structure or policies. They seem to be thrust forward on the sheer willpower and genius of the founder and the devoted associates, until the company either goes under or faces a crisis of leadership. It can be extraordinarily exciting to be involved in the initial stages of a company, and, ultimately, can prove to be very rewarding both professionally and financially—if the company survives. It is estimated that nine new companies fail for every one that manages to hang on. This volatile sort of environment frequently requires employees to work long hours under intense pressure, and it takes the kind of employee who can handle the often erratic behavior of the overtaxed entrepreneur-founder. Working for a new company involves an ever-present financial risk; you may find yourself out of work overnight. Nevertheless, for someone who is looking for a wide variety of experiences, who likes to operate without structure, and who is willing to trade risk for rapid advancement potential, start-up situations can be ideal.

When Beatrice completed her bachelor's degree in liberal arts, she found that she was not qualified for any particular job. She managed to locate a job with a new company that had only five employees. She was hired as a clerk and jill-of-all-trades. Once on the job, she set about acquiring many of the business skills that she lacked, such as knowledge of accounting. She also added as many technical skills as she could, such as computer programming. Then she worked on upgrading her skills and developed an understanding of corporate finance and the applications of the computer systems developed by her company. She quickly became indispensable. The firm grew to more than fifty employees in a period of less than four years; she became a vice-president; her salary increased 250 per cent.

II. Infant organizations that survive and grow, such as the one for which Beatrice worked, inevitably face a crisis of leadership, when, because of their success, they must begin to operate within an explicit framework in order to continue their growth. They reach a point where all the work that has to be done and all the decisions that have to be made can no longer be handled by the founder. The resolution of this crisis of leadership is called the *growth through direction* phase. In the start-up situation described above, Beatrice had ideally prepared herself to assist her company in moving into this next phase of development.

As a company grows, a structure must be superimposed on the existing anarchy. Systems have to be worked out and an effort made to be consistent. Policies have to be outlined and some long-range planning undertaken. The manager in a company in this second stage functions as a director and an administrator of policy. Since this type of company is still relatively small, there are few layers of individuals. It is possible to control the action directly, although it must now be exercised within limits agreed upon in policy formulation. The problem that is encountered and that ends this second stage of growth is that the policies, since they are relatively new and constantly being tested, are often found to be too constrictive. Ultimately a crisis of autonomy takes place.

When Harriet analyzed her career history, she found that she invariably chose to work for companies that were in their second stage of growth and had only about thirty to fifty employees. She usually had only one person over her and one level of subordinates. She could understand the needs of the company very well and was able to exercise a great deal of influence in helping the organization meet its goals. Her career problem in this type of situation was that there was little room to move up. The person at the top, to whom she reported, was most often the founder of the company. Although her jobs offered her much of the power and variety of experiences on which she thrived, she found that she was having to make lateral moves to achieve any advancement in salary and authority.

III. To have room to move *up,* Harriet needed to join a company in at least its third stage, *growth through delegation.* This stage usually accompanies a large spurt in growth, and decentralization begins to take place throughout the organization. Companies begin to restructure themselves by dividing into functional areas or logical segments, such as districts, product groups, or profit centers. A company at this stage has a lot of room for promotion, and line jobs proliferate, but a manager may have to do a great deal of moving around as the company reorganizes itself. Managers who work in companies in this phase need to thrive on rapid and frequent change. They also have to be skilled at and comfortable with delegating responsibility and authority, while still retaining accountability for getting the job done. If Harriet truly seeks more power, rather than the satisfactions she gets from working in smaller, second-stage companies, she must be prepared to relinquish some of her pleasure in fast response and direct control.

IV. Rapidly growing organizations eventually face a crisis of control, since decentralized units tend to get out of hand. A fourth stage occurs—*growth through coordination*. In this phase, a company begins to get much more sophisticated in the type of reporting procedures that are required. More checks and balances are instituted. Progress must be measured continually against corporate goals. Staff positions start to develop in companies that formerly were managed with a lean staff, largely of line executives. This situation is often an excellent one for someone who enjoys being a staff specialist, skilled in achieving objectives through meetings and team efforts. It requires the type of person who is willing and able to produce required reports rather than railing against them as a waste of time. Fourth-stage companies are not good places for someone who acts impulsively or who has strong entrepreneurial tendencies.

V. Fourth-stage companies eventually run into a crisis of red tape. Out of the morass of documents arises the fifth and final stage: *growth through collaboration*. Some of the most advanced management techniques are applied at this point in a company's growth. Maximum use of talent is sought. Fifth-stage companies are mature companies, where age and seniority of managers are pluses rather than minuses. These companies can be excellent training grounds for gaining experience in the workings of a fully developed organization—experience that may be later applied to help a younger company. Many excellent role models are found in companies that are in this stage, and they frequently have time to serve as mentors as well. Eventually, these large, often well-run corporations arrive at a crisis of psychological fatigue, which they may or may not pull out of.

What phase of development does the organization for which you work currently appear to be in? What stage of development would you choose to work in?

Do you like risk, particularly if the rewards may be potentially great? Do you thrive in an atmosphere that lacks structure, where you can just act to get things done, without having to clear decisions and conform to policy? You may be ideally suited to work in a stage-one company, one in its birth and youth phase.

A recent business-school graduate made this choice and traded security for the excitement and challenge of joining a start-up situation. Within the first year, the product flourished and the company was sold to a major corporation with a substantial financial gain to the young employee. Most people aren't this fortunate, but it can happen and sometimes does.

Do you like to organize? Do you prefer to be in a more structured environment than a new company? You might look for a situation in a company moving into stage two, growth through direction. Usually a lot of opportunity exists in this type of company, which is still developing, and its employees can have a great impact on how the company is structured. Many companies choose to stay at this reasonably small size, where they are large enough to be secure, but small enough to avoid developing too much structure. This is the sort of company that Harriet, who was mentioned earlier, generally chose to work in.

If you like to have many people working for you and to exercise a lot of power in managing and influencing them, an organization at stage three—the growth-through-delegation phase—may be for you.

"I really enjoy heading up my own profit center," reports Anna Belle. "I work out attainable profit goals, which are approved by the management, and then I'm pretty much left on my own as to how to accomplish those goals. It's a little like having my own company, but I also have the security of being part of a larger organization. There is no worry about money for the advertising and promotion budgets once my annual plan is okayed. There's a lot of challenge, and room for creativity, in trying to meet the goals I've set for my group."

Anna Belle is probably well situated in the phase-three company where she works and would be less happy in a more structured stage-four company. If you like a lot of structure and prefer to work within a known situation, you may choose to work for a company in the growth-through-coordination phase. It's also an excellent place for someone who really enjoys being an expert in a particular area and is suited to a staff specialist role.

It can be very challenging to work for a fifth-stage company—one in the growth-through-collaboration phase, which rewards maturity and experience, yet is able to embrace the newest management techniques. Do you enjoy a large corporate environment that seems to be well run and dynamic, which provides both security and challenge?

One of the truisms in business is that small organizations spend a lot of time in action and little time in analysis, while large organizations spend a lot of time analyzing and don't act much. Are you action- or analysis-oriented?

According to Dr. Greiner, most persons can work comfortably in an organization during one or, at most, two stages. It is the rare manager who can adjust to three stages in the same organization, or who is ideally suited for three different stages—even in different organizations. Harriet eventually decided she was happier working in smaller, less stratified companies, even at the expense of upward mobility. Beatrice left her company as it moved into the third stage, and she joined another firm. She, too, felt she could contribute most to a developing company, where she could do a wide variety of work and make a greater impact. Diane and Eva started their careers and gained their training in a mature, well-run fifth-stage company. They cannot imagine leaving to work for another type of organization, and they thoroughly enjoy the complexities in their own. Anna, who started with them, left after five years of experience with the corporation, and she formed her own company. She was never happy in a highly stratified situation, where her ideas were constantly being studied and restudied, but rarely implemented. She had to be her own boss, but she used her background to work in her specialty with stage-four and stage-five companies, whose operations she well understood.

Do your talents and ambitions seem to fit with the stage of development of the organization for which you work? If not, what stage might suit you better?

EXAMINE YOUR CAREER STAGE

Not only is the developmental stage of your company important to consider, but so, too, is the stage of your career in relation to the type of organization.

Stages of career development can be divided into three phases: (1) establishment, (2) advancement, and (3) maintenance. A good fit between the stage of your career and the type of company you work for can make a big difference in the ultimate level you reach.

In an article in *MBA* magazine, corporate controller Charles Jacob recommends that you evaluate companies to decide whether you are in the correct place at the right time, or whether you need to gain other experience. He divides companies into five categories, with the divisions based on the type of industry and the type of management.

Category I is made up of companies in mature industries, such as steel and most automobile manufacturers. Managers in these industries use proven methods, and there is little room for innovation. This sort of company can provide a good foundation for persons in the establishment stage of career growth, but will allow little room for fast movement or rapid achievement of responsibility. They do not seem particularly suited for someone in the advancement stage of her career, unless she wants to commit herself permanently to that industry and probably to that company as well.

In *Category II* Jacob places companies who, almost intentionally, set out to be training grounds—companies like ITT, Macy's, and Procter & Gamble. They use sophisticated management techniques and systems. They tend to overhire talented beginners, train them intensively, work them very hard, and expect many to move to other companies, leaving them with those employees who best fit their system. Senior managers in Category II companies usually are in their fifties and have advanced by slow degrees up the corporate ladder. Category II companies are excellent for people in the establishment stage of career development because of the large corporate experience they gain. There is little substitute for the experience gained early in the development of a career in either Category I or Category II companies. There is a nationwide network of graduates of these systems, and it is helpful to be a Procter & Gamble-trained person if you are in consumer products, or an ex-Macy employee, if your aim is to manage a department store. It's difficult to secure experience with these companies after the establishment phase because you have probably become too high-priced, and their policies are almost invariably to promote from within.

"Beware, though, of the golden handcuffs that can shackle you to some of these large corporations," advises a woman executive. "I had joined a major company that heavily recruited M.B.A.s, specifically to get that training and experience. I did well in the company. In fact, I found when I went to try to move to another company that might prove to be more exciting and where I could move up faster, that I couldn't match my salary or my benefits. Since I'm supporting two children, I couldn't afford to take a loss to change jobs. Most people can't. I'd advise people to anticipate these important economic factors and move before they get financially locked in . . . if a large company isn't where you plan to stay for your working life."

Category III companies are developing companies whose potential for success is great. These companies are often headed by youngish executives who came from Category I or Category II companies. There is usually not yet a fully developed middle-management level in these corporations, which gives lower level executives a chance to substitute drive and intellect for years of experience. Although Jacob feels that this category of company offers the best opportunities for management growth, he cautions against joining such a company without already possessing good managerial skills. He also points out another advantage to joining a Category III company. Their top management is committed to modern techniques, so it is relatively easy to promote new ideas. There is a risk in these situations, however, that you may advance to a level where your technical and management skills are not adequate for you to handle your job. So, while a Category III company may be an ideal type of organization for someone in the advancement stage of her career, the risk of failure is higher than moving up more slowly in a Cateogry I or II company.

Jacob identifies *Category IV* companies as organizations that need to adopt modern systems and techniques, but are not quite sure how to go about it. These companies experience profit problems and are challenging places to move into top-level management positions, if you possess the proper training and experience. These companies do not provide good lower- or middle-management experience, but can be ideal places for managers in the later stages of advancement.

The final group—*Category V*—suffers from unenlightened management. Jacob describes these companies as having market positions that were established years ago, and they are now making a profit in spite of poor management. He counsels managers to avoid these companies completely, unless they can go in at a chief executive level with a free hand, and can infuse new life into the organization, to help it avoid the inevitable downward spiral. Management in this type of company is afraid of talent, and it is no place for someone in the training or advancement stages of a career.

It is not easy to characterize companies by either method we've discussed because no single company precisely fits any description. However, you can probably place the organization where you are now working into one of Greiner's developmental stages and one of Jacob's categories. If you are considering changing companies, view the old and new companies from these perspectives to help you in making your choice.

When she was in her late thirties, Laurie returned to school following a divorce and acquired an M.B.A. Although she had worked part-time in her husband's small business prior to the divorce, she had no large corporate experience, such as that described as a necessity by Jacob. Upon graduation, she secured a position in a medium-size company in the South, where she believed she could gain a good deal of needed experience. The company was not terribly competitive, and life was fairly quiet and nondemanding, so she was able to turn the bulk of her energy to perfecting portable managerial skills. After two years in this position, she felt that she had learned all that this job and this company had to teach her. Although Jacob would most likely categorize her present firm as a developing company, or Category III, since it is expanding rapidly and there is room for her to move up, Laurie feels she needs additional seasoning in the development phase of her career. She wants the background and experience of working for a large Category II company in a highly competitive environment. Ideally, she'd like to find a position in one of the corporations included in *Fortune* magazine's list of the top five hundred industrials. She's particularly eager to find a position in a major northeastern city because she doesn't want to become too comfortable in the slower tempo of life where she is now located.

Laurie does not plan to stay with this second-career-step company very long either, since she views it largely as the completion of the establishment phase of her career. She is looking forward to making the move into the advancement phase. Even while she is looking for this next job she'll also be keeping her eyes open for a company where she might want eventually to spend the remainder of her career. She is looking for a developing company where she might move up rapidly, or perhaps a Category IV company where sophisticated management techniques are sought and where good advancement potential exists.

YOUR CAREER AND YOUR ORGANIZATIONAL FIT

Write out for yourself the answers to the following questions regarding the company where you now work:

1. Do I have a good understanding of the informal structure of my organization? (If your answer is no, describe what you are going to do about this lack of important information.)

2. Who in my company can help me achieve my career goals? (Put an asterisk by the names of those people who need to get to know you and your work.)

3. I do or do not like the business my company is in. (If not, why? If so, what do I like about it?)

4. There is or is not a reasonable fit between the goals of my company and the means they use to achieve them and my own beliefs and values. (If your answer to this question is negative, identify what penalties you think you may be paying for this ethical dissonance. For example, do you work less effectively than you might somewhere else? Do you lack maximum enthusiasm for your work? Are you unable to see yourself with this company or in this industry in the long run? Do you have any symptoms of stress that may be a result of this lack of fit?)

5. The company where I am now working is most likely in the following stage of development:

- First stage: Birth and youth
- Second stage: Growth through direction—beginning to establish policies
- Third stage: Growth through delegation—decentralizing
- Fourth stage: Growth through coordination—establishing controls over decentralized units
- Fifth stage: Growth through collaboration—maturity

(If you can, indicate whether your company is at the beginning, middle, or near the end of the phase.)

6. Through how many phases have I been with this company?

7. Do I find a comfortable fit between my abilities and ambitions and the stage my company is in?

8. What phase of company do I think best suits me?

9. What stage of career development am I in? Establishment? Advancement? Maintenance?

10. Identify your company according to Jacob's categories:

- Category I: Large, mature, old industry
- Category II: Large, aggressive, good training program
- Category III: Rapidly developing, lots of opportunity
- Category IV: Trying to change and become more contemporary
- Category V: No desire for change, living in the past

11. Does the category of your company seem to suit your stage of career development? If not, what category of company would you like to be working for?

12. Did you get good basic experience in either a Category I or a Category II company? If your answer is negative, is there anything you can do to make up for this deficiency?

The answers to these questions will give you some clues to help you address one of the most important questions that you will have in your career planning: Am I working in a company and in an industry that are appropriate for me, and where I will probably achieve my career objectives? Write down a tentative answer to this question. Review this question again when you've completed reading the book.

9

MENTORS, MODELS, AND SPONSORS

You can't make it in business on your own. Being successful in the corporate world is not only a matter of your experience and your ability to be in the right place, but it is also very importantly a matter of whom you know and who knows you.

Someone has to take the time and energy to tell you about the subtleties of your job, about the policies of the company. You can't succeed unless you know what's acceptable and what isn't. This information isn't written down, it's passed by word of mouth. You also must be recommended and supported for promotions; better jobs are rarely secured by ability alone.

Look around and see who can help you and at the same time look to see whom you can help. Complex business friendships and associations are two-way relationships; they are almost always mutually beneficial. Start building a whole network of people who can rely on you and who can help you.

In Chapter 8 you started to pinpoint the people who could possibly assist you in developing your career. In this chapter, we'll examine why mentors, sponsors, and role models can be of great importance to you, and we'll discuss the different things each one can do for you.

MENTORS

In order to understand the mentoring relationship, let's first define
it and then look at how it works to see how you might make use
of it.

In an article on the subject in *Business Week,* a mentor was
defined as someone who sees possibilities in a younger person and
helps bring that person along. In this article, Lynn Cullum of
General Electric is quoted as saying that a mentor "brings you
along, promotes you, makes sure you get rewards. He watches out
for your interests and will not promote you too far or too fast."
Business Week was one of the first publications to examine the
problems that women might have in finding other women to serve
as mentors. The article also pointed out that the situation seems to
be changing, though slowly. "Up-and-coming male executives
have always had a perk not usually available to young women executives: the services of a mentor."

Yet for women who are targeting the top, one or more mentors
would seem to be a very important factor in their ability to reach
their objectives. A survey on the subject of mentors conducted in
1977 by Heidrick & Struggles, Inc., a management consulting firm,
revealed that female senior executives averaged three mentors
each during their careers, and that 70 per cent of these mentors
were male. One of the surprising facts is that 30 per cent of the
mentors were female. This would seem to indicate that there are
more women at the top helping other women than we realize.

Whether or not you now have a mentor, male or female, the
more you understand about the mentoring relationship the more
comfortable you will be with it and the more effective use of it you
will be able to make when the opportunity arises.

Men Helping Other Men

Almost all information available on the subject of mentoring has
been gained from studying men mentoring other men. In his book,
The Seasons of a Man's Life, Yale psychiatrist Daniel Levinson

provides some specific information about male mentoring relationships. He describes a mentor's function as that "taken by a teacher, boss, editor, or senior colleague." The mentor is a teacher or advisor who is not "a parent or a crypto-parent. His primary function is to act as a transitional figure. [He] represents a mixture of parent and peer; he must be both and not purely either one." For this reason, as Levinson points out, the mentor is "usually older than his protégé by a half generation, roughly eight to fifteen years."

In describing the evolution of the relationship, Levinson says:

> a young man initially experiences himself as a novice or apprentice to a more advanced, expert, and authoritative adult. [Eventually] he gains a fuller sense of his own authority and capability for autonomous, responsible action. The balance of giving and receiving becomes more equal . . . their relationship becomes more mutual.

In his studies, Levinson found that the mentoring relationship typically lasted two or three years, with an outside limit of eight to ten years. The relationship frequently comes to an end because of some external event such as promotion, relocation, or retirement. Or, as Levinson describes it,

> Sometimes it comes to a natural end, and, after a cooling-off period, the pair form a warm but modest friendship. It may end totally, with a gradual loss of involvement. Most often, however, an intense mentor relationship ends with conflict and bad feelings on both sides.

Levinson says it is rare for a man to find a mentor after he reaches the age of forty. In a typical male career cycle, this represents the time when a man's career is approaching its maintenance phase. The time has come for him to take his own place as a mentor if he has reached a powerful enough position.

Men Mentoring Women

Although Levinson's study is limited to men, he does say a few words about women and mentors.

> One of the great problems of women is that female mentors are scarce, [but] some young women have male teachers who function

as mentors. This cross-gender mentoring can be of great value. Its actual value is often limited by the tendency, frequently operating in both of them, to make her less than she is: to regard her as attractive but not gifted, as a gifted woman whose sexual attractiveness interferes with her work and friendship, as an intelligent but impersonal pseudo-male, or as a charming little girl who cannot be taken seriously.

Levinson's conclusions are not very encouraging for a woman who is searching for a mentor, but, at least they provide some clues as to what to look out for in male-female mentoring relationships.

Gail Sheehy, in *Passages,* states bluntly that when a man becomes interested in guiding and advising a younger woman, there is usually an erotic interest that goes along with it. One young woman executive solved this problem by acquiring several mentors: "Men in my company just didn't run the risk of acting as a mentor to a woman because of the inevitable gossip that would result," she observed. "So, what I did was to prove my abilities to several men, in the hope that more than one would sponsor me for a promotion or choose me to work on a special project. When more than one man seemed to be championing me, it took the pressure off any particular individual. Eventually, I gained several mentors this way, and now I always try to have at least three. Any sexual implications have become so diffused that it no longer interests the gossips. I found another way that this safety in numbers works for me as well. When one of my mentors fell from grace, I didn't go down with him. I had other people to depend upon and was not too closely attached to any one person."

Sheehy also suggests in her book that "the relationship of guide and seeker gets all mixed up with a confusing male-female attachment. And it is this mysterious, ambiguous, potentially enriching, but possibly crippling, attachment with which many successful women and their mentors must cope." Another pitfall that Sheehy identified was that if a woman remained reliant on her mentor overly long, she became a millstone and usually had to be discarded. A woman who is unable to break away from a dependent relationship as she learns the business is not fully maturing in the professional sense. She becomes a drain on the mentor after a few years and takes the time and energy that could best be spent bringing someone else along. Furthermore, she is not taking on enough risk and responsibility in her own right.

"It's exciting to bring a talented younger person along in the organization, but I don't want to keep training and retraining," Henry, a senior manager, reported. "I expect my people to learn things quickly, then move on to something new. I don't know whether I attract women who are looking for another father and hesitate to leave their safe departmental home for greater challenge, but I seem to have difficulty encouraging some of the talented women who work for me to try their own wings. I just don't have time to keep giving them the reassurance they seem to need even after they've mastered the job."

Remaining overdependent is not always the case, however. A seasoned woman executive, in talking about her male mentor, said, "He acted as my mentor, my sponsor, and my role model at different times during the years in which we worked together. He took a great risk in giving me one particular promotion, but I proved myself and managed to live up to his expectations. Eventually I moved to another city, but we've never lost contact. We're still friends, and I'm still grateful for the opportunities and training he gave me."

Perhaps losing touch does not have to be the result of a mentoring relationship between men and women. The competition between men and women undoubtedly still has a somewhat different quality than competition between men, since the psychological implications of the elder male's being replaced by a younger male does not enter into cross-gender mentoring. Male mentoring appears to contain more of a parental, father-son struggle, which results in the older male's feeling threatened when the younger male is ready to take a fully adult role in the organization. While there may be less competition in male-female mentoring, Sheehy found that even here, ending the relationship was tricky. She states that men and women sometimes find their way back to a footing as friends "after a predictable period of strain. This requires an exceptional degree of sensitivity on both their parts."

Woman to Woman

Mentoring between women may prove to have different characteristics than mentoring between men, or between men and women. Women have not yet been thrust into the kind of open competition with one another for jobs that men have experienced for generations. Women have historically competed for men, not for jobs. This may allow relations to continue longer among women who are professional friends and helpers.

"It's great fun to help younger women," one woman mentor pointed out to me. "The ones I've chosen to indoctrinate into the finer points of the world of business I count among my close friends. It's nice to have friends who are younger than you are. It keeps you current and gives you a good insight into what's happening today. It was really shocking, though, when one of my protégées found herself mentoring someone else. It made me aware of the passing of time. I've often heard mentors referred to as godfathers. All of a sudden, I felt more like a *grand*mother than a *god*mother."

Don't hesitate to search actively for mentors of either sex. Try to find several if you can. Be aware, when looking, that, because of the time and commitment that are involved, it is not something that you can *ask* someone to do for you. Mentoring involves coaching and training others to operate effectively in the corporate environment, and it includes giving them inside information and special opportunities. It is one of the informal ways in which people are selected to be promoted and then given the background to be able to handle the more responsible jobs. Neither men nor women mentor someone they don't like because of the emotional involvement that is part of the relationship. Studies have found that some men choose to mentor younger men who are very similar to themselves or who are as they wish they had been. This may be another factor limiting the number of mentors available to women.

The absence of a mentor may prove harmful to your long-range career plans; and it's not easy, for reasons that we've already discussed, to find them. Yet almost all successful men can point to a specific person who acted as mentor. A recent *Harvard Business Review* article was entitled "Everyone Who Makes It Has a Mentor." Acquiring mentors would seem to be essential for women as well. Try to make yourself and your skills visible to those who might make suitable mentors for you. In the meantime, look for and utilize sponsors and role models.

SPONSORS

Don't get discouraged if you haven't yet developed any mentors. Sponsors can be very helpful, and you never know when a sponsor may turn into a mentor. A sponsor is someone who holds a job above yours by one or more levels, is aware of you and your talents, and will suggest you for assignments and promotions, even though he or she may not take the time to coach you in the ways of the corporate world. Most senior executives are busy doing their own jobs and protecting their own positions, but they have time to give able people opportunities for experience and exposure. In fact, it's part of their job to do so. A sponsor is seldom the person for whom you are working directly; that person—if he or she takes an active role in your upward mobility—is more likely to be a mentor.

In one major organization, Rachael realized that she could not be promoted to the next level without the authorization of the corporate president. Her boss didn't want to lose her and was unwilling to make her career aspirations known at a higher level. She explained the situation to another man at her boss's level. She told him that she had prepared an extensive report on a new position that needed to be created at the higher level—the level to which she wanted to be promoted. She explained that among the benefits of doing this would be the more efficient operation of his department. She asked him to read the report, and if he agreed with her findings and her proposal, to show it to the president. She was asking for little effort on the part of her sponsor. He didn't have to *do* anything if he didn't agree with the findings. If he did put forward the proposal and it was accepted, he would have another small feather in his cap and a more smoothly operating department. In fact, he did submit it, and Rachael did get the newly created position and promotion.

Her own boss's blocking her efforts is not an uncommon occurrence. While going around your boss in this manner won't work in all organizations, Rachael had a very good understanding of the informal workings of her company and the relative power of different individuals. The man she approached to sponsor her was much more powerful than her boss, even though they seemed to be on the same level, and her sponsor was a personal friend of the president as well. A sponsorship from him held weight, and Rachael had accurately assessed the amount of risk she was running, relative to what she was trying to obtain.

In another case, a very talented senior executive was trying to bring about needed changes in her organization. The senior vice-president to whom she reported believed in what she was doing and supported her case with the company president. Between them they planned the reorganization of the corporation as they felt it should be structured. While working on this project over several months, their interest in each other grew from intellectual admiration to an emotional involvement. The president, who was not in favor of their plans, had been waiting for an opportunity to get the company back on its old tracks. He now seized on their personal relationship as a reason to replace both of them—and he did.

Sponsorship or mentoring by someone who loses his or her job often causes you to go along with them, or at least to be considered among the "outs" of an organization. However, this is a gamble you have to take. The higher the level you reach in a company the greater risk you have of losing your job. And sometimes you lose your job largely because of who sponsors you.

One rapidly rising executive was hired as the senior vice-president of a subsidiary of a large conglomerate. It was the perfect career move for him. Unfortunately, just six months after he joined the firm, having been selected by the presidents of both the subsidiary and of the parent corporation, the chairman of the board decided to "clean house" in this particular subsidiary. This young man went along with both the people who had sponsored him for his position. He was considered one of their team and, as such, couldn't remain.

To succeed in an organization you have to find sponsors and, in most instances, ally yourself with a group. You also find yourself in jeopardy if that group falls from favor—but that's the way the situation often works. You must protect yourself by having portable talents, a good professional reputation, and active contacts who will help you relocate should that become a necessity.

Study your organization. Identify people who can help you and start looking for sponsors among this group of people. Let them get to know you and your work; you may even wind up with a mentor as a result.

ROLE MODELS

In addition to seeking—and hopefully finding—sponsors and mentors, you can help yourself learn the ways of the corporate culture by studying role models. Role models are persons whom you feel are doing things right. Observe them in an effort to learn from what they do, and adapt what you can from their behavior and actions. You will find role models among men and women, among peers and bosses and subordinates, and even among your friends and relatives. Think of the many characteristics you want to develop more fully, such as leadership skills, analytical ability, political savvy, and negotiating and persuasive powers. Observe anyone you know who has outstanding abilities in one or more of these areas. Don't expect one or two people to embody all the things you want to learn. Find lots of models, each for his or her particular skills. Managerial skills are complex, and it takes a great deal of observation of many people to develop all the required facets into a personal style that is effective for you.

Sometimes you do find models who embody most of the managerial mastery that you want to achieve. One executive woman described as follows her way of handling difficult problems: "Over the years, I worked for two people who always seemed to control situations with a minimum of effort and achieve the desired results. One was a man, and he was president of that company; and the other was a woman, and she was a senior vice-president in another firm. To this day, when I'm stuck, I reflect on how I believe they each would have handled my current dilemma. I usually manage to come up with an answer that works. Years later, I'm still using these two people, whom I consider almost ideal managers, as my role models."

Role models can help you decide what *not* to do, as well as illustrate what you should do.

A younger woman had been encouraged by an older friend's success at gaining an advanced education, while handling a full-time job as well. She attempted to follow this same route. But she observed that her role model's life seemed to get out of balance in terms of the physical and emotional drain caused by her intense involvement in both work and study. The younger woman was also aware that she possessed neither the physical nor the intellectual resources of her model. The younger woman re-examined her own priorities—she didn't want to follow her friend's pathway and end up exhausted. So the younger woman decided to slow down her pace and attempt to avoid too much stress and an unbalanced life-style. Yet she still pursued the advanced degree, her "dream" that she had identified by observing the success of her friend and role model. She cut back to part-time employment and located a graduate program where she could attend part-time as well. This added up to a full-time schedule and was all that she could comfortably handle, unlike her friend.

When you are studying role models, you'll find that you'll not only adopt part of their style but you will *adapt* it as well. You'll take what seems to be useful for you and fit it to your own personal and professional style. Adopting and adapting are excellent ways to learn to be more flexible in your professional style, which will result in your being more effective as an executive. We'll take a further look at your professional style and how to broaden it in Chapter 11.

THE IDEAL AND THE PITFALLS

The perfect situation for an aspiring woman is to find several mentors, with at least one of them a woman. Look among people who are perhaps half a generation older than you are, who are part of the organizational in-group, and who are willing and able to take the time to coach and train you.

Examine any male mentors you may be fortunate enough to acquire and try to avoid the classic stereotypes reinforced by Levinson's findings: that the male mentor regards you as a little girl, as a sex object, or as a person less able or brilliant than you really are. If you find yourself falling into one of these categories, gently ease yourself out of the situation—these roles don't develop senior executives.

Don't be discouraged if you don't appear to have any mentors. Learn from role models, find and make use of sponsors. And don't hesitate to mentor and sponsor people with whom you are working. You'll find you will gain as much from them as you give, and talented women, and men, too, need all the female mentors they can find. It's fun and it's rewarding.

10

YOUR EDUCATIONAL PASSPORT

Even the best mentors, sponsors, and role models can't help you obtain your professional goals if you don't have an adequate educational background and if you don't keep abreast of changes and developments in your field. Lack of education, knowledge, experience, and managerial skills were cited as the most serious deficiencies in female managers by more than half of the respondents to a 1978 survey of the executives of the American Management Associations' member organizations. By contrast, the traditional complaints—lack of self-confidence, emotionalism, and lack of interest or commitment to a career—were mentioned by a total of only 37 of the 972 respondents.

There is a very clear message here. Most women do not *yet* have the educational preparation that qualifies them for senior positions. Women need more technical and managerial education. Do you have this necessary background? If not, how can you get it?

GO GET THAT DEGREE

The first step in striving for a senior position is to obtain a career-oriented degree—law, business administration, accounting, engineering. There is a never-ending argument in favor of liberal arts college training, versus a more pragmatic discipline—but it really doesn't matter on which side of the issue you stand. Reality dictates that a professional education must be acquired somewhere along the line, either instead of, or in addition to, an education in the humanities. Without specific training in some aspect of business, you may never get on the corporate ladder at all, or you may find yourself completely blocked at your current level. A professional degree can be a boost up the ladder, or it can set you up for on-the-job experience.

Today a bachelor's degree is a basic requirement for upward mobility. But not everyone has been fortunate enough to have had the opportunity to attend college. If you did not, and if you truly want to move ahead, make a college degree your first priority. Don't be concerned about being out of step with the college generation; almost half a million women *over* the age of thirty-five are now in college. It's possible to get or complete a degree without leaving your job, although it takes a great deal of energy and dedication. Night-school opportunities abound, and they provide the additional benefit of meeting a new group of people who have needs, problems, and life experiences similar to your own.

Pioneer professional organizations (one example is the National Association of Bank Women—NABW) are creating new ways to help women gain necessary educational qualifications. The NABW sponsors bachelor's programs in several locations around the country. A degree can be obtained from recognized educational institutions by attending two-week institutes twice yearly for three years and pursuing courses locally to meet the school's total requirements. This program is proving to be very successful, and, not only are the 24,000 NABW members eligible to apply, but any man or woman in banking may be considered.

Often employers pay for the program in order to assist valuable employees in improving their skills.

If you did have the chance to get a college degree, do you feel you were really educated while you were in college? In the past, many women were sent to college largely to place them in an environment where they could find a suitable husband. Education was a secondary consideration. If, for any reason, you feel your education was inadequate, find ways to improve it now.

When you have a good education behind you and a bachelor's degree to show for it, consider studying for an advanced degree. Many senior male professionals and most younger men on a fast track to the top have either an M.B.A. or a law degree. Other advanced degrees, too, can be helpful, particularly if you choose to move up in a staff capacity. Economics, computer science, accounting, and engineering are among those that can be particularly useful.

One young woman, a violist with a master's degree in music, found that she didn't like teaching music. When her husband finished his advanced degree, she returned to college for a bachelor's degree in engineering, and is now working in the computer field. Another woman, the mother of three, discovered that she wasn't going to get tenure in the humanities area, even though she held a Ph.D. and had been teaching for a number of years. So she took some remedial work in advanced mathematics and began work on an M.B.A.

MATH ANXIETY

One reason that fewer women are getting technical educations than their male peers is that the women traditionally have not been sufficiently prepared in math. The woman Ph.D. mentioned above did not let this stop her; she set about making up for her deficiency. But, for many women, a math deficiency acts as a "vocational filter," according to sociologist Lucy Sells. Sells studied the educational background of a group of students applying to the University of California at Berkeley in 1977. She found that the absence of an adequate high school math background precluded the women from seven of the university's nine schools and colleges. Of the women in the group who entered Berkeley, only 8 per cent had four years of high school math. Without this prerequisite, the remaining 92 per cent could study only the humanities, music, social work, elementary education, guidance, and counseling.

Studies have shown repeatedly that until children reach the age of twelve, there is no difference between the sexes in their aptitude for math. Why, then, have women not continued to pursue studies in math, especially when it is recognized that lack of preparation will ultimately handicap them, or at least seriously limit their choices professionally?

A combination of subtle and not-so-subtle factors seems to be at work here. Women have had bad advice from parents and teachers. Many girls who were mathematically inclined were steered in other directions or, at the very least, not encouraged to pursue studies in these areas. This in part reflects a cultural myth that math is a masculine ability, and that there is something not quite feminine about really liking math-oriented subjects. As a result, girls are likely to avoid mathematical subjects "since girls aren't any good at them anyway." Therefore, most girls don't enroll in the more advanced classes at the high school level, and this places them at a disadvantage when they get to college. No wonder they become anxious about their "inability" to do math. The fields to which women are then limited are overcrowded, and they perpetuate the myth that women are only interested in the so-called "helping professions."

With the advent of the computer, even the social sciences now require a good quantitative background, particularly for advanced work. A study by John Ernest at the University of California at Santa Barbara shows that less than 10 per cent of Ph.D. degrees earned by women between 1972 and 1975 were in the fields of economics, math, computer science, physics, and engineering. These are not very encouraging statistics in a technological society that is becoming increasingly dependent upon the manipulation of data as a basis for decision making. Ernest concludes in his study that, "Men take more mathematics, not because they like it more than women do, but because, whether they like it or not, they are aware that such courses are necessary prerequisites to the kinds of future occupations they envision for themselves."

How are your math skills? How do you feel about your ability to use numbers in decision making? In long-range planning and projections? If you are not comfortable with numbers, what can you do to remedy the situation?

Remedial courses are available in many places, and you can often take courses through adult education programs in local schools. Stop avoiding math, and quell your anxiety about it by overcoming your lack of preparation. You'll probably even discover that you like it. One senior woman executive I talked with advises young women on the way up: "Learn to live with computers; they're here to stay."

GETTING YOUR ADVANCED DEGREE

Although the progress of women at the doctoral levels, in math and the physical sciences, has not yet made gains, women are rapidly closing the gap between male and female enrollment in schools of management. Many schools now have equal numbers of men and women enrolled, and sometimes there are more women. You will no longer be a rarity in these schools—although not all of your professors may yet have adjusted to this fact.

Anne Hyde, president of Management Woman, an executive search firm dealing exclusively with women, advises, "For women who want to be considered for top-level positions . . . an M.B.A. has become essential." It is possible that an M.B.A. or its equivalent in a relevant field, will soon be as essential as a bachelor's degree was ten or twenty years ago. It will soon be the groundwork education on which a career is built. Anyone holding an M.B.A. from an accredited institution knows just how comprehensive that education is. It is going to become increasingly difficult for someone without that perspective and broad-based business background to compete with those who have it.

But take heart. It is no longer necessary to take two years out of your career for graduate education. Most people cannot afford to do this, anyway. Executive M.B.A. programs are proliferating throughout the country. Their enrollments are made up of thoroughly experienced executives who attend school only on weekends or occasional weekdays. These programs are designed to allow the business person to continue his or her job, while getting a degree.

Joining the Network of Future Corporate Leaders

A full master's degree program is not the only answer. Many seasoned middle managers attend what are essentially cramcourse versions of M.B.A. studies in the form of advanced management programs. Few women have been accepted into such programs since few have reached high enough ranks in their organizations. This is changing, though slowly. Harvard University has graduated thousands of men from their thirteen-week Advanced Management Program, but, as of December 1977, only eight women had completed the program. However, there are middle-management and senior-management programs available at other institutions that accept a larger proportion of women.

In order to be eligible for these management programs, you must be selected by your company. Usually you have to meet other requirements as well, such as earning a salary above a certain figure, or being earmarked by the company for substantial advancement. There is often not a lot you can do about requirements such as those, except to be one of the fast-moving executives. But you should investigate these programs by writing to the major business schools sponsoring them, such as M.I.T., Stanford, and Harvard. If your company has never considered sending someone, you might suggest it. Or you may be able to maneuver yourself into exactly the program that will benefit you most.

A manager of a multinational corporation was told directly by his mentor that he was in line for a top managerial spot in the very near future. The rising executive realized that he lacked expertise in certain areas since so much of his training had been on the job. He also realized he suffered from some "tunnel vision" because most of his work experience had been gained at this company. When he asked for some additional training before assuming further responsibilities, they offered to send him to one of the short courses for senior managers. But he felt that he still needed more background than this would provide, and then, too, he really wanted to get an M.B.A. degree, as added insurance in the event he one day wanted to change companies. He had done some research and knew that one of the universities offered a one-year program for experienced managers, but they had to be recommended by their companies, who not only had to pay for the education, but also had to pay for their families to come along as well during that year. He sought the corporate permission and recommendation to enroll, and it was granted. He knew what it was he wanted and needed professionally and went after it.

Since these highly selective programs, which train proven people even more fully to become senior managers, are paid for by the corporations involved, they become extremely interesting to strive for. They are training grounds for future corporate presidents, and women have a lot of catching up to do in becoming qualified for these top positions. An added benefit of participating in one of these programs is the exposure to people who will later become internationally recognized leaders in their field. These senior people form a network, which is long-lasting and supportive. More women must gain the education and experience to join this network. If you can secure the opportunity to participate in one of these elite groups, make every effort to do so. They represent several steps—or a large boost—up the corporate ladder.

Ingrid will admit to her closest friends, "I know I'm under consideration for one of the management institutes and I know that if I get to go, I've already been chosen for a major promotion." She doesn't yet know if she'll get it, but her inside sources of information have revealed to her that she's being considered. Her knowledge of company politics also makes her aware of what it means if she does manage to catch that particular golden ring.

Once you're part of such a select, largely male group, it's not all smooth going. There are still residual problems that have yet to be solved. One of the women chosen just a few years ago for participation in an executive program was housed several miles away from the men. She didn't realize, until well into the course, that her fellow classmates were accomplishing the incredible amount of work loaded onto them by forming teams. She was having to do everything on her own, without benefit of group input, experience, and sharing. Even after she made this discovery, she couldn't do a lot about it because of the logistics of the situation.

Another woman, coming along a few years later in a similar program, discovered that group members were housed in small apartments, sharing a common living room and bathrooms. She learned, after being assigned to a particular group of male apartment-mates, that this was not the first group to which she had been assigned. It appears that the men and their families had received letters asking them if they minded having a woman in their quarters. Somebody in the first group objected, and she was reassigned to another apartment group.

Once settled into a large male group, yet another executive woman, Joyce, found that all seemed very comfortable and compatible, although the ratio of men to women was about 50 to 1. But, after the weeks progressed at a seemingly friendly and cordial level, a traumatic confrontation occurred when one of the class discussions centered on material dealing with a large financial settlement awarded to women employees as the result of an affirmative action suit. It seemed to Joyce that the men, in responding to this subject, released an enormous amount of stored resentment at women executives generally. And she also felt that much of their hostility was aimed specifically at her, as a scapegoat.

Even Joyce, a woman with twenty years of business experience, who is in line for a senior management position in a major corporation, was shocked by the depth and amount of resentment, fear, insecurity, and hostility felt by some men when they truly confronted issues regarding the inclusion of talented women in their already extremely competitive professional environment.

OTHER SOURCES OF EDUCATION

Education does not begin and end in formal institutions. Many seminars are offered by a variety of organizations. The American Management Associations (AMA), for example, offers seminars on virtually any topic about which a business person could need further education. These seminars usually last from two to five days and are given at locations throughout the country. Courses that confront the problems that women face as they enter formerly all-male bastions are especially helpful. The AMA is currently offering courses specifically for women on management skills, assertiveness training, self-improvement and interpersonal skills, and on the woman manager in a changing environment.

For years the NABW has run seminars for male managers on the issues that must be faced by both men and women in dealing with each other in the rapidly changing business environment. Both men and women managers benefit whenever anyone takes one of these seminars. The NABW also offers seminars that can be taken by women bankers on "The Process of Management" and on "The Management of Conflict and Change in the Organization." These two-day learning workshops are useful to anyone, whether or not she has a college degree. The same organization offers home-study units that can be taken individually or in groups. These are on many topics that will improve business skills, such as "Team Building," "Performance Appraisal," "Negotiating," and "Coaching Employees."

Professional associations offer annual or more frequent opportunities to keep up with your field. Many companies offer in-house training sessions. In most cases, the cost of the courses or professional gatherings is paid for by the employer.

Education is expensive. It is a valuable fringe benefit—take maximum advantage of it.

READ, READ, READ

As most executives know, continuing education does not take place only in the classroom. A minimum amount of reading must be done regularly to keep abreast of changes in your field and happenings locally and internationally. Usually this reading amounts to more than most people can cope with, but there are ways to handle this requirement. The first is to make sure that your reading pace is as rapid as possible. Studies show that most business executives read at a speed of less than 300 words per minute—a level below that of the typical college student. Do you know your reading speed? Test yourself with one of the books on the subject. If you need to speed up your reading rate, do so. The ability to absorb large quantities of material and retain it will be of great help to you.

Be judicious in what you choose to read, and what you read of what you choose. Many well-informed business persons "read" both the New York *Times* and the *Wall Street Journal* daily. If you *really* read either or both of these publications, it could easily keep you occupied for a major portion of the day. Instead, select those articles that seem to contain useful information and read them. Otherwise, just rapidly scan the rest of the publication to get a general idea of what's there.

A widely read woman banker merely cuts out articles of interest and puts them in a folder. She doesn't take time during her busy day to do this more careful reading. She saves it for her frequent plane trips, taking only a carefully edited collection of articles. This helps her pass her travel time in a productive and interesting manner.

Forward-looking companies, who seek to save their executives time and themselves money have evolved ways to help their people keep up with the vast choice of professional reading material. One major company circulates the table of contents of a variety of magazines. Managers need only mark the articles they want to read, and the company library provides them with a copy. A similar service, now available commercially, gives a précis of each article, as well as title and author. There are many creative ways to keep up with your reading in the limited time that you have. The important thing is to keep abreast of your field and events in general. And, whether or not you take a speed reading course, you'll find that the more you read, the more rapidly you'll be able to read. It's a skill that improves with practice.

Education is a never-ending process for self-fulfilled persons. The ability to read intelligently and glean the vital information is essential for any professional. It's necessary to keep up with new technology, new processes, new styles, and new concepts in order to keep up with your job and be able to develop new ideas. Education is a continuing effort and a rewarding one.

Education in the formal sense is only half of the twofold preparation that is necessary for a striving business person. The other half is gained from putting this knowledge to use through actual experience. In the next several chapters we'll discuss how, when, and where you might best gain this experience.

11

YOUR
PROFESSIONAL STYLE:
FIND IT, FLEX IT

The classic definition of the job of a manager is "to meet the goals of the organization through others." These "others" are the people who work for you, the people you work with, and the people for whom you work. How well you are able to influence these different groups of people is, to a great extent, a matter of your managerial style and your understanding of the style of others. If you have been working for any length of time, you probably have developed a pronounced style of relating to others, or, better yet, a repertoire of styles. You may not, however, consciously be aware of your style or the variations that you use to fit different situations.

Do you know what your dominant managerial style is? Are you aware of the types of people and situations that are easiest and, more importantly, those that are the most difficult for you to deal with? The clearer your understanding is of what you do and how you do it, the more effective you will be as a manager. Even your personal style is closely tied to your professional style: the way you dress, the gestures you make, your use of language, and the appearance of your office. These same personal factors offer helpful clues to the managerial style of others and can help you decide how best to deal with someone else.

IDENTIFYING YOUR PROFESSIONAL STYLE

One of the most useful methods of analyzing styles of behavior has its basis in Carl Jung's identification of the four ways in which people experience the world. Jung's research led him to the conclusion that people react primarily as a result of sensations, thoughts, feelings, or intuition. Your sensation ability tells you that something exists. Your thinking ability helps you analyze what that something is. Your feeling ability tells you whether you like it. Your intuition tells you, through hunches or guesses, what use you can make of it.

Most of us use a combination of all of these Jungian styles, but usually one dominates the way in which we relate to the world. This "dominant" style is the way in which we see and understand things most clearly and are the most comfortable ways for us to act. When you read through the descriptions of these four styles, try to identify which you believe to be your dominant style.

ARE YOU A DOER?

Doers are people who trust their senses. If they can see, hear, feel, taste, or touch it, then something is very real and important to them. Jung called such people "sensation-based" types.

If you are a doer, you "see it and tell it like it is." You tend to live in the present and are very pragmatic. You want to get on with the job and see the results. Doers are efficient and resourceful, especially in crisis situations. Doers seek action and will respond to ambiguity or anxiety by "doing" something. They seek fast and easily identifiable results.

Real estate, finance, and medicine are areas where the sensation-based action person is often found. Doers are also comfortable as entrepreneurs and in direct sales.

Doers tend to dress in functional attire and want things that work well and are efficient. They tend to have sparsely furnished offices—they are too busy to put in homey touches. If their walls are decorated at all, the decorations tend to be useful items, such as charts and maps. The office may appear to be disorganized because the doer doesn't take the time to keep things orderly.

Just by walking into her office, one could discern that Sally was probably a doer. There were usually lots of papers on her desk, as she was engaged in many things at one time. Her office showed no evidence of her personality, but was totally functional. She could have moved out at any time simply by taking her business papers with her. Her chosen field was real estate financing, and she was extremely successful at it. Her objective in business was to get the real estate transaction closed and move onto the next challenge.

From time to time, Sally would run into someone with whom she could not communicate comfortably—someone largely concerned with theoretical future plans. To a large degree, this had to do with her time perspective as a doer. Doers have difficulty projecting into the future. Nor do doers relate easily to people with a strong attachment to the past. It's the here-and-now that's important to them. This is why they are good in crisis situations and calm when handling emergencies.

ARE YOU AN INNOVATOR?

Intuitive types are creative people, who concentrate on the future, to the exclusion of the past and present. If you are one of these innovators, you tend to be visionary, to spend a great deal of time seeking new ways to solve problems. Ideas and concepts are what interest you most. You are imaginative. Innovators are comfortable in marketing or research, or they may be artists or inventors.

Offices of innovators are often imaginatively decorated with futuristic art and bright colors. You will frequently find round forms —such as round tables—in their offices. One successful designer bought an office building because it contained a round room where it was pleasing to him to work. A leading architect has as his hallmark round forms, such as balconies, in many of his buildings. He lives in a house that is essentially round and contains many curving forms.

There is a great variety of dress among innovators from the completely absentminded approach among those who feel that dress relates to today and doesn't have much effect on the future, to very outlandish styles that may relate in some way to the person's concept of the future.

Innovators frequently have difficulty with people who are relators. Relators see things in terms of the past—particularly their own past. The innovator and the relator approach the world from two entirely different time perspectives and have difficulty finding a common meeting ground.

WHAT IF YOU'RE A RELATOR?

If you operate primarily from an emotional base, you are likely to be warm, affectionate, spontaneous, and have a strong need for friendships. You are good at communicating with people and getting them to do things. You will be more concerned with the people you work with than with tasks, goals, or profits. Psychiatrists, nurses, teachers, social workers, and personnel managers are frequently relators.

People in direct sales are often relators with a secondary style of a doer, or vice versa. The relator's ability to sense what others want and need helps him or her to care about and meet the needs of other people—an essential skill in selling anything successfully over a period of time.

Relators seek clues from past events about how to act in the present. When you hear someone tune in to what you are saying by interjecting a statement like, "Well, that reminds me of when . . ." you have a pretty good clue to the fact that you are probably dealing with someone who is a relator.

In a successful law firm, the walls of the founder's office are covered with pictures of his children and grandchildren. His desk has memorabilia from milestones in their lives, as well as in the life of the firm. It's a pretty good guess that he's a relator, even though lawyers usually tend to be analyzers. Most of the specialists who work in his firm are indeed analyzer types. His role, then, is to hire the right type of people and to motivate them. He is almost a public relations officer for the firm, and he keeps the clients happy on a personal level.

Relators will often have cozy touches, such as family pictures, plants, and a coffeepot. They will usually offer refreshments if they can when you visit them. Their offices may appear to be in disarray, but underneath the apparent disorder, they are generally well organized. They like to have a lot of historical information on hand when they have to make decisions. Their great attachment to the past may also show up in their office decor in the way of old maps, antique furniture, or accessories.

Someone operating from a strong base of feelings will tend to dress in bright colors, talk a lot, and often be quite humorous. They will usually start a business conversation with a personal discussion before getting down to the matter at hand. Relators have trouble dealing with doers, who want to get on with the job without taking a look at what implications the past has for current action and decisions.

WHAT IF YOU'RE AN ANALYZER?

As an analyzer, you are involved in all three aspects of time: past, present, and future. You need to know the history in order to understand the present and project the future. You tend to be systematic and well organized. You emphasize reason and logic and are deliberate in your actions. Law, corporate planning, accounting, systems analysis, and engineering are fields where you find people who emphasize their thinking abilities.

People who are primarily analyzers are good administrators, organizers, and planners, since they like to arrange things in a logical fashion and plot them out in procedural steps.

Analyzers tend to dress conservatively and often choose geometric patterns over circular or abstract designs. They will be color-coordinated, but not colorfully dressed. They most often have very neat offices with clean desks—everything organized and in its place.

Whenever she had a problem, Jenny had to trace it back and find out its causes in order to understand it. Then she had to review exactly what happened, and, finally, she confronted the person involved with the history and present state of affairs in order to plan to prevent this particular problem from occurring again. She is an analyzer and must go through each step in order to handle a situation. By contrast, a relator would be most concerned with how the problem was affecting the people involved, a doer would select another means of acting and get on with it without worrying about why the problem arose, and an innovator would seize the opportunity to try and find a totally new way to approach the problem.

Actually, no one is purely one type. Everyone has traces of each style, but in most of us one style tends to develop more than any other, so that it dominates our behavior. We also usually develop a secondary style to use when our dominant style doesn't work, or which we use when we are under stress. Do you change your style if problems arise? Do you know how you change it?

Successful business people very often are doers or analyzers. As they move up the corporate ladder, they also learn to operate as relators and as innovators, as well. The ability to alter your style to fit the style of the people with whom you are working can be learned. And it has to be learned.

In groups of women who are given tests to analyze their basic Jungian styles, typically 60 per cent will have relating as their dominant style. It is interesting to speculate that the reason so many women appear to be relators is that they have been conditioned to be so. It's encouraging also to observe that when the same test is given to a group of experienced businesswomen, usually only one or two people answering the questionnaire will show a dominant style of relator, and it's a pretty safe guess that they work in personnel. Experienced businesswomen have learned to alter their styles or have developed a different dominant style— usually that of doer or analyzer—which proves more useful in the business setting. Being primarily people-oriented rather than task-oriented can be counterproductive if you are striving for a senior position in management. You have to be *both* goal conscious and able to motivate your subordinates to work in that direction.

FLEXING YOUR STYLE

Go back and read through the four descriptions again and try to identify the types of persons with whom you have the most difficulty dealing. See if you can understand better how they operate—particularly with regard to their sense of time. Practice making suggestions in a timing that they will understand, at least when you first start talking to them. Give a relator a little of the history of the situation, tell a sensor what is needed now, suggest to an innovator what should be done, and do a little bit of each thing when making a presentation to an analyzer.

Dr. Robert Pearse, business psychologist and professor of organizational behavior at Boston University, tells management groups, "If you want to be an effective manager, you must ask yourself what changes you have to make in your professional style. Your style profoundly affects the way you listen and what you hear. It affects the way you perceive the world and the way you make decisions, but you can learn to communicate on another person's wavelength. You can deliberately train yourself to think and respond well to people whose styles are different from your own."

Understanding Other People: Pull Out Your Antenna

People give clues to their style not only in their actions but also in the way they dress, what their offices look like, and even in their telephone manner.

Relator types tend to be informal, warm, and friendly on the telephone. Doers tend, on the other hand, to be brusque and abrupt on the phone and need to control the phone call so that it won't get off target or take too long. Analyzers tend to set up ground rules for a phone conversation, so that it will cover all the necessary information and they express little emotion over the phone through lack of voice inflection. Innovators have a telephone style that is also impersonal and aloof, as if their concentration is elsewhere. And it most likely is.

Take time to observe all the clues you can that other people give you and practice adjusting your style to theirs.

Consider the case of the young woman executive who dresses in a relatively quiet, tailored fashion. Her clothing, however, is obviously quite expensive. She is always impeccably groomed. She arrives at work in a Mercedes sports car. Her bearing exudes confidence, and she speaks and moves slowly and precisely. There is little indication of spontaneity about her. She doesn't have to act assertively. Everything about her sets up an aura of command and control. People tend to be slightly or even totally awed by her. Her outward style and symbols are very effective in her situation. It helps her to establish herself as a ranking executive in the financial community where she works and in an organization that has never had a woman at her level before. She projects a strong and memorable identity with the persons with whom she deals. She quickly establishes her position in ways others don't usually take time to analyze consciously. From this position of both strength and credibility, she starts her negotiations, which are usually successful.

Relative to the four types of personal style, this financial executive's dominant style is that of a thinking person—an analyzer—and you probably won't be surprised to learn that she has a law degree. Her secondary style is that of a doer. She has trouble adapting to people who operate from a feeling base and even with those who operate at an intuitive level.

Another woman in the same organization dresses in quite similar tailored clothes, but of undetermined cost and quality. There is no atmosphere of wealth about her, and no one could probably describe the kind of car she drives to work, even though they often see her arrive. Her office is always somewhat in disarray, although she can immediately put her hands on what she needs. She is slightly absentminded and often acts or reacts impulsively, particularly if there is not a lot at stake. But she rarely loses a power struggle where the outcome is important because all the people who work for her and most of her peers actively support her. They find her warm, helpful, and approachable. Her peers usually owe her favors and respond well to her cooperative method of working. She has analyzed both the style and the motivations of her superiors and is able to state her case by appealing to their needs in a way that they can understand. Her fundamental style is that of a relator, with a heavy dose of doer in her secondary style. As you may imagine, she has difficulty dealing with her corporation's lawyers, who operate from a sense of logic without taking into account the variables about people that she feels are so vital in handling any problem. If you were working with these two women and wanted to influence them, you'd need to approach them very differently.

More than likely, both of these women will develop their ability to act satisfactorily in situations where they are not now totally at ease, because they are constantly seeking to improve their professional effectiveness and continually looking at new ways at understanding themselves and their relations with others.

Dr. Pearse advises, "An extreme style change can confuse the people around you. People who work with you anticipate what you are likely to do, based on how you have behaved in the past. It's for this reason that you should just temporarily flex your style —that is, just modify it enough to be more suitable to a certain person or in a specific situation for a short period of time.

"It's difficult to make major personality changes, which is why you should be working at something that suits your natural personal style. If the two are not reasonably compatible, you'll have a lot of difficulty in really progressing."

MULTIPLE STYLES

Many persons who are now senior managers either had a basic style that combined large amounts of each of the four ways of reacting, rather than one clearly dominant style; or, over the years, they matured into management generalists, and they gradually grew in the areas where they were less developed. It's not difficult to flex your style when you can act comfortably out of any of the four modes, and it doesn't confuse the people who work around you—they are used to seeing you react in various ways.

A middle manager, who headed up a local organization of a

worldwide company, knew all the people who worked for him
well, and he understood their styles and motivations. He could
predict how they would react. He engendered deep loyalties because of his genuine concern for their welfare as well as his dedication to the goals of the company. He was a feeling type, a relator, but he was also by nature an analyzer and an innovator. He
saw that things were done in an orderly and logical fashion with a
concern for an historical perspective. He always saw what had to
be done now and ensured that it was taken care of. Yet, he never
lost sight of the future and often solved difficult problems by a
creative leap forward. He serves as an excellent model of someone
who works well from all four Jungian areas of action and who
easily flexes his style to suit the needs of the situation. It was no
surprise to his staff that he progressed through the ranks of the organization and eventually became chairman of the board. Most of
his original group still works for him and rose through the company as he did.

In addition to beginning to understand your professional style
and be better able to deal with other people, there are many other
resources you should possess to be an effective executive. In the
next chapter we will take a look at some of these important skills
you should have or should set about acquiring.

PART III

EXECUTIVE RESOURCES

12

MANAGING TIME:
THE FINITE RESOURCE

Everyone starts out with the same basic and limited raw material: only 168 hours in a week. Study after study shows that the typical senior executive works a fifty- to sixty-hour week. That's a big chunk out of the weekly ration of time. Unless work is also done on the weekends, it amounts to a ten- or twelve-hour workday. These impressive figures do not take into account commuting time, which realistically must be calculated on a door-to-door basis. Studies done on working women show that they usually do 80 per cent of the regularly recurring household chores, such as cooking, cleaning, shopping, and laundry. Often as many as 100 hours are accounted for by working women when they total their weekly office hours, commuting time, and household tasks. If they also require eight hours of sleep a night, this only leaves them with twelve hours a week to spend in nurturing meaningful relationships, in recreation, and in doing whatever else they might want to or have to do. It's no wonder that executive women make statements like "I have to get by on four or five hours' sleep most week nights"; "I find I get a migraine headache once or twice a month and have to stay in bed a day or so to recover"; "I'm always tired and can never seem to catch up"; "I can do with very little sleep for a couple of nights when I'm on the road, but then it catches up with me."

If striving professional women are to accomplish what they set out to do, more time has to come from somewhere. Many of them borrow from their sleep time, only to have to repay this loan—plus interest—later. A better way is to understand and use the principles of time management and make more effective use of the time you have available. Most working women have already developed many creative ways to make good use of their time to meet even the minimum requirements of living. Fortunately, there are some additional ways to improve your time utilization so that you may increase the opportunities for professional advancement as well as improve the quality of your life.

CHOOSING YOUR PRIORITIES

A busy professional woman who is also a wife and mother made the fundamental observation about time management: "I don't need to learn to manage my time—I need a course in *life* management." You can't manage your time well unless you have looked at your life priorities and values and know what gives you the most satisfaction. You've already made a good start on this when you read the first section of this book. As time-management authority Alan Lakein puts it, "Life is a never-ending stream of possible activities, constantly being replenished by your family, your teachers, your boss, your subordinates, as well as by your own dreams, hopes, desires, and by the need to stay alive and functioning. You have so much to do and so little time!" However, on the encouraging side, he states, "There are constraints on everyone that make free choice impossible in all situations. But you are free to choose much of the time. . . . We all have plenty of time to do everything we really want to do."

With that in mind, the first step is to decide what it is you really want to do. You've done some very concrete thinking about that in Chapter 7. Go back and review your notes on "My Dream." Is there anything else you can add there at this point? With an idea of your dream in mind, your next step is to set about doing that which will help you toward achieving your dream in the most effective manner possible.

EFFECTIVENESS AND EFFICIENCY

An article in *Fortune* titled "Keeping the Clock from Running Out," points out that executives make *effective* use of their time. "Not efficient use of their time . . . because efficiency merely means 'doing the job right,' while effectiveness means 'doing the right job right!'" In his book *Managing Organization Conflict,* Professor Stephen Robbins describes these concepts another way: "The administrator is concerned with attaining goals, which will make him effective, and with the least allocation of scarce resources, which will make him efficient."

Women have perhaps been encouraged to be efficient at the expense of being effective. Since in the past women's salaries were generally low and their positions largely clerical, they could be encouraged to be perfectionists at their tasks. The price of their time was not a significant factor. As women move into the higher ranks of organizations and their time begins to become an expensive resource to the company, women must now look closely at where their time is *best* spent in meeting the goals and accomplishing tasks.

The marketing director of a company had come up the secretarial route and was still an excellent typist, since she found it easier and quicker to create advertising copy at the typewriter. During one organizational emergency, she was deeply involved in interpreting some market research data for the president, which he needed in a hurry. The senior vice-president to whom she reported needed a report out for a client that same day, and the entire secretarial staff had been decimated by the flu. Her boss asked her to type the report so that it would be out on time.

The marketing director was not entirely pleased at being asked to fill in for the clerical staff, but it was her nature to be cooperative and to perform tasks as directed. Then she stopped and thought as a manager, "What are the organization's priorities and where is my time best spent? Also, what are the cost factors involved?" The president needed the data results; her boss needed the report typed right away. "My salary is approximately four times that of our secretaries and even higher than that of a temporary clerical worker. It just isn't reasonable for me to spend my time typing. No one else can interpret the research data and if I don't do that now, I'll find myself working overtime, which is not sensible." She estimated the time it would take her to type the report and showed her boss precisely how much it would cost the firm if she pinch-hit for the absent secretaries. It didn't take any persuading to have him authorize the personnel department to get some temporary clerical help—even if they had to hire them to work all night at overtime cost. What might have been more efficient for her boss was clearly less effective both for her as a manager and for the use of the firm's resources.

There are constant conflicts to be resolved among your tasks, the firm's goals, and the precious resource of time. The use of the four fundamental tools of management—planning, organizing, controlling, and evaluating—can help you to resolve these conflicts so that you can choose the right thing to do—and do it right, making maximum use of the scarce resource of time.

THE PARETO PRINCIPLE

Before you take a look at where your time is now going, it is well to understand the Pareto principle. Vilfredo Pareto was a late-nineteenth-century sociologist and economist who postulated that the significant items in any group constitute only a small percentage of the total group. This is the origin of the 80-20 principle: that 80 per cent of your results are accomplished with 20 per cent of your time. The corollary of this principle is that 80 per cent of your time is spent in producing 20 per cent of your results. You need to identify what 20 per cent of your time is put to the most constructive use and free up some of the time that is being used less productively. To do this, you must first analyze where your time is going and then plan to use more time where you produce more results.

Your Time Study

You may think that you just don't have enough time to stop and analyze where your time is going. But you'll find the time you invest doing this will ultimately be counted among the 20 per cent of your time expenditure that produces 80 per cent of your results. There are many ways of keeping track of your time. One of the simplest ways to do this is to enter on your desk calendar at regular time intervals exactly what you have been involved in doing for the past fifteen minutes or half hour. Be honest. Write down what you have really been doing, not what you think you should have been doing. If you have a secretary, she can keep the time log for you. It will probably be more accurate and objective.

Since there is no typical week for most people, it is best to keep this log for two weeks and then summarize it. You'll find that you are wasting time in certain areas about which you were very well aware. You'll also find some surprises about your use of time. Often what we think is wasted time in the form of unstructured activity is actually time we use either in recovering our energy or doing some creative thinking and problem solving. But you'll also unearth some time wasters. Look at those long and hard and see what you can do about them. We'll have some suggestions for you later in this chapter.

One time-management firm has computerized similar time studies for executives. At random times during the day, a black box placed on the executive's desk will beep. The person then presses a button to indicate what she is doing at that moment. Eventually the computer produces a printout that gives a summary of the use of the executive's time. This method is expensive, but takes little effort on the part of the person being studied. Whether you have assistance from a computer, your secretary, or have to jot down notes on your own, an accurate picture of how you are actually using your time is information that is essential in order to plan how to do more of the things that really matter to you.

Making Lists

All busy people who use their time well either are blessed with total recall or have learned to keep orderly, accurate lists of things they must do. These lists of tasks are often called "To Do" lists. If you don't already make use of one or several "To Do" lists, start now. If you already use such lists, become more systematic about them. Keep them in the same place and use them at the same time on a continuing basis.

Fortune devoted an entire page to Roy Ash's handwritten "To Do" list when they were discussing how he managed Address-ograph-Multigraph, a major office equipment manufacturer. Ash calls this list his "brick pile" and uses a yellow pad to keep a running list of issues that have to be resolved. He sums up his overall company goals for these items to "Rethink, redesign, rebuild, and re-earn." These goals are ambitious, but they are reachable because someone defines, plans, and carefully writes out the steps that have to be taken toward them. Here are some of the items on Ash's list for the one particular day examined by the magazine:

Improve French management and operations

Set up intracompany transfer pricing responsibility

Completion of Spain rearrangement

Restore AM Belgium profitability

Separate U.K. sales and manufacture

Analyze relative profitability of different duplicating products

Get parts management under control and orders filled on time

His total list contained forty-five items, all directed toward making his company profitable.

Alan Lakein would have referred to this as Ash's "A" list, his most important goals. After listing such goals, Lakein advises setting priorities on which activities are most important and numbering them in the order you plan to attack them. He recommends that you also have a "B" list of medium-priority items and a "C" list of low-priority items. Each of these lists should be ranked in the order that you feel you should accomplish the tasks.

Some people prefer other names or concepts for their lists. They may make them out according to what is urgent, what can be set aside temporarily, and what can be avoided. Still other executives find that it is more useful to have their lists compiled for different time periods, such as monthly, daily, and weekly. However you find "To Do" lists work for you best, use them. You'll find you save a great deal of time, and intellectual energy, by writing things down.

A well-known movie star, wife, and mother also runs a successful business. She divides her lists according to whether the task relates to her home, her business, or her acting career. At all times she has these three lists with her. "I couldn't function without my lists," she states. "Once I've written something on a list, it's 90 per cent accomplished. I don't have to clutter up my mind remembering what I've got to do. If I turn my attention to my family, I just look at my list and either do the things I've jotted down, get someone else to do them, or forget about them. The point is to get them crossed off the list."

Another busy woman reports, "I write out my urgent list each morning. It's usually about twelve or so items long. I find I get to only about the second or third item on the list by the end of the day, so it's terribly important for me to be very careful what I put first. Then I carry over the things I didn't get done onto the next day's list. Everything I have to do that isn't urgent gets put in a folder that I go through once in a while when I get caught up—a rare occurrence."

The Tyranny of Urgency

The "tyranny of urgency" from which this woman suffers is the situation for many busy people. The items at the top of the list may be the only things that get done. There is a constant stream of urgent tasks. Beware of letting the tyranny of urgency affect your ability to turn your attention from time to time to long-range planning and the accomplishment of long-range goals. What often happens is that managers spend too much time on technical and human problems, putting out the fires, and too little time in the conceptual area of deciding what should be done from a longer-range point of view and then planning how to get this done.

For this reason, lists in different time periods are useful. Tasks have quite different orders of priority when viewed from different time perspectives. Time allowed for creative thinking and for planning are vital elements in the successful accomplishment of your professional goals. Time must be set aside to do this in uninterrupted blocks.

Long-Range Planning

Many graduate schools of business administration teach a course in management policy, planning, and strategy toward the end of their programs. This course is devoted to the development of the corporation's long-range plan. The higher up you get on the corporate ladder, the more likely you are to be involved in planning processes that have a five- or ten-year perspective. For senior corporate executives, this larger view must take priority over the day-to-day emergencies if the company is going to be around in the next decade.

Here, as elsewhere, though, you must maintain a sense of proportion between short-term, urgent projects and long-range planning. A young corporate president was so obsessed with the need for long-range planning that he was rarely available to consult with his corporate staff on vital decisions that required immediate action. His associates became frustrated, and many left the company for jobs in a more balanced environment. The firm floundered for a long time because the president was so caught up in policy making that he didn't pay enough attention to current operations. The business never achieved the success that originally appeared possible.

First Organize, Then Delegate

In order to organize your time you must know where your time is now going. The essential information for establishing control over your time is the two-week summary of your present use of time. Once you have this background and you have begun to use "To Do" lists, you are well on your way to organizing your time.

The next step is to know your priorities. What is important for you to accomplish? By when must this be done? You need to have clearly established goals for your job and for your career. You did this in Chapter 7. Keep these objectives in mind. They are what enable you to decide what to do in order of its importance to you.

Goals often conflict and you have to know what takes priority; and then take the decision that will move you toward your most important goal.

To a large extent organizing your professional activities means finding out what you can delegate to others and then influencing them to do it. As we've pointed out before, the art of managing is the art of influencing others to achieve the goals of the organization. As you will see at greater length in Chapter 16, this is the definition of managerial power. The extent to which you are able to do this is both a measure of your power in the organization and your effectiveness.

Look over your activities list for the two weeks you studied. How many of those jobs could have been done by someone else? Why didn't you delegate the task? Working through others can be a difficult lesson for many women to learn since they have often been trained to do things for someone else. Women have been raised to be "doers," rather than "motivators of others" and "users of power." To be a successful administrator you must learn to delegate to others whenever possible, even if they don't do the job so rapidly or so well as you would do it yourself. Not only do you gain extra time for yourself, but you are training and developing your subordinates in the process, which will enable you to delegate still more to them in the future.

"I always push my people to take on more than they feel they can do, or to try something new," says Janet, a successful manager in a hospital. "I always give each person a chance at learning the job of the next step up. For example, the secretaries get a chance to do some interviewing of new employees. This way they begin to learn techniques and to see if they like the work and want to move up in that direction. I give the interviewers a chance to do a rough cut at the part of the departmental budget. The only way to learn the budget on an annual basis is to try doing it and see where you make errors when the final results are in. While it took some of my time to train my people and encourage them to take the risk of trying new things, in the long run it saves me time. If an interviewer is sick, one of the secretaries can fill in for the day. This means I don't have to do it. When I compile the pieces of the budget that have been estimated by several of my people, it takes me less time to complete the final draft. Not only that, but I probably turn out a better product in less time, too, because it is the end result of the thinking of several experienced people."

Try to pick out one activity from your list and decide to delegate that activity—even if it initially means you will have to take some time to train someone else to do the task. Estimate how much time you can save in the next six months by relieving yourself of that task.

Circadian Rhythm

Another way to gain some extra time is by closely studying your own circadian rhythm. Circadian rhythm is the ebb and flow of energy that you experience throughout the day. Are you a night person? A morning person? Do you do your best work at 3:00 in the afternoon or is it a low period for you? When do you like best to be with people? When do you prefer to be alone? Learn your times of peak activity and performance. Try to schedule your activities to conform to your body's natural rhythm and organize your schedule around it. It will help you get more done in less time.

One university dean who teaches and is also the financial planner behind a complex corporation says that the only way he is able to write—another in the long list of his successful activities—is to get up early and write for two hours before doing or thinking about anything else. Another executive in the computer industry says the only time he can find for writing books—and he manages to turn out one a year—is at airports and on airplanes.

In the first case, the university dean applies his early morning concentration, and preference for being alone, to his books. In the second, the computer executive finds he is too distracted by all the activity around him on airplanes and in airports to do heavy thinking, so he focuses his remaining energy and concentration on what for him is a lighter task: writing his books.

"One of the recurring jobs in our area is reviewing the archives every six months," complained a busy bank executive. "It is undoubtedly my most disliked task. I haven't been able to give it to anyone else because people move in and out of the department so rapidly that no one has a large enough overview to make a reasonable judgment about what can be thrown out and what has to be kept. I've finally discovered that the easiest time for me to do this job is when I'm physically tired. I can sort through the files while I'm sitting at my desk. This takes less energy than being out on the floor working with people. Hating this chore so much has forced me to figure out ways to give part of the drudgery away. I'm starting to have the printouts color-coded when we receive them to indicate their usefulness and longevity. This way I hope that I'll be able to direct someone else to pull all the output marked with a certain color and dispose of it."

This manager is suiting the job to her energy level. She's organizing it to be able eventually to delegate all or part of the task. She'll ultimately save herself both energy and time.

Setting Up a Schedule

When you have your tasks identified and organized on a priority basis, you next want to work at controlling your time. Scheduling activities is the way to do this. With an idea of how your time is actually being spent and a good idea of how you would prefer to spend it, you can set up a schedule. The most important thing about scheduling is to make it flexible enough to be realistic. This means leaving a certain amount of time unscheduled. Some people may need only an hour a day to take care of unforeseen problems; other administrators may have to leave half the day unscheduled. Once you begin scheduling your activities, stick to your schedule. Learn to say no. Arrange specific times to meet with other people and postpone impromptu get-togethers, which are often more social than productive. Productive meetings during working hours are usually the ones that are scheduled for a specific purpose. Learn the art of deflecting interruptions. How you do this depends a lot on your personal and professional style.

"My people know that I like to review problems in the afternoon," explained a busy woman. "I've made it clear that I am available on appointment for any departmental problem after 3:00, but that I'd rather not be disturbed for meetings in the morning unless it is an emergency. These are my ground rules and I have made them explicit to each of the people working for me. This way I'm free to do all my paper pushing in the morning and my secretary can work on it in the afternoon. I get the mail out the same day usually and have rough drafts ready for me to read over while I'm on the train home."

"It wasn't easy for me to learn to ask someone to come back later since I enjoy so much being friendly and socializing on the job," another woman executive explained. "I have so little time to be with friends outside of work, and most of my friends are in the office anyway. But after I got my last promotion, I found that I was taking work home with me much too often. I determined that I had to get more done in the office, so I am learning to say things like, 'I'd love to talk with you now, but I must finish this report first. Could we make an appointment?' My relationships at work are becoming less spontaneous, which is a pity, . . . but my brief-case is lighter at night, and my husband is complaining less."

How to Avoid Distractions

Studies by Henry Mintzberg, a professor of business, published in his book, *The Nature of Managerial Work,* show that the average senior executive spends only about six uninterrupted minutes at a typical undertaking—not much time to do any real creating or problem solving. Apparently, upper-level management is involved in so many different tasks, and so many people need their time and attention that it is very difficult for them to spend any length of time on any individual task or with any single person. This kind of constant interruption can cause a great deal of time loss because of the necessity of stopping and starting various undertakings several times. Start-up time usually means lost time.

Do you find yourself moving rapidly from one thing to another, rather than carrying important tasks through to completion? Can you compartmentalize an important project and block out other distractions? Or are you consciously or subconsciously looking for an interruption because you are bored with what you are doing or lack concentration? Or are the demands of your job such that you cannot plan enough time in blocks to work efficiently, which was frequently the case for the managers that Mintzberg studied. Diagnosing why you have a problem in carrying things through to completion is a giant step toward recapturing some of the time lost due to fragmentation. You'll find that it is helpful to look at not only *why* you are so often deflected from the task at hand but *how* it happens as well.

Interruptions fall into two general categories: external and internal. External interruptions, such as phone calls, visitors, meetings, can be major handicaps to the effective use of your time. Many of these are necessary and can't be avoided, although they probably can be better controlled to minimize their negative impact on your effective use of your time. Internal interruptions are the result of a lack of concentration, or a lack of interest, or both. Following are some helpful techniques for managing both these external and internal distractions.

1. Arrange your office or work area to avoid visitors. Close your door when you do not want to be disturbed. Face your desk away from the door when it is open, or if you don't have a door. Work out of the office on important projects that require continuous concentration.

2. Use your secretary to screen calls and callers. If you are fortunate enough to have a secretary, use him or her to help you avoid interruptions. Tell him or her when you want to make time to see people and when you need to be protected. More than one canny woman executive has developed a variation of her natural voice. Then, when she has to answer her own phone, she screens out unwanted callers by acting as her own secretary and message taker.

3. If you have a secretary or use of a word-processing center, learn to use dictating equipment. You can dictate about four times as fast as you can write. If you have a secretary, she or he won't have to waste valuable time taking dictation when you could be putting the information into a machine for later transcription. Using a machine comfortably is a rapidly learned skill that can save you a great deal of time.

4. Develop a "do it now" philosophy. Avoid procrastination. It often takes longer to think about something and put it off than it does to think about it and do it. Analyze things that you put off. Can they be delegated? Usually procrastination is a symptom of the fact that you don't want to do it, or that the task is too com-

plex. If the latter is the case, see if you can't break the job up into several pieces and get on with the first step toward completion.

5. Try to finish the things that you begin, or give them to others to complete when they've reached a stage where the finishing up can be delegated. Attempt to handle each piece of paper you deal with only one time. Look at it, decide what to do with it, and dispose of it.

6. Manage visits and meetings. When you're in control, set a time for them and a time limit on their length. Learn ways to end these get-togethers gracefully. Get up from your desk; have your secretary call you by prearrangement; simply state that you have to bring the visit to a close. Even meetings you don't control can sometimes be shortened by your informing the leader that you must leave at a certain agreed-upon time, but this can be done only *before* the meeting is underway. By scheduling your time, you know what you need to be doing and when, making it much easier to get other people's cooperation in the matter.

EVALUATING: LOOKING BACK FOR BETTER PLANNING AHEAD

Being an effective manager means you must constantly check your results against your desired objectives. You must allow yourself time to review your objectives. One woman has a contest with herself. "I have a daily activity sheet and another list that contains long-range goals. I take great pleasure in crossing completed activities off my daily list. I have even a greater sense of accomplishment when I can cross off a monthly goal. As an added time-saver, I keep both these lists in permanent form in my desk diary. I go over my lists twice a year to see what I have accomplished. Then I write a summary for my boss. This helps me evaluate what I've done and gives my boss an accurate summary of what part of her department has been achieving. Without these lists, I'd tend to forget many of the things that got done and done well. You usually remember most distinctly the problem situations—not the productive routine. This information helps me a lot with my future planning, too. Based on this past experience, I can see what is realistic to attempt to do in a given time."

R. Alec Mackenzie has pointed out in his useful book, *The Time Trap*, that, on a national average, administrators only get done about 30 per cent of what they set out to do each day. You should be able to improve your percentage by putting into practice the major changes in your behavior that have been suggested in this chapter:

1. Study how you are presently using your time.
2. Decide where you want to make changes.
3. Plan on paper what you are going to do.
4. Give priority to the items on these lists in terms of your goals.
5. Schedule your time.
6. Stick to the schedule.
7. Use every timesaving tip that works for you.
8. Evaluate your use of time on a regular basis. Your ultimate goal is to invest your time in ways that pay the biggest dividend for you and your organization.

There are two final suggestions to help you achieve the maximum payoff for the investment of your scarcest resource: your time.

9. Avoid the "paralysis of perfection." Not every task has to be done well, contrary to what your parents may have taught you when you were growing up. Some just have to be gotten out of the way. Others don't even have to be done at all. Other people can only suggest to you what you should or might do. You are free to choose whether to do it, or at least how well to do it and how much time to expend in the effort.

This leads us to our last suggestion, a vitally important means of saving time:

10. Be decisive. People waste time by weighing endlessly the factors involved in a decision. Women, in particular, tend to

overanalyze, rather than make a decision, take the action, and live with the risk entailed.

The next chapter is devoted to a method that will help you become more decisive and more able to see and accept calculated risk.

13

DECISION MAKING IN ACTION

At every step along the way in managing your life and your time, you will be required to make decisions. The more skillful you become at decision making, the more time you will have available to carry out your decisions and to accomplish your goals.

Managers must constantly decide not only what to do, but when and how to do it. Women have sometimes been handicapped in business because in the past they've been uncomfortable about being decision- and action-oriented. They have often been encouraged to let someone else decide for them, to be passive more often than active; and then, to execute the results of someone else's decision. This doesn't work in a managerial job. The manager is the person who must make the decisions.

Good Managers Think Carefully and Quickly

Effective managers have learned to be decisive. They are practiced in making decisions and living with the consequences. They place great value on rapid decision-making to save time. Even though they think and act quickly, good managers still make carefully thought out decisions because these are more easily defended than impulsive decisions, if they turn out wrong. By using a logical process, you'll then know why you did something, and this information will help you make a better decision the next time.

ACCEPTING THE RISK

All decisions carry with them some degree of risk. Sometimes we are prevented by our colleagues from taking what seems to be too great a risk. But most of the time, managers simply study the problem, decide what to do, and plan how to do it. It is usually better to have a decision made and in the process of being carried forward, than to have it pending. While there is risk involved in carrying forward a decision, there is also risk in postponing facing an issue—in doing nothing—unless you've decided that to do nothing is the best course of action, and you can defend this decision.

We All Make Mistakes

Managers are expected to be right in their decisions only a little better than half of the time. Once you realize this is what you are aiming for it becomes easier to be decisive and to take risks.

"Actually," commented a senior vice-president, "I find less risk in the decisions I make at my level than when I was dealing with less complex issues and smaller sums of money. When I make mistakes now, I can cover them more easily. And I make mistakes. We all do. Accepting your own fallibility is a lesson you have to learn if you are going to make it in business. You also have to learn how to avoid letting the results of your errors become obvious, and how to stop what you are doing, if it turns out to be a mistake, and start again."

TWO-STAGE DECISION MAKING

A clear-cut system for making decisions will help you to make the right decision, to defend your positions, and to correct mistakes if things go awry. One useful approach is the two-stage method of decision making. Making a decision is a very complex process, but it becomes easier and faster when you realize that every decision is made in two stages: (a) deciding *if* something must be done, and (b) deciding *what* to do.

The method uses the following steps in helping you think out your decisions:

1. Analyze the problem.

Decide what is wrong, and what is the desired resolution to the situation. What do you want to accomplish? Writing out this information is helpful. The process of writing out the details helps you clarify your thinking and also to be more objective later when you are evaluating the results of your action.

2. Establish a deadline for making your decision and for putting it into action.

The deadline will help you determine how much time you have to work on the next four steps.

3. Look for possible solutions.

Generate as many ideas as you can. At this point, it is often helpful to sound out other people, to get fresh viewpoints, or, if the problem is a complex one, discuss the matter at a meeting. Write down the alternatives, but don't evaluate them at this stage because you will block creative thinking.

4. Evaluate the alternatives.

Eliminate those that are unrealistic because there isn't enough time to accomplish them or because they would be too expensive to carry out. Take the remaining possibilities and extend them, mentally, to their logical conclusion. See which ones will give you the right results. Estimate the relative cost of each.

5. Decide whether you really have to do something, given the available feasible alternatives.

Often when you have thought through a situation to this stage, you will feel that either (a) it is best not to do anything about the problem; or (b) you should postpone making a decision about the matter until a specific time.

If your answer at this point is that you should not do anything, either set the matter aside permanently or plan for another review at a later time. If you are going to look into the problem again, establish a specific time and plan to start the whole process from the beginning. Inaction on a problem by *ignoring* it is actually a decision by default, which usually will return to haunt you again and again, using up both valuable time and energy. It is much more efficient to face the issue consciously, examine it thoroughly, and then make a clear choice not to do anything. This enables you to forget the situation permanently or until you have scheduled a re-review.

This is the end of the first stage of decision making. In most cases, your answer to whether you must take some action will be "Yes, something must be done." If this is your answer, you then move on to the second stage of the process: deciding what to do.

6. *Choose one of the alternative solutions.*

7. *Do it; put your decision into action.*

There is no point in deciding what you should do if you don't do it. This amounts to precisely the same thing as deciding in step 5 to do nothing *after* you have made a conscious decision that something has to be done.

8. *Evaluate your solution while it is being executed.*

Make sure your course of action is bringing you closer to the goal you outlined in step 1. If you find that things aren't working out the way you anticipated, you can generally stop the action. You should then reanalyze the whole situation from step 1 since you are now dealing with more information. Also, many factors may have changed since you first faced the problem. If you find you must attack the problem again, consider it as an entirely new challenge.

Understanding that every decision has two choice points, rather than one, helps you avoid confusing *whether or not* something should be done, with *what* you should do. Skill in decision making comes from working this eight-step procedure into your thought process. Practice applying it in both your personal and professional life.

Don't Be a Victim of "Analysis Paralysis"

Gathering information in the decision-making process is costly in terms of time, effort, and money. For this reason the amount of information generated is usually less than you feel you need in order to make a fully informed decision. It's axiomatic that most management decisions are based on inadequate information. Therefore, you must become skilled at making decisions and taking action based on the limited information and resources available during the time allotted to work on your problem.

You must be willing to take the risks that these limitations involve. Women, in particular, tend to overanalyze a problem. They are usually skilled at analysis, but often avoid making a decision and taking action while seeking the security of additional information. They are afraid of being wrong. They become victims of "analysis paralysis" and can't move to step 6 in the decision-making process. They can't decide what to do. Or they decide what to do and then hesitate to take the action, which is step 7. Men, on the other hand, sometimes have a tendency to move right to these two items. They make a decision and act on it, in what has been described as the "gunslinger" style: acting first and then later checking to see if they attacked the right target in an appropriate manner. But the goal for both women and men is the same: to find a reasonable balance between analyzing a problem and acting on the results of the evaluation.

The father of a businesswoman who balances analysis and action well taught her: "All people can expect from a good decision is to feel that they made the best decision at the time, given their resource limitations." This philosophy has enabled her over the years to make rapid personal and professional decisions and to act on them without agonizing over decisions that later proved to be less than perfect.

DECISION MAKING IN ACTION

Margaret, the director of a large clinic, had a rapidly increasing problem with the lateness of many of her staff. She realized that she had to face the problem because it was causing the clinic to operate at a decreasing level of efficiency. Her goal was to eliminate as much tardiness as possible and get the clinic off to a timely start in the morning. She determined specifically that she wanted to cut the number of employees coming in late each morning by at least half, so that all sections could begin operating promptly when the clinic opened. As things stood, certain areas got off to a late start and caused the whole clinic to get further and further behind with their appointments throughout the day.

The operation of the clinic was coming up for its semiannual review the following month, so Margaret gave herself a week to work on the problem and to decide what to do. This left her with three weeks until the review to implement the solution and get the operation running more smoothly.

The problem of tardiness, like any other, is complex, and Margaret had to study all the contributing factors, all the excuses. Many of the employees had to commute long distances in heavy traffic. Part of the clinic was staffed with hospital residents and interns who had other duties that often kept them working late into the night. Margaret considered possible solutions. These included:

- Docking the pay of latecomers
- Withholding raises from employees who were chronically late
- Threatening to fire habitual offenders
- Filing a formal report on tardy interns and residents
- Discussing the situation with the group and trying to work out a solution with their help

In evaluating these choices, she realized that docking the pay wouldn't work because some of the employees would rather come in late than earn full pay. Furthermore, she didn't control the paychecks of the professional members of her staff. She believed that withholding raises would demotivate employees who were currently doing a good job; it would cause them to be less effective once they did arrive at the clinic. Firing serious offenders would mean that she'd have to spend valuable time in locating and training their replacements, *if* she could even locate replacements. The interns, for the most part, did not like working in the clinic, so filing formal reports against them would only increase their resentment.

There was no question in Margaret's mind that something had to be done. Then, moving on to step 6, she decided to call a meeting of the staff and discuss the problem with them. She realized it might not produce quite such dramatic results as some of her other ideas, but, on the other hand, it wasn't likely to worsen the situation. And she believed that a solution reached by consensus had the best chance for success. She was also determined to learn more about the problem at the meeting and find out why the lateness had become so widespread so quickly—an aspect she didn't fully understand. Then she'd have additional information in the event she had to deal with the problem again in the future.

At the meeting, Margaret encouraged an open discussion and a sharing of information. Many of the employees didn't realize how much their own tardiness was affecting the work of others, and inconveniencing the patients as well. Margaret found out that there was major construction on a main route to the clinic, causing traffic tie-ups on certain mornings. She also learned that the hospital was short two interns because of illness. This meant that those on duty had even more night work than normal, and were therefore tired and slow in getting to work at the clinic in the mornings.

Once these facts came out into the open, and the staff understood the problem in its larger context, Margaret was able to develop a workable plan. She had the employees form partnership teams so that, at all times, at least one of the two would be in on time. If one member of the team expected to be late, he would get in touch with his partner, who would then redouble his efforts to get to the clinic on time. An unexpected benefit of this group meeting and studying the problem together was a stronger relationship among the staff—a great team spirit. They enjoyed being consulted about the problem and participating in planning to alleviate it. Margaret didn't quite achieve her goal of a 50 per cent reduction in lateness, but she did get the clinic off to a timely start in the morning, and this was her larger objective.

Margaret used the two-stage decision-making model to solve her problem. The steps outlined for decision making are a useful aid in working out virtually any problem, regardless of its complexity, and regardless of whether it is a professional or personal problem.

THINKING POSITIVELY ABOUT RISK

To get ahead in the corporate environment, not only must you be able to handle risks that come naturally with the responsibilities of your job, but you must also recognize risk opportunities. You are in competition with many other people at your level in the company and, if you want to move up, you must show that you are more creative than your peers in moving the firm toward its goals. You must identify and then take risks that will accomplish this. Richard Byrd, author of the book, *A Guide to Personal Risk Taking,* calls this kind of risk *dynamic risk.* He defines dynamic risk as that risk that is related to managerial innovation, as a risk taken to make a gain. The other sort of risk that managers take, only to the avoidance of potential loss, he calls *static risk.*

When a conservative European company purchased an American firm, the vice-president felt that there were now enough funds available to capture a larger share of the U.S. market. But this would mean spending a great deal of money, and making sales projections that were much larger than the small growth that the company was accustomed to. He discussed this with the president of the company, and finally they decided to go ahead with the plan. Both of them took a dynamic risk. They planned to institute new policies, redo all their promotional material, institute new programs, and thereby aggressively seek to increase their share of the market.

They could easily have settled for improving sales only slightly or raising the annual rate of increase of sales by only 5 or 7 per cent. They were not content with this type of goal, which would represent a static risk—avoiding a performance that was worse than anything the company had done in the past. They felt in this case that it was more dangerous to take a static risk than a dynamic risk because they were in a highly competitive market, where the two major contenders were constantly innovating. They felt that now was the time to make major changes, to see a major increase in their share of the market. There were also other reasons. They were now part of a very large organization, and if they proved effective in their present positions, and obtained visibility, there was room for them to move up. They were able to achieve an 18 per cent growth in sales the first year and almost a 19 per cent gain the second year by their creative efforts, their willingness to take a risk, and by very hard work.

Successful managers have to be dynamic risk takers. Static risk takers are better off in bureaucratic positions, where longevity on the job is the major factor in upward mobility and salary increases. But, as Byrd cautions, you must take your dynamic risk only where *you* can influence the outcome, not where the result is merely a matter of chance.

Psychiatrist David Viscott, in his book, *Risking,* points out that "in every risk there is some unavoidable loss, something has to be given up to move ahead. . . . Many people are terrified by any possible loss and try to avoid all risks." But, as he continues, "not risking is a sure way of losing. If you do not risk, risk eventually comes to you. . . . If a person postpones taking risks, the time eventually comes when she will either be forced to accept a situation she does not like, or she'll have to take a risk unprepared." Richard Byrd tells us that, "one motivational factor common to us all is fear. The biggest fears that drive us are those of failure, of what other people will think, of uncertainty." This bears out Viscott's theory that we must take risk or we will surely lose, because not risking in the corporate environment eventually means failing to move ahead. Harvard psychologist David McClelland thinks that managers are motivated by "the desire to achieve, to be accepted by others and to have power." Dynamic risk is perhaps motivated by McClelland's positive factors, and static risk, by the fears Byrd describes.

The two senior managers who took the dynamic risk of setting very high sales goals were apparently motivated by McClelland's positive factors. They did achieve in their own eyes and those of the people who work for them as well as the parent corporation. Their power position and ability to influence both their subordinates and their superiors were also increased. The price they paid for this was two years of extremely hard work—much harder than if they had not determined to take the risk. Had they not taken the risk, they probably would have been replaced when the company failed to hold onto modest annual gains in the face of their competition.

Bearing the Weight of Responsibility

Virtually all positions of responsibility require constant dynamic risk taking. Consider the situation of a manager of information services who has to select and purchase several million dollars' worth of computer equipment for his company. He has to choose between two very different types of equipment that are not at all compatible. This means that his decision, once made, cannot be moderated or reversed. He has sought advice from specialists in the field: about half recommended one type of system, while the other half urged him to buy the other system. Eventually one of these computer systems will turn out to be more suitable than the other, but he can't wait to find out which one. He must equip his company now, but a strong industry trend won't become apparent for several years. The responsibility for making this decision and spending this money rests squarely on his shoulders. No one can tell him what he should do. "The buck stops" with him. If he makes the wrong decision, he will adversely affect the profits of the corporation for many years to come. He has no fall-back position to minimize the risk, to make it static.

He is a stable, self-confident, experienced manager who can live with this amount of risk and responsibility. Nonetheless, he has paid the price with some serious physical stress symptoms in the form of high blood pressure, which he had not previously had. He'll probably return to normal when the level of stress over the decision goes down. But this is the price he has to pay to do his job and to prove himself for the senior management position for which he is in line. Do you want the level of responsibility that a risk like this decision entails?

On a less rarefied, but probably equally complex level, a marketing manager described her annual problems in choosing a marketing direction for the company and committing large amounts of the corporation's time and money to those ends. "So much money is committed on so few hard facts every year. I'm the one who has to make the decision to go with a certain marketing philosophy and I have to direct the promotional activities to support it. Marketing, like any creative activity, is very subjective. Little is known, really, about what succeeds and what fails. But the decision is up to me. It's a continuing strain. Furthermore, I must motivate my ad agency to do their best creatively. To do this, they must be convinced that the direction we're going in is the right one. And I've got to sell it to the president of our company as well. Not easy, when, in truth, I'm not sure myself. Sure, there's always market research information to back me up, but I know that if you ask the wrong questions or use badly designed questions, you don't get real answers. You get what people think you'd like to hear, not a prediction of what they'll actually do. You have to take research results with lots of grains of salt. It all really boils down to my making a decision in a very ambiguous environment."

How well do you handle ambiguity? How well do you handle uncertainty? Making any decision involves uncertainty about the outcome. Can you handle the type of uncertainty that the information systems manager will experience during the next several years or the uncertainty described by the marketing manager?

PLANNING DYNAMIC RISK

In considering whether you should take a dynamic risk, there are some factors for you to look at. First, you should consider whether to take such a risk; then, if you decide to take it, what to do to minimize the possibility of loss.

Take a dynamic risk because the potential gain seems to outweigh the amount of risk you feel is involved. Estimate the odds; analyze what you believe to be your chances of success. Look at the cost of failure. What will happen to you if the risk you take turns out badly? What might happen to you if you don't take the risk?

If you decide you will take the risk, plan your actions carefully. Use the eight-step decision process to decide what to do. Get impartial advice from people with no stake in the outcome. Plan carefully. Set personal limits as to how long you are willing to continue to take this risk. The corporate managers who set such ambitious sales goals would probably not have continued on that path a second year if they had not proven the risk worth taking— and a reasonable one as well—during the first year.

Have a backup position in case your risk turns out badly. Know when you can stop the action and what else you can start doing. Every decision you make involves a risk and every decision involves change of some sort or other. Another aid to managing dynamic risk situations well is to be adept at handling change.

In this chapter we've looked at decision making and risk taking. In the next chapters we examine how to manage change, and the conflict that almost inevitably accompanies it.

14

HANDLING CONFLICT AND CHANGE

One of the fine arts of management is being able to bring about change, and then managing the conflict that inevitably accompanies it. Like the chicken and the egg, change and conflict follow each other in an unending cycle. Good managers can use the conflict that comes from change as a catalyst to bring about still more change for the better. In a book called *Work in America,* author John Gardner says that "we must meet the challenge of altered circumstances. Change will occur whether we like it or not." And change brings with it conflict, as people and organizations attempt to alter themselves to adjust to the change. Managers must be able to plan for and manage both conflict and change.

A CHANGE IN ATTITUDE

Prior to World War II, industry did not necessarily view change positively, nor conflict as potentially useful. Most managers regarded conflict as disruptive and destructive, and change as threatening. Administrators often acted in an authoritarian manner to preserve things the way they were, and to eliminate or discourage conflict. After the war, companies became more complex, due, in a large measure, to the vast technological developments made during World War II. The unquestioning respect for authority began to lessen, a more democratic and participatory style of management evolved, and conflict came to be more accepted as a normal part of organizational life.

In recent years, a further evolution in thinking has brought about the realization that conflict, as a form of human interaction, is not solely negative. While it can be destructive, conflict is now recognized as a useful catalyst, forcing further change and adaptation. As the rate of technological, social, and cultural change continues to accelerate, it becomes increasingly vital for managers to be able to help their organizations adapt to this change.

James Cribbins, in his book *Effective Managerial Leadership,* states that managers "are paid to become more effective and to operate increasingly effective organizations." They must be able to innovate: to develop new ways of making the company more productive, efficient, profitable, and competitive. Since doing this requires a liberal measure of change, they must also be able to help the people who work for the company adjust to changing conditions.

How AT&T Changed

Change comes about in three ways: by evolution, by revolution, and by careful planning. Almost all organizations are constantly making slow adjustments—they are changing by evolution. Revolutionary changes occur when things have gotten so bad that something drastic has to be done and done quickly. But generally the most effective way to manage change is to anticipate changes that will be necessary and then to bring them about in an orderly, logical fashion—to plan change.

Even massive organizations like American Telephone and Telegraph Company experience all three types of change. For many years, very gradual, evolutionary change took place within this giant organization, which employs more than 900,000 people. Gradually the system was grinding to a halt because the need to service a rapidly growing population of users was outstripping the ability of the system to cope. In the late sixties, it became increasingly difficult to get phone calls through to major metropolitan centers during office hours.

Fortunately, the system had a well-trained management team that was able to analyze the operational and equipment problems and by some revolutionary methods bring the system up to standard. Two other forces began to come into operation about this time, which brought about further revolutionary changes. Where the corporation had previously had a virtual monopoly on telephone service throughout the country, new legislation gradually allowed competitors to enter into the telephone equipment business. Additionally, equal employment opportunity legislation was being enacted and enforced in the early seventies, and a major suit against the company forced them to open upper-level management jobs to women, and to offer equal pay for equal work.

With the pressure of increasing competition from other firms, AT&T, for the first time, found it was having to market its services and equipment to consumers. However, without a staff of trained marketing executives, management realized they were quite unprepared to handle this revolutionary change. Contrary to their previous policy of promoting from within, they had to hire managers from the outside. Women managers in the company who had an interest in marketing and who wanted to move rapidly up the corporate ladder were sitting in ideal positions in the mid-seventies. Both men and women employees are now finding opportunities in this newly enlarged area of the corporation, since a great deal of attention is being given to the profitable marketing of services and equipment. Planning for continued upward movement of women managers is also in progress.

While you probably won't be involved in such large-scale, revolutionary or planned changes, it doesn't hurt to be aware of major industrial changes, some of which might help you pinpoint unique opportunities for advancement or avoid unexpected obsolescence.

Blueprint for Positive, Creative Change

It is also wise to examine your own feeling toward change. Do you enjoy it? Do you seek it? Would you prefer to keep things as they are now? Is your nesting instinct so well developed you would choose to stay in your present situation rather than seek a new job or employer or a new way of doing things? As a manager on the move up, you will need to welcome change and enjoy managing it. James Cribbins has some suggestions that can help executives to plan and execute change systematically. He suggests that you:

1. Work as much as possible within the ongoing situation.
Try to make the changes evolutionary, rather than revolutionary. This is done by anticipating change and planning ahead for it so that it can be gradual rather than a "firefighting" operation.

2. Make only necessary change.

3. Get support for change.
Involve the people who will be affected in the planning stage as soon as you can. This will go a long way toward gaining their acceptance. Get feedback from the people involved and improve on the change if you can.

4. Plan the introduction of the change in every detail.
Phase it in gradually.

5. Don't try to rush or push people into acceptance.
Give them time to adjust.

6. Anticipate both rational and irrational resistance.
Cribbins points out that negative reactions to change—"resistance and resentment"—come "largely from feelings rather than from reason." Look at the resistance for clues as to how the change can be improved. Conflict that results from change can pinpoint problem areas.

7. Alter the course of events if things aren't working out well.

Although these suggestions sound straightforward and practical, it is amazing how rarely managers and companies utilize these ideas, which could be so helpful in preventing negative reaction, or in diffusing it when it does occur. One company announced that the executive vice-president was going to be transferred to head a subsidiary operation elsewhere, but did not mention who would take his place or how operations would be restructured. This manager was very well respected, and all the people who reported to him were quite anxious about the change until several weeks later, when the final plans for restructuring were formalized and made public. Meanwhile, rumors were rampant. Other corporate executives who might have been in line for this corporate plum were hoping that they might receive the promotion. They were all disappointed; the company was reorganized, and the job was left unfilled. It will take some months—perhaps even years—until the negative emotions generated by this poorly handled change disappear and the company is back to normal.

In another company, Sallie, a rapidly moving woman executive, was promoted into a difficult troubleshooting job. She applied her excellent problem-solving abilities and high energy level to the job. Within eighteen months, she had the most severe problems straightened out. Then she began to hear rumors that the department was going to be eliminated, primarily due to her success. She particularly enjoyed working for her present boss and was learning a lot from her, and was therefore anxious about her future. Sallie asked her boss what she thought would happen to both of them; her boss had no idea either.

One day, Sallie's boss was moved to another department as a minor promotion; Sallie was merely moved to another office, without being assigned any specific responsibilities. After about ten days spent in finishing up details from her old assignment, Sallie was given a promotion, but was assigned to work for a man for whom she did not want to work. She has been looking for another job since that time because she feels the company has no interest in her needs or aspirations, that it simply moves people mechanically according to its needs. She feels that management doesn't value her particular talents and doesn't really care whether she stays with the firm or leaves. All of this may be largely her emotional reaction to a change that was very ineptly handled.

Badly handled, change brings about a lot of unnecessary conflict. Well handled, change tends to cause conflict in those areas where further constructive change is needed.

CONFLICT: PERSONALITIES AND RESOURCES

How Much Conflict Can You Take?

In the late fifties, Janice, a young woman, took an executive position in the clothing industry: "I knew I had to change to another line of work because I just wasn't used to such vociferous disagreements. They seemed to go on constantly. My family had always solved things very quietly without raised voices or name calling. I was never able to learn how to shout back at someone when we got into a disagreement—I couldn't even get my voice heard in the fray. It took a tremendous toll on me emotionally, and I was always surprised to see the combatants emerge from the most pitched battles as firm friends as ever.

"Eventually I found a position with a large textile corporation where I could use my garment-industry experience and where people behaved, at least on the surface, much like my family. But I soon realized that just as many conflicts existed here as in the company I had left—if not more—since things rarely were faced and sorted out. The open disagreement that I was so uncomfortable with in my first job was probably much more effective in bringing about needed changes."

Fortunately, the company Janice joined didn't have to make rapid changes and the climate of the corporation was more suited to her personal makeup, so her progress continued rapidly.

How do you feel about conflict? What emotional response does the idea of conflict awaken in you? What words would you use to define conflict? Are they negative or positive words? What are some of the conflict situations in which you currently find yourself? Can you envision any positive changes coming about as a result of facing these conflicts? Or do you feel that "nice girls don't fight"?

Conflict can occur within yourself, between you and another person or other people, or between you and the company. You experience intrapersonal conflict when your roles clash—when you need more time for your professional life, yet your husband and children need that same time from you and, probably, you also need that time for exercise or just to relax and do nothing. Janice experienced interpersonal conflict with the people on her first job, and she wasn't used to this face-to-face emotional confrontation as a method of problem resolution. Sallie felt a conflict between her needs as a professional person and the organization's needs to fill certain positions with worker-managers to get the job done.

Resources: There's Never Enough to Go Around

Besides the emotional aspect of conflict, which can be mitigated to a certain extent by knowing yourself and choosing a working climate that suits you, there is another aspect of conflict that is unavoidable. This is the conflict caused by the fact that all companies have limited resources. People and groups within an organization necessarily have to compete for their share of these limited resources in order for the corporation to operate efficiently. To the extent that you can focus on the facts of the problem resulting from disagreement on the allocation of resources and minimize the emotional content of the situation caused by differences in values, attitudes, insecurities, resentments, and a variety of ego problems, the better will be your chances of using conflict constructively.

When a large bank installed a new computer system, it found that the various departments did not have sufficient time on the computer. The mortgage department needed the computer to get bills out to their customers and process payments. The commercial loan department needed the computer to get information for and about its customers in order to process their loans. The savings and checking departments had to get statements to their customers on time. To compound the problem, printouts showing total interest paid for the year had to be produced and sent out by the end of each month, as required by federal regulations. The fundamental problem was clearly a case of a very scarce resource: computer time. But it was aggravated by the departmental managers fighting over it. Each manager believed and tried to prove that his or her department's needs took precedence.

Every company attempts to achieve its goals and maximize its profits with a minimum use of resources. There is never enough of anything to go around—staff time, computer time, supplies, or anything else. This is even true for abstract resources such as recognition, attention, prestige, and power. Once you realize that competition is natural and conflict inevitable, you will feel less threatened by it and will be able, instead, to concentrate on handling conflict in a more impersonal and less emotional manner.

Playing the Game of Constructive Conflict Resolution

Some people even seem to enjoy corporate battling and appear to set up conflicts deliberately, perhaps because they so often come out on the winning end. Michael Maccoby, a psychoanalyst who has studied businessmen extensively and published his findings in a book titled *The Gamesman,* terms this type of person a "jungle fighter." A "gamesman," on the other hand, is a "person who loves change and wants to influence its course . . . [who] likes to take calculated risks and is fascinated by technique and new methods." This is a good image to bear in mind if you are targeting the top.

Whether you seek out maximum opportunity to bring about change in the corporation with the conflict that follows in its wake, or simply go about attempting to resolve conflict when it occurs in the normal course of events, it's useful to have a good idea of what you are doing.

Knowing some of the "rules" can help you to play the game of constructive conflict resolution more successfully, to influence the outcome, and to enjoy the challenge while you're doing it.

1. State the problem in terms of your goal, not in terms of a possible solution.

Try to identify *what* you are attempting to accomplish, not *how* you plan to go about doing it. When a problem is stated in terms of a solution, other possible means of resolving the situation are discouraged, or eliminated.

For example, if the executive in charge of the bank described earlier with the shortage of computer time states her problem as a need to divide the available time more equitably between the departments, she eliminates other approaches to the problem. Maybe some of the work could be done more efficiently without the computer. Perhaps this is a necessary short-term solution while the bank is expanding its computer capability. She would be better advised to state her goal as finding ways to meet both the needs of the bank's customers and to comply with federal regulations. This is really what she is attempting to accomplish.

2. Have a clear understanding of the issues involved in the conflict.

Meet separately with the parties to the conflict and hear what everyone involved has to say about it. Giving people a chance to voice their needs and concerns fully helps to minimize emotional tensions. Listening to everyone's point of view helps us to understand the conflict fully and come up with better ideas as to how to resolve it.

3. Differentiate fact from opinion and attitude, and concentrate on the facts.

Get the historical facts concerning the situation, as well as the present facts. This can save you from making the same mistake that might have been made in the past. It often helps unearth some additional causes of the conflict that are not readily apparent from an examination of present conditions. You might find out that two managers in the bank don't like each other and try to sabotage each other's work rather than cooperate in a smooth work flow. This might be an underlying cause of some of the argument about computer time. Often you will find that emotional conflicts are at the root of the problem, rather than a conflict over scarce resources.

4. Treat everyone equally and be consistent.
Favoritism will escalate the emotional aspect of a conflict.

5. Identify the obstacles to achieving the goal.

6. Look for and identify issues of agreement between the people who are in conflict.

7. When possible, divide the problem into smaller parts so that you can encourage cooperation a step at a time.

8. Establish with the people in the conflict the criteria for a successful solution.

This usually means further elaborating on your goals so that they will meet the needs of the people involved in the conflict to the maximum extent possible. What you are looking for whenever possible is a solution where everyone wins. If they can't have everything they want, they must at least feel they have gained something.

Describing some of the obstacles to the people involved often goes a long way toward helping to set realistic and acceptable subgoals with the parties involved. Explaining that it is not possible for the bank to acquire additional computer time for nine months will encourage the managers to think up different ways to meet their departmental needs, at least on a short-term basis.

9. Get everyone to believe that mutually acceptable solutions are possible.

10. Try to achieve a solution in which everyone wins, at least a little.

A compromise means that everyone gives a little and gains some. Sometimes you can find a solution that satisfies everyone; but when you have a solution where one side clearly wins and one side clearly loses, you set the stage for a continuance of the conflict.

11. Evaluate the solution.
Make sure it will bring about a more effective organization.

A WINNING SOLUTION

In a large consulting organization, each hour had to be accounted for by every employee and charged to a specific job. The reports had to be completed by a certain day each month, so that a summary could be prepared for the executive committee. The accounting department complained that the consultants were uncooperative about getting their reports in on time. As a result, the monthly summaries were late or lacked necessary information. The consultants complained that the accountants constantly bothered them for endlessly detailed information, and that they didn't have enough time to do their real job, that of consulting.

When a new woman came in as comptroller, she determined to

resolve this continuing conflict between her people and the consultants. At the same time, she wanted to make some needed changes in the systems of the company. She met with the consultants and then with the senior management to get a clear idea of the problems and what was needed to solve them. Finally she met with the accounting department staff to develop possible solutions. Eventually they worked out a shorter, simpler reporting form—one that could later be computerized. Then, the summaries could be produced more rapidly and updated with less manual labor. The changeover to a computerized system brought with it great strains until everything began to operate smoothly. The accounting department weathered the storm of adjustment well because the new comptroller planned for the change and anticipated many of the problems and conflicts that inevitably arose.

The comptroller was particularly concerned when she observed that one of the managers in her department didn't have any interest in learning about the new computer system. This employee felt she had gotten along without mechanical assistance during the twenty-five years she had worked as a bookkeeper, and she saw no reason to change now. This rejection of change is an attitude sometimes found among managers who have been doing the same job for an extended period of time. As far as this inflexible bookkeeper is concerned, I doubt that she'd be successful on this job or on any other. The ability to change is necessary for the survival of people, as well as of organizations. The active desire for change is an essential element in the makeup of people who seek more responsibility and greater challenge.

AMBIVALENCE ABOUT CONFLICT AND CHANGE

It has been said that "The answer is technology. What is the question?" Yet the application of new technology to old situations often results in an enormous amount of upheaval and conflict. Handling this kind of conflict is not easy. The comptroller we described above was experienced, so she knew what to expect. And she realized that the eventual results would be worth the troubles encountered along the way.

Attitudes to conflict and change are complicated by the fact that our society, our organizations, and we ourselves are often ambivalent about these issues. Ours is a society that values change and leads the world in technological advances, yet some of our major institutions appear to strive to preserve the status quo. Churches and universities, for example, do not appear to be forces in bringing about equal opportunity for women to achieve leadership and senior positions.

Many companies will say they support change and even encourage constructive conflict; yet when you look closely at who is rewarded by promotions, you find it is not the people who champion change.

Finding the Right Climate for Change

Before you decide to become a catalyst for change where you work, study the climate of your organization. Does change appear to be sought and valued? Is conflict encouraged as a means of bringing about effective change, or is it discouraged? Is conflict kept hidden? Are you rewarded for bringing problems out into the open, or do you get the feeling that the people to whom you report would just as soon "let it ride"?

Rena worked in a very successful small organization largely controlled by the original entrepreneur who had founded it. She was dedicated to efficient operations and to encouraging open discussions and conflict resolution. It was these skills that had, in fact, made her an upwardly mobile manager. In her new company, she found that disagreements were never resolved. This made the organization less effective and created an unpleasant work environment, too. Moreover, she found the president didn't want to hear about conflicts—whether they were interpersonal, or caused by a shortage of resources. He felt that his company was sufficiently profitable, and he wasn't really committed to further growth. He felt that anyone who didn't like things the way they were could go work somewhere else. Frustrated in her talents, Rena eventually did just that.

On the other hand, few industries have to deal with as much rapid change as the fashion industry, where Janice (mentioned earlier in this chapter) worked. The open conflicts frequently found in this industry enable companies to adjust quickly to the vagaries of style. Rena might find her abilities much appreciated in this environment. The attitudes of companies and industries toward the value of change and conflict depend upon the nature of the business, the feelings of the people in charge, and the pressures on the company to change.

Know your own attitude toward change and conflict as well as that of the people with whom you work. There's a gap between how we would like to behave and what we actually do.

Most People Would Rather Avoid Conflict

In his book, *Managing Organization Conflict,* Stephen Robbins states that "the goal of management is not harmony and cooperation—it is effective goal attainment." However, he shows how, in a business game with a particular group of people, harmony will take precedence over effectiveness. In this demonstration, a deviant member is planted, unknown to the other team members, in the group. This "devil's advocate" brings a large measure of conflict and disagreement to the group, which is involved in a problem-solving exercise in competition with other groups. Invariably, the group with the deviant in it ends up with the clearer analysis of the problem and a better solution than those arrived at by the other groups. But the final stage of this exercise requires each group to drop one member before continuing on to another "business game." And it is almost always the deviant member who is dropped. Even in this artificial situation, designed to teach the value of conflict in effective problem-solving, the group behavior shows a desire for peace and tranquillity at the expense of creative conflict.

Abraham Maslow, the psychologist who contributed so much to our understanding of motivation, pointed out that "in our society there is a fear of conflict, of disagreement, of hostility, antagonism, enmity. There is much stress on getting along with other people, even if you don't like them." While this is true for men, it is even more true for women, many of whom have been conditioned to be peacemakers and to avoid open conflict.

Know yourself and your comfort level with conflict; observe the group of people with whom you work to see what their tolerance

level for conflict is. Consider what your organization values and
rewards in this regard, and don't avoid conflict when it can be useful and creative.

CREATIVE CONFLICT

Team Solutions Are Better Than Individual Solutions

There is another business game that leaves a lasting impression on
contemporary managers. This game assumes you are stranded in a
desert or in the Arctic with a group of people and a few pieces of
equipment; your chances of survival are slim. You have the choice
of several courses of action and can use only some of the available
equipment. First you make individual choices, and then the group
as a whole must choose what to do and what to use. Despite the
disagreements and conflict between the team members, the consensus is almost always much more effective than individual solutions. The group's decisions invariably ensure their survival,
whereas the solutions of individual team members frequently turn
out to be dangerous to the group as a whole. This exercise teaches
a healthy respect for the beneficial effects of conflict.

Robbins says that good managers must "recognize the absolute
necessity of conflict, acknowledge the need to explicitly encourage
its functional component . . . and emphasize conflict management
as a major responsibility of all administrators." As a manager, you
will need to be skilled in planning and implementing necessary
changes and handling the resulting conflict because, as Cribbins
puts it, "three things are certain about the future. It will be radically different from the past; it will be somewhat different from the
present; it will be rather different from what we expect it to be."

15

LEADING AND INFLUENCING OTHERS

In order to be able to do your job as a manager, you have to be able to influence other people; you have to be able to get them to work toward the goals of the organization. The ability to influence other people, to lead and manage them, comes from a combination of skills. However, some people manage to rise in the corporate structure and become senior executives, while others, who work equally hard, or even harder, remain in supervisory or middle-management positions. The vital question is: Are those people who become leaders born with a special charisma, or a particular set of traits? Or do they develop and perfect top management skills during the course of their lifetimes? Hundreds of studies have been undertaken in search of a definition of the "leadership personality," and in search of universal leadership traits. None of the research has uncovered any consistent, inborn pattern that distinguishes leaders from followers. What happens, rather, is that people acquire the skills that make them effective leaders.

We've already looked at some of the skills that need to be developed as executive resources if you plan to become a leader in industry: wise expenditure of your time, decisiveness, the ability to seek and to take risks, and creativity in handling both change and conflict. In this chapter, we'll concentrate on some of the additional skills that you will want to develop in order to become an effective leader, manager, and administrator.

One of the most useful descriptions of the kinds of skills that are required in a leader, which was introduced in Chapter 3, has been provided by Robert Katz in an article in the *Harvard Business Review* titled "Skills of an Effective Manager." Katz views managerial skills in three fairly distinct areas:

1. Technical skills, which include knowledge of the mechanics of the particular job for which you are responsible.

2. Human skills, including the ability to motivate the people who work for you, to be a good team member yourself, and to be a good subordinate as well.

3. Conceptual skills, which include being able to analyze what needs to be done and how to go about doing it.

At the Top, It's Conceptual Skills That Count

One woman corporate president interviewed for this book was at one time the treasurer of her organization. As treasurer her technical skills were of utmost importance—skills which enabled her to analyze the financial condition of her company and see that the financial reports were accurate. Now, as president of the company, she must use additional skills. She must motivate the people who work for her. She must inspire the confidence of the stockholders and appear in public as the major figurehead of her company. Furthermore, she must now take a longer-range view of where her company must go and what they must do in order to continue to be successful five and ten years in the future. As treasurer, she was very much involved in analyzing the corporate financial history to determine what they could reasonably do in the short term. As president, she must delegate this work to others and concern herself more with the conceptual aspect of her job. She needs to devise long-term business projects. Then, with the help of the people who work for her, she must move the company in the right direction.

According to Katz, the relative importance of these three sets of skills varies with the level of administrative responsibility. At lower levels, the major need is for technical and human skills—you need to know how to do the job and how to work well with people. At higher management levels, an administrator's effectiveness begins to depend more heavily on conceptual skills. Planning, organizing, and decision making become increasingly more important. At the top of an organization, conceptual skills become the most important. Katz believes that as executives move up in an organization, the need for technical skill decreases in almost direct proportion to the growing need for conceptual skills.

CONCEPTUAL SKILLS: LEARNING TO LET OTHERS DO IT

The ever-increasing need for skills in the conceptual area has important implications for upward-striving women. Historically, women have neither been encouraged nor even allowed to become involved in long-range planning or in the decision making that affects resource allocation and the profits of a company. It has been largely in the areas of technical and human skills that women have excelled and have been allowed to excel. It has been, therefore, a self-fulfilling prophecy that women are good at and indeed *very* good at first-line supervisory jobs because they tend to be good with people and carry out tasks well; and they have been rewarded for this. Most women in business have not been trained to develop the conceptual skills necessary for assuming the senior-level positions. It takes a great deal of experience to develop this kind of ability. And you must have the opportunity to delegate much of the technical requirements of your former position. Because women have been rewarded for doing a good job, they have often found it difficult to learn to "let others do it." But, as we've often pointed out in this book, an effective manager must change from a doer into a motivator. She must be able to stop using her highly developed technical expertise and start concentrating on gaining experience in planning and policy formulation in order to have the perspective necessary for top executive positions.

One Woman's Giant Step

Lucy understands this need very well. She had several years of business experience where her technical skills were all important. First she was a top-notch executive secretary; then she became an administrative assistant and developed more technical skills in the computer area, as well as in corporate accounting. She was perfection itself, and right arm to the company president. But there was no chance that she would rise in the organization. She was too valuable for her technical skills, and she realized she would never have the opportunity to gain responsibility at a higher level, nor to gain experience in long-range planning. She secured a scholarship for a two-year M.B.A. program and, when she graduated, she immediately set about making up for her lack of concrete policy experience. She joined a consulting company that specialized in strategy consulting, and now she is getting a great deal of experience compressed into a few short years. She travels internationally, analyzing a variety of companies and making recommendations for long-term business strategy—what products or services they can most profitably offer in the future and how to go about doing it.

"It's really quite a shock the first few times you see a large company start to change direction based on your recommendations," Lucy reported. "Sometimes they even start to do this merely on the strength of your preliminary findings, before you've had a chance to fully digest all the information and come back to them with a final, formal report. It's quite a responsibility.

"I find I'm not only getting the policy formulation experience that I was seeking but I'm also getting a lot of experience in dealing with people at a high level in business. I thought I was pretty good in getting along with my coworkers in my former jobs. But getting information out of the senior managers in order to get my consulting work done has proved a real challenge. Often these executives seem to be jealously guarding their private kingdoms within the corporation. They are threatened by anyone who might make some recommendations for change. But I've got to get the information, and it's got to be an accurate picture of what the situation is, in order for me to produce a good plan. It hasn't been easy but I'm learning. My guess is that the same thing happens to corporate presidents—that they often have trouble getting exactly the information they need, particularly if things aren't going well. We need to know when to look more closely and to read between the lines. I'm learning to pick up these signals on my current job."

Lucy is rapidly developing conceptual skills and human skills with her experiences as a consultant. Another way you can do this is by moving around in your company and gaining experience in different departments—at your present level, or, better yet, by moving up the ladder. Ideally, you should try to gain experience in marketing, finance, and in production. Real experience in these three vital areas is a large boost up the ladder to the senior positions. Most people are deficient in at least one of these areas.

TECHNICAL SKILLS: OVERCOMING THE "CLEAN-UP" SYNDROME

In the area of technical skills, women frequently continue to value perfectionism at the expense of gaining other skills, and usually at the expense of the momentum of their careers.

In a long discussion with her boss, Alma told him that she would like to complete work on some details that had been left pending by her several predecessors. She asked her boss how he felt about her taking time to clean up these small matters. She would have to take some time away from the creative work needed to acquire new business—the primary responsibility of the new job. Her boss agreed that it would be an excellent idea to wind up these minor matters and that he'd like her to take the time to do it.

When she was discussing this situation with a friend, Alma admitted her need for perfection and her discomfort at allowing loose ends to clutter up her performance. She realized that her expectations for herself included having all the things for which she is responsible completed and done well. Her friend pointed out that there must have been reasons that the men who preceded her in this highly visible department were able to leave these fairly nonproductive details in their inactive files. She also suggested to

Alma that these men moved onward and upward in the organization nonetheless. "Don't you think you might reconsider some of your priorities?" Alma's friend asked. "It's understandable that your boss would be happy to get these things finally out of the way because someday his boss might ask about one of them. But is completing them the best way to use your time on the job? What's going to make *you* look good and get *you* promoted?"

Not surprisingly, Alma also found a lot of detail work left undone on current projects for which she was given responsibility. Alma knew very well how much she needed to see things done thoroughly, properly, and completely. Such lessons learned in childhood can be very hard to unlearn. It is reasonable to predict that Alma will spend all the time necessary going after new business aggressively. She will also finish off all the incomplete and inaccurate work that she inherited. She'll work longer hours and harder than the men who held the job before her. She can probably get away with this at her present level—but, before she can do more senior jobs, she will have to learn to establish priorities better and to live with her less-than-perfect technical completion of all jobs. In her job, as in most, there simply isn't enough time to handle every single detail.

HUMAN SKILLS

Listening, Looking, and Body Language

In the human-skills area, women generally have an advantage, which they can capitalize on if they develop these abilities in the business setting. Women often have an opportunity to develop insights into how to work with and influence other people. Their male counterparts may not have needed to develop this kind of understanding or may have had little interest in doing so.

The chairman of the board of a corporation found it almost uncanny that one of his vice-presidents, a woman, could predict people's reactions. He often consulted with her privately so that he could better anticipate the results of some action he was contemplating. He also gave her special tasks that involved getting people to do things, where others had been unsuccessful. "I really like people," this vice-president stated. "I get to know them: what they like, what they dislike. I listen to their professional problems. Sometimes it's hard to separate these from their personal problems, but I let them know where I draw the line. I'm not a social worker or a mother confessor, but I am interested in the people who work around me. A small glimpse into their personal lives from time to time only helps me to understand them better on the job. I steer the conversation back to the work setting as soon as I can, but I've usually learned something useful before it gets there.

"I'd say that listening is the most important way to understand what motivates a person to do a good job. People will usually tell you what they want, if you'll only listen. We're often too caught up in our own work and our own problems we don't stop to listen, or we listen but we don't really *hear* what they say.

"Looking is the other faculty that I use a lot. I watch what people do with their bodies, and I watch their facial expressions. I ask myself if their gestures and expressions match what they are saying. If they don't, I'm inclined to trust the body language, and I'll start asking questions to find out what they really feel or are really thinking."

For a few years, this vice-president had considerably more work to do than her male counterparts because she had to do her job and give advice on human relations problems as well. The president often asked her to troubleshoot in solving particularly knotty situations. Once she had to oversee the removal of personal secretaries from all the vice-presidents and substituting a word-processing service plus one administrative assistant for every three senior executives. This move was unpopular with her peers and the secretaries, but she accomplished it to everyone's satisfaction.

This is the kind of change that can bring with it a great deal of conflict unless you understand what it is that each person wants and needs out of his job. This woman has this kind of knowledge, gathered from years of working with and listening to the people around her. Ultimately her success both with her own work and these additional assignments resulted in her getting the job of executive vice-president.

IMPROVING YOUR SKILLS

Human and conceptual skills are often closely interrelated, and improving either one will often have a positive impact on the other —if you're aware of the need to develop in both of these areas. If you accept the premise that a leader is not born, but gradually develops as he or she acquires the necessary skills, then all men and women have the potential to enter the ranks of corporate leadership. The old axiom "working hard to get there" may well be true, but you should be discriminating. Work hard on those skills pertinent to the level of corporate leadership to which you aspire. Alma, whom we described in this chapter, is still more involved in just "working hard" and hasn't yet realized that she should direct her efforts to doing her job well *and* moving ahead fastest. She's still devoting time and energy to "doing the wrong things right." Expertise in methods, processes, procedures, and attention to minute details are the marks of a skilled technician. The ability to view the company and all its diverse functions as a whole—and then plan, establish priorities, make good decisions, and get others to work toward your goals—is what ultimately separates the leaders from the followers.

MOTIVATIONS: THE FIVE-LEVEL PYRAMID

The art of leadership is largely the art of motivating and influencing others. Despite the many studies of motivation, there are still no answers as to precisely what motivates someone to do something. However, many important guides to understanding behavior in this area do exist. Abraham Maslow formulated some very helpful ideas on the relationship between need and motivation. Maslow postulated a hierarchy of needs, based on their importance in our lives. We can be motivated by higher-level needs only when lower-level needs are satisfied.

At the base of the pyramid of needs are the physiological

needs: warmth, food, and shelter. The next level of needs are those related to your safety and security—those connected with your physical and economic well-being. If you are reasonably healthy and are able to work at a fairly secure job, you will then be motivated by the third level of needs, which are social: the need to be liked, to be accepted, to be part of the group.

If you feel you are adequately accepted socially, you are motivated by the fourth level of needs, which Maslow termed ego needs and which includes such things as the need for achievement, development, self-confidence, status, and recognition. Finally, someone who is reasonably satisfied with herself in the area of ego needs will be motivated by the need for self-actualization. This is a term that Maslow developed to embrace the idea of self-realization, of self-fulfillment—of using your abilities to the fullest.

Each of these levels flows into the next; to a certain extent, they overlap. Rarely are the needs in any area fully met. Rather, as your more basic needs are satisfied, you go on to seek fulfillment at the next higher level. As James Cribbins explains in *Effective Managerial Leadership,* "The lower level needs are more demanding, but those farther up the hierarchy are more enduring and effective as motivators." The desire to fulfill needs at all levels is the force that impels employees to do their jobs. If you can understand what needs people have already satisfied and what level of need they are presently working to satisfy, you will be better able to provide the right kind of rewards that will encourage them to set their sights on higher levels of need.

Professor Cribbins enlarges on Maslow's definitions and ideas. He identifies important motivators as:

1. The need for attention and approval
2. The need to belong and conform
3. The need to participate and contribute
4. The need to be different
5. The need for independence
6. The need for development
7. The need to experience success, adequacy, and self-esteem

When Needs Conflict

At any given time employees are likely to be meeting needs on several levels simultaneously. Ellen has a responsible middle-management job that she's good at. She gets an adequate salary and lives comfortably. She doesn't have to worry about food, shelter, or medical care. But, because of the constant danger of cutbacks in her department, she fears that her job is in jeopardy. As it is now, she is very short-staffed and has virtually no hope of getting additional personnel. She is worried about this, and as a result the job is taking a heavy toll on her health. There is, however, a countervailing security need that keeps Ellen on this job. In three years' time, she will be fully eligible for the company's pension plan, and she'll have a retirement income to show for the many years of hard work she has invested in this company.

Ellen does not like the person to whom she reports and, in her present company, she has no opportunity to move up. Her social needs are met at work, since she and her coworkers have a close-knit group—the result, largely, of sharing the disadvantages of being both overworked and insecure in their jobs. Ellen's social needs would be better met if she liked and respected her boss, or if she could at least relate to him more comfortably. Her ego need for achievement would also be better met if she felt more a part of the organization as a whole and believed she was making a positive contribution to its success.

Here is a situation in which social needs merge into ego needs, the next higher level. For her own pride and self-respect, Ellen would like to feel she is doing a good job. Unfortunately, she is doing a job she doesn't even like in order to satisfy her security needs with the retirement income. To her way of thinking, these safety/security needs virtually dictate that she stay where she is until she gets her pension. The only thing that would force her to leave sooner would be serious stress symptoms caused by the many unresolved conflicts. In her case, ill health might outweigh the carrot of the future retirement benefits.

The majority of Ellen's higher-level needs—ego and self-actualization—have to be met outside of work. She takes courses that add to her professional skills and she does volunteer work, where she feels her efforts are appreciated. When she has served out her additional three years, she's almost certain to leave the corporation and seek a job where she will have an opportunity to fill more needs at the higher levels.

Ellen was being demotivated. She didn't feel she was getting approval, nor did she feel she was contributing. She had little opportunity to have her ideas and experience incorporated into future planning in order to straighten out continuing problems. She rarely experienced any feeling of success. Ellen was promoted to the position she now holds against her express wishes. In her former job, she had much more opportunity to be independent, to solve problems on her own, and to see satisfactory results. It would have been much easier and less stressful for her to wait out her remaining time in that job. She might even have remained with the company. She received a substantial salary increase, but her higher-level needs were not met as well in the new job as they had been in the old one.

This is an illustration of the fascinating fact that when lower-level needs are met, attempting to further fulfill that level of need does not necessarily increase motivation. If an employee considers her salary ample and has raises that keep up with the rise in the cost of living, increasing her salary further will not necessarily increase her motivation. This is particularly true if there is a decrease in satisfaction in other areas, such as the opportunity to develop and really to use all her talents. Giving her additional challenge and responsibility is much more likely to motivate her and keep the motivation sustained for a longer period of time.

Where Do You Fit In?

How are your needs presently being met? What safety, security, and social needs are unmet? Does this affect your ability to seek out challenges and take on more responsibility? Consider the needs of the people who work for you. How are their needs, in Maslow's terms, being met?

Maslow considered self-actualized people to be healthy psychologically. To further elaborate on what I pointed out in Chapter 3, Maslow said that self-actualized people have a:

- good perception of reality
- greater tolerance for ambiguity

• greater acceptance of themselves, others, and the natural world.

Further, self-actualized people are:

• spontaneous and natural
• autonomous and free to be individualistic
• creative and original

All of these would seem to be reasons to attempt to meet as many lower-level needs as possible, both for yourself and the people who work for you, so that the challenges of the job can really help people utilize their talents to the fullest extent possible.

In an interview given to the Boston *Globe* in June 1979, Matina Horner, the president of Radcliffe College, said, "Success isn't the money or the privileges. It isn't the might and the mighty. It's being able to do things you deeply care about." Dr. Horner would certainly appear to be a self-actualized person.

Dr. Horner makes another point in that article. She says that she is willing and able to fight for what she believes in. The article describes "Horner's astute aggressiveness at high-powered Harvard-Radcliffe meetings" as "legendary." She isn't afraid to use power in influencing people to accomplish what she cares deeply about. In the next chapter, we'll take a longer look at the place of power in organizations.

16

THE PLACE OF POWER

Power in a business context means your ability to influence people and your willingness to exert your influence for the good of the company. David McClelland, a professor of psychology at Harvard University, has studied in great depth power and motivation in organizations. He has determined that power is a constructive motivating force for leaders of organizations, but only when it is "disciplined and controlled so that it is directed toward the benefit of the institution as a whole and not toward the manager's personal aggrandizement." He says that an effective manager's power motivation "refers not to dictatorial behavior but to a desire to have impact, to be strong and influential."

How do you feel about power? Are you comfortable about acquiring and exercising power? The whole concept of power is controversial because of the many definitions of the word, but let's focus on the concept of productive power because it is really the only type that belongs in business.

WOMEN AND POWER

Even when people agree with this relatively nonthreatening definition of power, the controversy often reappears when power, as exercised by women, is considered. As Dr. Jean Baker Miller puts it in her book, *Toward a New Psychology of Women,* "Women start . . . from a position in which they have been dominated" and they "do not have a history of believing that power is necessary for the maintenance of self-image." She goes on to say that women are inexperienced "in using all of their powers openly." Yet, she continues, "the issues of power have to be faced." These issues certainly have to be faced by women seeking to move up in the corporate world. If you were raised not to seek and exercise power openly, you probably learned methods of getting things done that were indirect approaches to the problem. You probably learned to manipulate. This has often been—and continues to be— a useful means of achieving goals for people who are uncomfortable with being strong and direct. Sometimes it even works in business situations. But you can't really acquire sufficient power in an organization if you have to be devious or manipulative, or if you are uncomfortable with the idea of having a direct impact on people.

Rose Marie was a woman in middle management who worked for a man who did not permit her to disagree with him openly. He seemed to have been conditioned to view women as homemakers and as people subservient to him. Both his mother and his wife reinforced this bias in their dealings with him. Rose Marie had to get her department's work done by planting ideas in his head and letting him think they were his. Or by enlisting the aid of a male manager who was permitted to have a different opinion. The president did not believe that a woman could come up with the facts to support a plan of action different from the one he thought appropriate. Rose Marie clearly saw that she would probably never be able to move into a senior position where she could really exercise power because of his stereotypic view of women. She eventually left the company to work for a firm in which both men and women treated her as a professional. Here she was allowed to pull her own weight, have her own opinions, and influence others to go along with them.

Power is a complex force in business that comes from three main sources: (1) the power of position, (2) the power of person, and (3) the power of knowledge.

THE POWER OF POSITION

The power that an executive derives by virtue of the authority entrusted to him or to her in a particular job is an important, well-defined power source. Each position in the organizational chart carries with it the responsibility for performing certain tasks and the authority to see that the tasks are carried out. Implicit in this is the power to reward and to punish. Yet, as anyone who has received a substantial promotion will attest, positional power must be earned; it is not just a mantle that you put on when you are chosen to fill a certain job. While the job description spells out the power that comes with it, unless you can demonstrate an ability to handle it, the people around you will very skillfully begin to erode the power that was yours by right of job description. Power is a scarce resource in corporations. By their human nature, it seems, peers and subordinates are ever seeking to enlarge the scope of their power or to avoid being controlled.

"The Vultures Come Out"

"When I was promoted to the highest level ever attained by a woman in our company," said a senior manager, "I was continually tested, as any person would be who was put in my position. In addition, I was challenged by all the men I worked with to see if I, a mere woman, could handle the responsibility. If you are going for the top corporate jobs, you've got to realize that there is only so much power to go around. There is a constant power struggle going on. Any power you can get from someone else enlarges your own power base. Nowhere is this more evident than when a new person takes a job. The vultures are out. It's so subtle. You ask someone for a report by a certain time. They test you by not turning it in, or by turning it in late. Withholding information is a common way of exercising power. They look to see what you do about getting the information and how you handle yourself. Your subordinates will often neglect to do something they should do but don't want to do, and wait to see how you react, and how you get them to do it."

"It's not only women who have trouble exercising the authority that comes along with a position," a recently promoted man reported. "A man or a woman will be tested. You've got to be extremely careful when you are new in a job. The person you're replacing probably exercised more power in certain areas than required by the job description, and gave up some in other areas. You're bound to have to restructure the handling of the job based on your own strengths and weaknesses."

Taking Stock of the Situation

This man continued, "You have to move somewhat cautiously at first, yet at the same time you have to exert as much legitimate power as you can to avoid losing any of it. I try to get as much history as I can from the people who work for me and from people who know how the department has been run. Is Harvey always careless with figures, yet accepted anyway because he is so creative? Is June always late getting things done, but can be absolutely depended on to have a first-rate report when it is completed? Where do I have to apply pressure and where should I go easy? I want to know these things before I come down too hard on people.

"I begin to move when I have the information I need. So the people around me soon get to know me and get an idea of what it will be like working for me.

"Another man in our organization has quite a different style. When he gets a promotion, he sits back and questions and observes for quite a long period of time—often as much as three months. Then he moves—and he moves swiftly and decisively. That's not my style, but it surely works for him. However, people are very apprehensive when he's put in charge of their department. There's not much give-and-take when the decisions are made and the power exercised."

Pitfalls: Fancy Titles, Less Power, Downgraded Salary

It's even more difficult for women who are moved into positions for which they are not truly qualified because the company wants to meet certain equal opportunity guidelines. If you suspect that this might be the case in a promotional opportunity you are offered, don't let the company give you a title, while using your inexperience as an excuse to remove some of the power and the responsibility from that position. Instead, ask for training in the areas in which you lack experience. Identify specifically what you feel you need to know to do the new job well; what it is that will give you the confidence you need to move up with assurance. Is it a course on computers? A knowledge of statistics or some other technical background? Or is it in the area of human skills that you feel uncomfortable? Have you had a course on the theory of management? Do you feel you need or want one? Or do you feel inadequate in the area of direct selling? Perhaps your new job requires a great deal of conceptual thinking, of long-range planning, and budgeting. Go after the skills you lack.

Don't let the position be downgraded in salary either. This is a common phenomenon because women moving up are likely to have been underpaid to begin with. They probably came in at a lower salary level or didn't make as many salary moves as some of the men. But, bear in mind that salary is a reflection of the power of the position. Find out what the salary range is for the job and what the last person was making. These are reasonable questions to ask. Don't accept less than a figure that's in the job's salary range and based on your experience. Don't let the job be downgraded salary-wise because the position is going to a woman. In Chapters 24 and 25, there are some additional suggestions for securing salary and perquisites suitable to a position you are considering.

If You're Not Ready for a Position, Don't Back Off—Get Help

"I took a senior vice-president's job, which I know I was offered only because I'm a woman and I'm black. I also knew I didn't have enough background or experience to handle the position. But I wasn't going to let that stop me. A move up for one woman is a help to all of us. I believe women should take advantage of every opportunity open to them. After all, men don't necessarily feel confident either when they take on a new job. They just don't talk much about their insecurities and are more experienced in taking lots of risks.

"The important thing for me was to secure the agreement of the company for some crash courses. I outlined a specific training program, complete with the timing of both seminars I wanted to take and travel to our other corporate offices to get acquainted. I felt they'd be reluctant to let me go once I started the job, so I outlined a brief program and completed it before I began the assignment. Now, after two tough years, I've fully mastered the job. I'd certainly recommend to other women that they take any job opportunity they can get. But that they fully prepare themselves to do a good job. It's our responsibility both to take higher-level positions and to carry them out well."

Another woman, commenting on her move to a middle-management job from that of executive secretary, said, "My company got three equal opportunity points for moving me from a secretarial job straight into middle management: I'm female and of Oriental extraction, which gives them two points, and then they get a third for promoting a secretary to an executive job. I didn't know the first thing about managing people, but I'd spent fifteen years with this company. I knew most of the people and virtually everyone knew me. I had lots and lots of favors that I could ask to have repaid when I took my new position. I'd been able to grant things to others in my former position as secretary to the chief executive officer. Now it's my turn. When I need help, I ask for it and I get it.

"My new status is great fun for me. I'm learning how to be an executive through trial and error, but I'm also planning to take some management courses to learn still more. It's nice to have this challenge. Actually, I'm finding my new job much easier than catering to 'the great man's' whims. I had lots of power derived from the fact that I was the secretary to the president, but it wasn't really my own. I prefer being able to use my own strength instead of his."

Every Woman's Success is a Beachhead for Other Women

Every woman who takes a higher position and makes the effort to ensure that she gains the background to do the job well helps other women up the ladder. Her success helps to break down the prejudice that women are uncomfortable with power and can't exercise it openly.

It isn't always easy to be in the limelight, as the ex-secretary and the newly appointed vice-president were. It probably will take them even more effort to succeed than a man, because they are being watched more carefully. Not only do the observers analyze their ability, but they also draw general conclusions from what they see. Can secretaries make the switch to management and perform well? Can a woman take a senior management job and handle it competently?

If you find yourself in a high-visibility job where you may be establishing a beachhead at that level for other women, recognize that you probably will have to work harder at the job for a while than a man who might have been given the job—he wouldn't have to prove that males can handle that degree of responsibility and power. Determine beforehand if this is the kind of situation you are going into and what it will entail. It's almost always worth the strain of the scrutiny if you are targeting the top. It will be your chance to prove yourself in a highly visible setting.

It's easier if you are seasoned and have the necessary experience to fill a position. Even so, you may still have to show that you can be as good as a man.

PERSONAL POWER: GETTING TO KNOW AND LIKE PEOPLE

The ex-secretary mentioned earlier talked about using her personal power when she got promoted. Personal power is derived from the people with whom you work. A boss can give you more power than your position usually entails if you perform well and can be counted on. Subordinates may work better for you than for someone else if they respect you, like you, or relate well to your management style. Your peers may help you get things done more easily for these same reasons and because they know they can count on you for help as well.

In the case of the ex-secretary, her peers liked and respected her. They were happy to see her get a good opportunity and knew she'd be easy to work with. She had built many close friendships during the years she had worked with the firm, and now she could depend on them. She also had the advantage of knowing the history of so many of the people in the company, which helped her in being able to deal with them appropriately.

The ability to succeed in an organization is often based on whom you know, who knows you, and who likes and supports you. It's the personal power you can gather around you because of your management and personal style.

He's Not Liked, But He's Respected

Often it's gathered not necessarily because the person is liked, but because he or she is effective. The ambitious executive mentioned earlier who had the well-justified reputation of sitting back and observing and then moving swiftly to rearrange his department, wields a lot of personal power. People in the organization know how he acts when he takes over a new area; they make an extra effort if he is assigned as their manager because they want to keep their jobs. He is not liked, but he has the respect—albeit grudging —of the people in the organization, because he gets the job done.

To reiterate an important point made in Chapter 3, Dr. David McClelland, in an article in the *Harvard Business Review* about power in organizations, states that a "top manager's need for power ought to be greater than his need for being liked by people." He further defines a good manager as one who "helps subordinates feel strong and responsible, who rewards them properly for good performance, and who sees that things are organized in such a way that subordinates feel they know what they should be doing." A manager who is able to do those things will command a great deal of personal power. She will be well respected, even if many of her actions require her to be firm and demanding.

EXPERT POWER: FROM COURSES, READING, PEOPLE, QUESTIONS, EXPERIENCE

According to McClelland's description, to perform as an effective manager it also helps to have a substantial amount of the third type of power: that which comes from knowledge and experience. Knowing how to do your job is the third important element in your sum total of power sources. If the people who work for you or with whom you work have evidence of the fact that you are skilled in doing your job, they will perform better for you.

"It's very nice to move up to a position where you supervise people doing a job that you have mastered," a fast-moving young woman said. "You have complete understanding of the job and can easily oversee what has to be done from a technical point of view. If you were known as being especially good at the job, as I was when I was a loan review analyst, it's even easier to train and supervise people. But you've also got to learn to be a manager somewhere along the way. You need to learn how to tell people when they are not doing their jobs well. You need to know how to correct them, how to tell them how to improve, without antagonizing them. My job is not to be liked, it's to get the work out. That's a hard lesson to learn, but a necessary one.

"Once I learned how to manage people, I found that these skills were transferable and I didn't have to limit myself just to a supervisory position where I had excellent technical experience. I've just been promoted to an entirely different area, which will give me line experience and help to make me a generalist. I'm planning to be a vice-president of this company—the youngest woman vice-president they've ever appointed. I have to get a broad range of experience and learn to transfer my skills, not get stuck as a staff specialist."

Be sure to become expert in terms of managerial skills in addition to technical competencies. It's your managerial abilities that will enable you to move up. You'll get your expert power from reading, from course work, and from experience. You can also get it from other people. Ask questions. Most staff specialists are

only too happy to give advice and to work with you in their particular areas of expertise. After all, that is what they are paid to do.
Don't hesitate to seek help and advice. McClelland has found that
it is a mark of maturity in managers if they are not defensive and
are willing to seek advice from experts. It's often a lack of self-
confidence that causes us to fail to admit that we don't know
something. The mark of adequate expert power is to identify what
you need to know and to be able to do and then set about acquiring these skills.

RISKING POWER TO GET MORE

These three elements—positional power, personal power, and expert power—make up an individual's power base. In the words of
social psychologist Abraham Zaleznik, they add up to the "total
esteem with which others regard the individual." But there is risk
in the exercise of power. In an article titled "Power and Politics in
Organizational Life" in the *Harvard Business Review,* Dr. Zaleznik states that we must be willing to risk our power for the sake of
the success of an undertaking, if we want to retain our power
base. Zaleznik describes the effective manager as an individual
who "knows he has power, assesses it realistically, and is willing
to risk his personal esteem to influence others. A critical element
here is the risk in the uses of power. The individual must perform
and get results." Power not exercised is eventually lost.

It's necessary to be aware of your power within an organization
and to hold onto it, while at the same time trying to acquire still
more power.

MAINTAINING IT

Power is one of the limited resources available in organizations;
there is only so much to go around. In order to protect your place
in the scheme of things, you must be prepared to maintain your
share of power in the face of competitors who want to build them-

selves up at your expense. There are some techniques that can help you avoid erosion of your power base, and at the same time help you to move ahead in your company.

1. Form strong relationships with people above you whenever possible.

This strategy gives you protection and helps you gain added strength by association with higher-placed and more powerful people. The close relationship between the former secretary, mentioned in this chapter, and the chief executive officer strengthens her power position, since people know she can get his attention if it proves necessary.

If you are merely trying to protect the position you are now in it is often safer to keep a low profile; but if it's a promotion you're after, you must become visible. You have to take chances by doing things that will be rewarded if they succeed. This is the kind of risk that was taken by the woman manager in Chapter 9, who surmounted the obstacle of her boss by using one of his powerful peers to present her report. She risked a good deal by writing the report and by going around her boss. But she would probably have been permanently prevented from promotion if she hadn't. If she had failed to secure approval for her promotion, it might have been so uncomfortable for her to remain in her old job that she would have had to look for another job. She had calculated all these possibilities and was willing to expose herself to the risk. She used her personal power—her relationship with a strong, highly placed executive—and she got her promotion, which greatly enhanced her positional power.

2. Understand the informal power structure of your organization and use it.

As we suggested in Chapter 8, keep an organization chart up-to-date, with names of people connected with dotted lines to show informal working relationships. Women are often on the fringes of some of the informal systems because they are not "one of the boys." Figure out how to work your way in, or set up a parallel system of your own. Take the initiative—invite people whom you would like to get to know better out to lunch, or for a drink after work.

One woman surprised the head of a department by doing this. She was having continuing difficulty with some of the people he supervised, and she wanted to solve the problem. She didn't seem to be able to do this during office hours; he was always too busy to really investigate the problem in depth. She used the semisocial opportunity to get at the root of her problem, and the two people gradually formed a mutually helpful business relationship. Her direct communication with this man enhanced her personal power and helped her do her job more effectively.

3. Develop strong peer relationships.

Your ability to get things done very often depends on your sources of information. Find out where the informal sharing of information takes place and become part of this network.

One woman said she has developed "the fine art of hanging around after meetings. You don't find out what really happened in a meeting and what it will mean to you and your work until the meeting is informally reviewed afterwards. I just hang around unobtrusively so I can be part of the impromptu discussion that usually follows any significant meeting."

To do your job well, you also have to be able to ask special favors of people from time to time. Help your peers when you can. You are then in a position to call on people who owe you. Help your peers when you can, but be sure to ask for help in return when you need it. Don't be the nice person who is always ready and willing to assist others, but rarely calls in the debt. Make it clear from the beginning that you will ask for your quid pro quo.

4. Develop loyalty among your subordinates.

Manage in a day-to-day style that develops loyalty. Be predictable and be fair. These qualities engender respect, particularly when combined with evidence of your ability to get things done. And they demonstrate your power.

5. Know what kind of performance is rewarded by your company and make sure your efforts are directed toward these ends.

6. Anticipate change.

Be aware of what's going on and project what's likely to happen.

7. Be willing and able to move elsewhere if you have to.

Be confident that you can move up or out—this will give you additional strength in your current positions.

USING IT

Power, its sources and its exercise, must be confronted, understood, and enjoyed if you want to achieve higher positions in business. As Zaleznik states: "Organizations operate by distributing authority and setting a stage for the exercise of power." It's no wonder that individuals who are highly motivated to secure and use power find a familiar and hospitable environment in business. The greater your understanding of the elements of power in organizations and your knowledge of how to use it effectively to achieve their goals, the greater will be your chances of success in the business environment.

17

EXCHANGING INFORMATION

How many times have you thought you explained to someone what to do, only to find that your instructions were misunderstood, or not heard—and, as a result, that the job was left undone, or was poorly completed? Learning how to communicate clearly and completely is an essential skill for managers, since they must generally accomplish their tasks through other people.

It has been estimated that we spend 70 per cent of our waking hours communicating: talking, listening, reading, and writing. That statistic alone should encourage you to develop your ability to communicate well, both in person and in writing. But there is also another reason you should be concerned about effective communication. The only way you can understand other people's needs and hope to influence them is to be able to send and receive messages accurately. Let's look first at the messages you send other people.

SENDING MESSAGES

Women often have more trouble communicating with other people effectively than they do perceiving accurately what is being communicated to them. To be a successful manager, you must develop your sending skills so that you say what you intend to say in a manner that the receiver understands.

Written messages seem to cause women less difficulty than communicating in person. In their education, women have been encouraged and allowed to excel in English. It's fascinating to watch a room full of men and women taking the qualifying examination for entrance into graduate schools of management. The test is about equally divided between verbal and mathematical skills. For the most part, the women agonize over the mathematics sections and breeze rapidly through the verbal skills areas. Just the reverse is true for men. The median test scores reflect this difference in learned skills very clearly.

Putting It in Writing

Just because your written skills may be fairly well developed and you can write grammatical English, don't rest on your laurels. You still have to perfect your skills in business English. You have to learn to make things happen as a result of what you write. You also communicate a great deal of your management style in the tone of your written communiqués.

One woman executive received a substantial promotion the day after a new president took over her company. When she got to know him better, she asked him why he had the confidence to give so much responsibility to someone he didn't really know. "Easy," he replied. "I reviewed your memos and correspondence from the central files. You communicate very effectively and, perhaps even more importantly, the tone of your writing was just what I felt we needed in the position in which I placed you."

Another woman described writing a long and detailed report on a complex matter and handing it to one of her peers to incorporate into a larger business document. "He took what I had written and made it much clearer, much more concise, and certainly more easily readable. I was really given something to think about because I was quite confident in my ability, but I saw how much more I had to learn, after he worked over my material."

Would you get the promotion you want if the new corporate president reviewed your business writing? Can your peers express things in a clearer and more persuasive fashion than you can? Do you have confidence in your business writing ability?

Here are some suggestions to help you perfect your power to influence others through the written word:

1. Write simply.

Use short sentences. Keep the verbs active whenever you can. Remember that attention is in short supply in the corporation—it is one of the scarce resources.

2. Unbend from some of the grammar rules you learned so thoroughly in school.

Use dashes, triple dots, fragments of sentences, capital letters—anything that will get you extra attention or hold the readers' attention once you get it. You are not trying to get an A in English from your fifth-grade teacher, you're writing to business people who have a very limited amount of time to absorb what you are trying to communicate.

3. Edit yourself.

Keep unnecessary words to a minimum in the interest of time. Avoid buzz words and jargon when you can. They don't read well.

4. Then, get an editor.

If you are writing something important, find someone who can edit it for you. The first rule of communicating well in writing is to have a good editor. When one executive complained to a professional writer about how much she disliked writing business reports, the writer replied, "That's because you don't have the privilege of an editor." Give yourself the "privilege" of an editor; if the report is of real value to you or the organization, don't try to edit yourself.

5. Develop a style for your writing.

Be somewhat informal and communicate some of yourself in the material. Use other people's names in the body of the copy, if you are addressing someone in particular. Write conversationally; it makes better reading.

Face to Face

Communicating in person is more uncomfortable for many women than committing themselves in writing. Personal communication may take place between two people, in meetings, or in formal presentations. While some people may appear to have a natural ability to discuss, direct, persuade, and negotiate comfortably and easily, for most people interpersonal communication is a skill that they have developed as a result of experience and hard work. They have a sense of confidence that comes about only as the result of lots of successful experiences. Furthermore, you don't usually see the stress or anguish that even some of the most polished performers suffer. Stage fright serves to energize many people, and most people seem to suffer it to some extent. In a television interview, Sammy Davis, Jr., vowed that if he stopped being desperately nervous before a performance, he'd stop performing. He needs and wants that adrenaline flowing in order to do his dynamic best.

To improve on your ability to communicate in public, here are some helpful suggestions for public presentations:

1. Don't eat or drink anything except water just before your appearance.

Coffee or tea will make you more nervous. Starches and dairy products tend to make your mouth dry. Alcoholic beverages—especially beer—make you salivate.

2. Prepare your material.

If you are confident of your information, you can deliver it more confidently. Index cards are excellent for notes. They don't make a noise, and they don't cover your face. If they are 5" x 8", they are large enough for ample notes.

3. If you are using visual aids, try them out ahead of time.

They won't work at least 50 per cent of the time. Be prepared for this and plan a fail-safe, so that you can perform well even without the visual aids. The head of a major ad agency had a very professional presentation planned before a very large group. When she was about to begin, she discovered that none of the visual equipment would work. She lost face and probably several potential clients by stalking off the platform. Her behavior was unprofessional, and she disappointed the group that had come to hear her. Do your own double-checking of equipment and be prepared if it fails to work.

4. If you harness them, nerves work for you.

Use isometric techniques to release nervous energy. If you are sitting, press your feet into the floor. Press your hands into the chair arm or pull up underneath the arm with your fingertips, whichever is unobtrusive. Press the table or the sides of the lectern if you are using one. You'll find one or more of these techniques steadies you and gives you some additional strength to draw on.

5. If your voice tends to quaver, take several deep breaths before you begin to speak.

6. Have water and cough drops on hand in case you need them.

7. Keep your feet and body as still as possible.

Many people react to nervous tension by some rhythmic motion (often in time with the heartbeat), such as nodding their heads, swinging their feet, or swaying back and forth in a chair. Observe this in other people and see how distracting it is. If you have too much tension to discharge through isometrics, get up and walk if possible. Walking is an excellent attention-getter.

8. Project to the people in the back of the audience.
Ask them to raise their hands if they cannot hear you.

9. Don't be overly serious or grim; smile occasionally.

10. Invite participation if you can.

11. Short, colorful sentences are better than long, complicated ones.

12. If you go blank, just pause.
The best speakers do this for emphasis. Look at your notes, think, then begin again. Don't say, "ah," "er," or apologize.

13. Plan your exit material carefully and end on an upbeat note.

"WOMEN'S INTUITION"

Messages are constantly being sent and received by a variety of means. What a person is saying and doing may be at odds, or these activities may reinforce each other. There are hundreds—if not thousands—of body language cues being given out by people all the time. You may not even be aware of how you are picking up information about what is really going on. How often have you heard someone say he would do something—and you knew perfectly well he had absolutely no intention of doing it? Many women have trained themselves to respond to the less obvious physical clues in a situation, even without realizing they are doing so. Someone's face may express a negative emotion, or their head may be shaking from side to side, while verbally they seem to agree with you. Someone may be reassuring you about the outcome of a situation, while he is talking to you with clenched fists.

This close observation of another person's total behavior and the resulting ability to predict what will happen is what has long been referred to as "intuition"—especially "women's intuition." While it may seem to be unconscious, or intuitive, it in fact is something you do consciously—it is a matter of watching, listening, and learning from both the words and the action that are going on around you, and then applying this knowledge. It stems from an interest in people and a need to anticipate what someone will do and to understand why.

In her book, *Toward a New Psychology of Women,* psychiatrist Jean Baker Miller observes: "There is no question that most women have a much greater sense of the emotional component of all human activities than most men." She points out further that this is a "basic ability that is very valuable." You will often find this same ability well developed in men who lead organizations, or in their closest aides. It's not a skill that's limited to women; it's just that women have spent more time developing it!

"I understand the dynamics of what's really going on at our staff meetings much better than the men do," relates a woman manager. "I can usually predict what someone will do, when the men have absolutely no idea what might happen. For me, it's almost as though people are books that I've read before. I might be missing some pages or some chapters from a particular book, but I've got a pretty good idea of the ending anyway. And the older I get, the more I find this to be true. This kind of insight helps me to understand how I can get people who work for me to do what they have to do."

An international woman executive feels that the most difficult thing about working abroad is not being able to read gestures and facial expressions automatically, to get a sense of what's going on. "Gestures and expressions mean very different things in different countries. I didn't realize how much I relied on them to tell me what someone is really thinking until I started working in several different countries. For me, being cut off from familiar body language—clues to people's motives and thoughts—constitutes culture shock. I found myself totally misreading situations until I discovered why it was happening.

"Dealing in a foreign language has a similar effect. Each language has nuances of meaning that you rarely can fully master in a language other than your own. I almost always try to deal either in English or in a language that is secondary to the person with whom I am working, so that they are at a disadvantage equal to mine. For example, if I'm negotiating with a German-speaking Swiss who prefers not to negotiate in English, I will choose French as an alternative, because then we are on an equal footing. Otherwise, he has the upper hand. Communication is every bit as much how you say something as what you say."

Use your ability to understand what others are communicating to you and continue to develop this talent by intellectualizing it as much as you can. Expand your conscious knowledge of body language whenever you can. Pay attention to your own body and how you use it. Besides increasing your understanding of what other people mean, it will help you to reinforce what you are saying with your own body language and enable you to communicate more accurately.

One of the most important places to be able to communicate effectively and to understand what is going on is in business meetings, the subject of the next chapter.

18

MAKING MEETINGS WORK

Some of the most important communicating situations you face as a working executive are meetings. In many companies, most of the executives' time is spent in meetings—so much so, in fact, that they have to get a lot of their other work done outside regular business hours.

Sarah, a superstar in her company, either comes in at 7:00 A.M. or stays until 7:00 P.M. to handle her paper work and planning. Almost all of her time between 9:00 and 5:00 is spent in meetings. Sometimes she is a participant in these meetings and sometimes she runs them. In addition, she is often involved in pre-meeting discussions, which help her to prepare for the get-togethers. The only possible way for her to stay on top of her paper work is to put in at least two extra hours per day. And her situation is not atypical.

With meetings such an important part of many executives' work day, and frequently an integral part of their success, it is well to understand the dynamics of meetings and how you can shine at them. In this chapter we'll take a look at what really goes on in meetings and how to plan the various roles you may have to take on, with particular attention to learning how to chair the proceedings successfully.

WHAT'S GOING ON

There are two things at work simultaneously in any meeting: the first is the substance of the meeting—what's on the agenda; and the second is the vested interests of each participant in the meeting. The ego involvement and needs of each person in the room, including the chairman, is, by far, the most important factor in determining the success or failure of the meeting. When you learn to find out where all the participants stand, and what they need from the meeting, who is allied with whom, what old hostilities and vendettas are being aired, you'll be in a much better position to have the meeting turn out the way you want it to.

The Pre-Meeting

One of the best ways to find out what will really happen at a meeting—apart from a discussion of the formal agenda—is to talk about it very briefly beforehand with as many of the other participants as possible. Sarah does this as a matter of course. You can often learn where others stand on the issues and what may keep the meeting from reaching a satisfactory conclusion. You can sometimes enlist other people's support for your point of view—lobbying doesn't take place only in the nation's capital.

If you are in charge of the meeting, you can informally ask others to introduce key issues that would better come from participants than from you. You can also request that certain extraneous issues be avoided in order to keep the meeting on target. As the chairman, you can use these informal pre-meetings to prepare the stage so that the meeting can accomplish what it is supposed to in a minimum amount of time.

The Status Arena

Business meetings are events where people can acquire more power or lose some. Meeting participants are always concerned about their strength, their power, and their position relative to other members who are present. Understanding that other people are protecting themselves can help you to anticipate when someone might abruptly change his or her position. Or, when he or she might lash out even when, or perhaps because of the fact that, they have just been proven wrong. Beware of your own ego involvement in a particular stand. Are you supporting it because *you* want to be right or because it appears to be the most appropriate course of action. Avoid pushing yourself forward just for ego gratification. Learn to separate reason and fact from emotional reactions. A calm presentation of fact and logic will go far to set you apart as a contributing member of the meeting.

The Substance

Meetings are usually held for one of five reasons. Having a clear understanding of the purpose of a meeting will help you avoid giving inappropriate responses. The five reasons for meetings are: (1) to disseminate information and share knowledge; (2) to consider a problem and generate ideas about how to solve it; (3) to decide among possible choices; (4) to plan how to carry out a decision that has already been made; and (5) to set up rules and regulations for enforcing decisions already in action. In any one meeting, it is difficult to accomplish more than one of these purposes unless the situation is quite simple. Usually you are better off limiting a meeting to one of the areas and addressing another issue at a subsequent meeting.

WHAT'S YOUR ROLE?

In addition to observing each participant's needs, knowing the purpose of the meeting, you should also be very clear about your own role in the meeting. Make sure you know whether you are expected to take charge, to be an expert witness, or to be a participant. Regardless of which of these three roles you play, your competence in public speaking will greatly help you. If you are inclined to nervousness, use some of the techniques outlined in the last chapter to harness this nervous energy to your advantage.

These tips are not just for platform performances; they're for any occasion when you want to project your opinions and your competence.

Participating

If you are asked to be a participant in a meeting, you are undoubtedly asked because it is expected you will have something to contribute. Prepare thoroughly before the meeting. Know where you stand on the issue in question. Come armed with facts that will help you win your point of view and achieve the outcome you desire.

Meetings frequently give you a chance to be noticed by people with whom you don't normally have contact. Do your best. Be ready to make useful contributions and voice them.

Analyze what's going on in the meeting in addition to what is being said. Watch the body language. Often this gives you valuable information about who holds the power in certain areas and who is allied with whom.

Whenever you can, help the person who is running the meeting to keep it on target; he or she may repay the favor at some meeting where you are in charge.

Barbara, the only woman at her level in a major industrial corporation, described the difficulties she had at meetings where she found herself the only woman: "I felt that I stood out too much. This made me hesitant to say what I had to say. I had never been reluctant to participate before. But now I really felt like the odd 'man' out. Since I couldn't let this continue and pull my weight fully in my new job, I had to decide on a course of action. I decided to get to know several of the men on the various committees with me on an informal, more personal basis. I figured if I was comfortable with some of the meeting members, I could go back to my usual behavior of being a strong participant myself, and get things to turn out the way I believed they should. I lunched with these men, stopped by their offices at slow times to chat informally. It worked. When I knew some of them better and thought of them as coworkers, as people, and began even to count on some as friends and supporters, I gained some confidence. I started to speak up again. I no longer felt that it was 'them against me.'"

Making Your Point

There's a three-step method that will help you to win your point at meetings, even if you are the only woman: (1) state your position clearly; (2) support your position with one or more pertinent facts; and (3) restate your position. If you don't re-emphasize your position—if you omit the third step—where you stand often gets lost in the sea of facts you have presented.

Sarah was participating in a meeting to decide what to do about a large tract of one-family homes that wasn't selling as anticipated. Her position was that the promotional budget had to be increased from $100,000 to $150,000 in order to get the sales that were needed to keep the project profitable. She presented the following facts to support her position:

1. 25 per cent of our potential market in the immediate area has been lost because the factory in this town has not expanded at the anticipated rate. Local advertising was cheap, but there is no one left now to advertise to.

2. We can regain a number of prospects equal to the number we have lost by enlarging our advertising area to encompass the two major towns within a 25-mile radius of the development.

3. Advertising in the papers and on billboards in these larger towns to reach these prospective buyers will cost us 50 per cent more than what we had originally budgeted.

She continued by restating her case: "I believe we must increase our advertising budget by 50 per cent if we wish to maintain our sales rate at two homes per week."

Visual Aids

Visual aids that illustrate the points you are making will help you convince other people and will help them to understand what you are saying more clearly.

Sarah used a chart that showed the breakdown of the former $100,000 budget, along with the population it was expected to reach. She used a second chart to show how the population had changed and how a replacement population could be reached with the larger budget. Her third chart showed the breakdown of the $150,000 budget. She showed these charts after she made her points. This gave her a further chance to restate her position and to reinforce it.

Make sure you use visual aids whenever you can. But make sure the visual aids are *simple* illustrations of what you are saying. Depending on the complexity of the situation, you can carry on your discussion while referring to the visual or show the visual after you have made your point. Be sure that the visual emphasizes your point and doesn't detract from what you are saying. Make certain that everyone can see it. Remember the ego involvement of each person in the meeting. If they can't see your visual aid, you've probably lost their support. Move the visuals around or ask the people to move, if you have to.

Sarah passed out copies of her three charts, since the meeting was simply a creative one in which the purpose was to figure out ways to get the sales back up to meet the goals. She wanted the charts to continue selling her position after the meeting had adjourned. Do this when you can. Get a simplified version of the visual information into people's hands for their own records and for them to think about after the meeting.

If you can arrange to demonstrate something, do so. People remember what they see better than what they hear. They remember what they do even better than what they see. Having visual aids or letting people try something can help you in your position at meetings. Visual aids and demonstrations are important if you are a participant; they are equally important if you are called in as a specialist.

Appearing as an Expert

Sometimes your part in a meeting is to provide background information. Get together with the chairman or whoever has requested your participation and find out what kind of information you are expected to provide. Plan the kind of visual aids that will be most effective in getting your information across. Know ahead of time the purpose of the meeting and whether or not you are expected to give an opinion, or simply to present facts. Coming to a meeting as an expert can give you an excellent opportunity for visibility and recognition if you present your material in a succinct, logical, and interesting fashion.

Ms. Chairman

As you move higher in the organization, you will find yourself more and more often in charge of meetings rather than being just a participant or an expert witness. It takes practice to acquire the skills necessary to run meetings successfully. One of the most important of these is to learn how to prepare for the meeting thoroughly before it takes place. Most meetings succeed or fail at this stage. Since the truly productive part of most meetings lasts only about one and a half to two hours, it's essential to do a lot of work ahead of time to ensure that everything runs quickly and smoothly when the people get together.

Here are some additional suggestions for preparing for and chairing successful meetings:

1. Prepare thoroughly.

The rapid and successful conclusion of a meeting often depends upon the completeness of the preparation. Include the following in your preparation:

(a) A clearly defined statement of purpose for the meeting. Be sure you know why the meeting is being held and what you expect to have accomplished by the time it ends.

(b) A prepared agenda. It is useful to put items under specific headings, such as "For Discussion," and "For Decision." Note a suggested time allotment for each category, or even for each item within a category, and stick to the allotted times. After all, discussions can go on indefinitely.

(c) A total scheduled meeting time of two hours or less.

(d) Only a manageable number of people included. In an article in the *Harvard Business Review* titled "How to Run a Meeting," Antony Jay suggests that between four and seven people is ideal, ten is tolerable, and twelve is the outside limit of participants.

(e) Get all needed information ready. Distribute background material before the meeting so that participants can read it and think about it. Keep written material to be distributed at the meeting itself at a minimum. If you have to provide last-minute information, translate it into charts and other graphic illustrations that are understood more quickly.

2. Recognize the importance of the physical setting.

A round table implies equality of status and encourages open discussion. Face-to-face seatings across a table tend to encourage conflict. If a rectangular arrangement is necessary, seat adversaries next to each other to discourage unnecessary interpersonal conflict. It's much harder to disagree in this position. To encourage anyone's participation, or the strength of their position, seat them near you.

3. Handle the substance of the meeting by keeping the group moving toward the objectives.

Refer to the agenda and restate the goals of the meeting to the participants if necessary. Virtually everything said at a meeting falls into the following categories: questions, answers, positive reactions, and negative reactions. Answers are of three basic types: fact, opinion, and suggestion. With these distinctions in mind, you will find it easier to handle the group.

4. Manage the people in your meeting.

Generally, a good meeting elicits creative suggestions from the participants, but people sometimes hesitate to volunteer an idea because they don't want to become targets of criticism. Invite participation from all members; encourage the shyer members, since good ideas don't necessarily all emanate from a group's most vocal members. Try to keep the meeting atmosphere cordial, but encourage constructive conflict—disagreement over ideas. Discourage emotional disagreement by distinguishing fact from opinion.

5. Get results from your meeting.

Group decisions are based on compromise; everyone will have to concede a little. Avoid imposing your own solutions on the group. Try to stay with your original time schedule. If the meeting drags on without appropriate resolution, adjourn the meeting and begin again another time. In any event, close on a positive note; state what was accomplished.

6. Prepare a report on the results of the meeting.

This can be long or short, but it should be an end result of any meeting for the purpose of identifying the value and achievement of the meeting.

WHAT MEETINGS CAN DO

"A meeting defines a team or a group," Antony Jay states. This group "creates its own pool of shared knowledge, experience, judgment, and folklore . . . [which] greatly increases the speed and efficiency of all communications" among group members. "A meeting helps every individual understand both the collective aim of the group and the way in which her own and everyone else's work can contribute to the group's success. A meeting creates in all present a commitment to the decisions it makes and the objectives it pursues."

Business meetings are vital means of gathering information, sharing information, creating new solutions, making decisions, deciding how to proceed, and ensuring that companies operate the way they were intended to. As an executive on the rise, it's important that you master the art of making meetings work both for the organization and for you.

19

LESS STRESS,
MORE ENERGY

For the professional woman, an excessive amount of stress seems almost inevitable. Not only does she have to cope with the same difficult, high-pressured environment that has produced serious stress symptoms in so many men, but at the same time she has to overcome a good deal of her feminine cultural conditioning. She has to deal with overt and covert antagonism caused by her redefining her role in society and competing with men. Moreover, if she has a family, she usually has to continue to fill her traditional role of nurturer since there is rarely anyone to replace her in this area. But who nurtures her?

Since there probably isn't anyone around to take care of you or to see that you take care of yourself, it's mostly up to you. You need to observe what causes you undue amounts of stress, decide what to do about it, and set about managing the stress level in your life.

WHAT IS STRESS?

Stress can be either a friend or a foe, depending upon its magnitude, intensity, and duration. Dr. Hans Selye, founder of the International Institute of Stress, calls the things that cause stress in our lives "stressors." There are many stressors in our lives and they come from many different sources, yet all elicit essentially the same biological response in the form of chemical changes.

In small doses, these chemical changes, which manifest themselves in such overt symptoms as a more rapid heartbeat, perspiration, a spurt of energy, can help you to run and catch the last commuter train that gets you to work on time, or to stay at work a couple of extra hours and get the year-end report done. But prolonged stress may manifest itself in symptoms that are negative, such as insomnia, headaches, irritability, feelings of anxiety, and excesses in drinking, smoking, or eating. When the symptoms are this severe, it's a sign that you need to control your stressors better. If you don't, you may cause irreversible damage to your body in the form of high blood pressure and heart disease, diseases of the kidney, arthritis, allergies, and diseases of digestion and/or resistance. As a professional woman, you must learn how to make stressors work for you while at the same time avoiding the harmful effects of too much stress—what Dr. Selye refers to as *dis*tress.

There appears to be an optimum amount of stress for each person—a certain amount of tension and stimulation that spurs one on to creativity, change, and progress. Too little stress can cause boredom, fatigue, and frustration. It's up to you to become increasingly self-aware in order to find the optimum stress level for yourself and to find ways to manage your stressors and your reaction to them so that you will not experience distress.

MANAGING STRESS

In order to manage stress, the first step is to identify your stressors; the next step is to decide what is fixed and what can be changed, and then to do something about those factors that can be altered. The third step is to take steps to minimize your distress.

Find Your Stressors

One helpful way to identify the sources of your stress is to examine these four areas: your environment, your job, your relationships with other people, and your own internal problems. Environmental stressors are such things as cold, heat, noise, allergens, smog, lighting, an uncomfortable commuting situation. Organization—job—stressors include such things as deadlines, business travel, work overload, frustration in achieving your goals, ambiguity in assignment, and role conflicts. Interpersonal conflicts—your relationships with people—occur both at work and at home, and your intrapersonal conflicts—your internal problems—you carry with you everywhere. Intrapersonal stressors might include such things as your competitiveness, your need for perfection, your ambition. All of these stressors interrelate to some extent, but it is often easier to pinpoint what is bothering you if you look into these four areas separately.

In your notebook where you are working on your career development plan, make a separate section devoted to minimizing stress and maximizing your energy. List as many stressors as you can identify in your life under these four categories of environment, organization, interpersonal, and intrapersonal. By doing this you'll find that you're focusing largely on the negative causes of stress in your life. But, as Dr. Selye found out, things that cause you happiness and joy can also cause you stress and even distress. You need to take note of them as well.

Life Events

Thomas Holmes and Richard Rahe, two doctors at the University of Washington, have found that important life events contribute significantly to distress. Furthermore, the impact of these events can be roughly measured. Doing this can be very useful in helping you to plan for and manage stress.

Identify for yourself those stressors that have happened to you within the past year. If anything has happened more than once, multiply the number of points assigned by the number of times it happened to you. Then add up the total of your points.

Schedule of Recent Events

LIFE EVENT	MEAN VALUE
Death of spouse	100
Divorce	73
Marital separation	65
Jail term	63
Death of close family member	63
Personal injury or illness	53
Marriage	50
Fired at work	47
Marital reconciliation	45
Retirement	45
Change in health of family member	44
Pregnancy	40
Sex difficulties	39
Gain of new family member	39
Business readjustment	39
Change in financial state	38
Death of close friend	37
Change to different line of work	36
Change in number of arguments with spouse	35
Mortgage over $10,000	31
Foreclosure of mortgage or loan	30
Change in responsibilities at work	29
Son or daughter leaving home	29
Trouble with in-laws	29
Outstanding personal achievement	28
Husband/wife begins or stops work	26
Begin or end school	26
Change in living conditions	25
Revision of personal habits	24
Trouble with boss	23
Change in work hours or conditions	20
Change in residence	20
Change in schools	20
Change in recreation	19
Change in church activities	19
Change in social activities	18
Mortgage or loan less than $10,000	17
Change in sleeping habits	16
Change in number of family get-togethers	15
Change in eating habits	15

Vacation   13
Christmas   12
Minor violations of the law   11

Drs. Holmes and Rahe found by studying thousands of people that if during one year the points totaled 150 to 199, the person had about one chance in three of becoming ill; when the points totaled 200 to 299, the person had a fifty-fifty chance of getting sick; and if the point total was more than 300, there appeared to be an 80 per cent chance of a major illness occurring within the next two years.

Holmes and Rahe studied people who were already seriously ill and looked back into what had happened in their lives in the past in order to develop their point system. The total score you arrive at is not intended to be predictive of the fact that you may become ill, but it is a useful indicator of whether your stress level is slight (under 150), moderate (150-199), heavy (200-299), or severe (over 300). If it is over 150, you may want to take a hard look at any further changes and try to postpone them for a while or avoid them altogether. You'll notice that many positive and happy events rate high in the point scale—such as marriage, pregnancy, and job change.

Marcia completed her doctoral degree after four years of very hard work and took a full-time job; her husband also got a better job and increase in salary. During the year, her father became extremely ill, had an operation, and died six weeks later. In the midst of all these changes, the dream house that Marcia and her husband had been waiting for came on the market, and they bought it. It was only later that Marcia realized that the house purchase in the midst of all these other major life changes was not a very good idea. She simply did not have the energy to move her household, but she had put herself in the situation where she had no option. If she had looked at her point total on the schedule of recent events, it might have persuaded her to put off buying a house and moving until a calmer period in her life came around.

Change What You Can

Stress requires adjusting and adapting. When you have to bear too many stressors at the same time or within too little time, your flexibility is greatly diminished and the effects of stress are greater. Take a look at the stressors you have identified in the four major areas and the items on the Holmes and Rahe schedule of recent events. Look for items that you can change, minimize, eliminate, or delegate. Make some choices that will cut down on your stress level.

Star the items that are causing you excessive amounts of aggravation. Is there anything you can do about any of them? Remember, you don't have to do it all; you are not Superwoman. Decide what you won't do, what you can eliminate; choose some things to do less well or less often. And don't feel guilty about these choices. Guilt is a negative use of energy and a source of stress as well. Learn to concentrate your time and your energy on what is really important to you.

In reviewing your stressors, you more than likely also identified quite a few that you can't change, that you have to live with. The secret of managing this fixed stress is to learn to take care of yourself and to minimize the negative effects.

Time for Yourself

Allow yourself time for relaxation, for exercise, and for adequate health care. Know yourself and what gives you the most relief from stress symptoms.

Relaxation techniques are helpful to many people. Dr. Herbert Benson of Harvard University outlines meditation techniques in his book, *The Relaxation Response*. Yoga has helped many people with its combination of mental and physical exercises aimed at reducing tension. Regular and reasonably strenuous forms of exercise, such as aerobics, tennis, jogging, ballet, help many people to reduce their stress level, while at the same time equipping their bodies to handle a reasonably high level of stress without distress. Find out what you enjoy and what makes you feel good, and do it.

Adequate rest and good nutrition are musts for everyone who wants to perform well on the job and have enough energy to lead a balanced life. A good balance in your life will enable you to harness stress for optimum results: to solve problems, meet deadlines, deal with change and conflict, and be creative.

ENERGY

Without exception, every successful professional woman surveyed for this book included "lots of energy" near the top of her list of requirements for success. What do we mean by energy?

Energy is the force, mental and physical, that you possess that enables you to get things done. Although successful people may appear to have more energy than others, it is more likely that they have learned to manage their energy carefully and to achieve maximum results from its expenditure. You, too, should regard your energy as one of your vitally important resources for getting things done.

Even those fortunate people who may be endowed with more than the normal share of energy can accomplish still grander feats if they understand their sources of energy, and replenish themselves regularly. Understanding where your energy comes from is essential to managing it. Physical and mental energy are the two distinct types one usually thinks of, but there are two more that are helpful to consider: nervous and emotional. For some tasks you draw on all four kinds of energy at one time; for others you use only one or two. If you are conscious of what kind of energy you are drawing on, you can control its expenditure and replenishment better and get things done more easily.

Conducting an all-day seminar probably requires most of your intellectual capacity, is certainly physically tiring, and taxes your nerves and emotions as well. You'll need to find ways to replenish your energy in all four areas in order to perform well the next day or the next week because you're probably overdrawn in one or more of these areas. Solving a tough technical problem often taxes only your intellectual energy, but if the problem defies solution and you become irritated, frustrated, or angry, you'll be using up emotional energy as well. If there is too little time to solve the problem and you become tense, you'll find it a drain on your nervous energy.

Knowing what kind of energy you are drawing on and where you still have a good supply will help you to plan your activities wisely and will show where you need some resting and recuperating.

Physical Energy

Are you feeling particularly well and fit, or have you been ill-treating your body by not getting enough exercise and rest or not eating sensibly? What environmental factors may be affecting your body? A seminar leader flew into a city heavy with smog to conduct a tough training session. She later recounted, "Even though my co-leader warned me to take it quite easy and not put forth as much effort as I'm used to doing, I didn't heed the warnings. By midmorning I felt quite faint and had to leave the room several times. Thank goodness we teach in teams, and she had experience in pacing herself in this city where the carbon monoxide content is actually dangerously high."

Intellectual Energy

Have you been concentrating on solving a lot of problems lately, dealing with some very complex issues, having to learn a great deal in a very short time? Have you ever felt that you'd rather not have to learn or decide anything for a while? What enables you to turn off your thinking machine and give it a rest? "For me to go into idle, I have to go to the ocean," a hard-driving executive told us. "The minute I smell the salt air, I begin to relax. Then I can go get my brain out of gear. I don't know what will happen to me if I have to work away from either coast—say in Chicago—but I guess even there I could find something that would help me to stop thinking for a time, something that would be diverting and help me get back my perspective. But I'm glad I can go to the shore each weekend from where I live now."

Emotional Energy

Have you been living in a highly charged emotional state, either due to irritation, anger, or more pleasurable sources, such as the discovery of a new love or the marriage of one of your children?

Or have your emotions been in a reasonably calm and steady state? The expenditure of emotional energy—feeling sad or happy —can leave you depleted, as the Holmes and Rahe survey illustrates so clearly. What helps you to become calmer and get back your equilibrium? Masking your real feelings can require a great deal of emotional energy, and you may find yourself called upon to do this at work, if you want to keep your job. Frustration is almost endemic in business, since you can't always have things your way, or be with people you like. Boredom, too, can be an emotional drain. What restores your emotional balance?

Nervous Energy

Are you doing anything that exerts a continuing drain on your nervous system? Does your environment put a strain on your nerves? Are you contributing to nervousness by your eating habits, by drinking too much coffee or other caffeine beverages? Getting energy from stressing your nerves can sometimes be beneficial to keep you going in the short run, but almost always is damaging in the long run.

"We had a terrible year," reported one executive whose office was in midtown Manhattan. "They were building right across the street from my office, and it required blasting into bedrock several times a day. You'd hear the warning whistle for the blast and then sit there for several seconds or sometimes several minutes until the blast went off. It always shook my whole office. We thought they'd never get through. I was a nervous wreck that year; almost everyone in the office was more edgy than normal. It seemed like the last straw on top of all the other stress producers in the city. I coped by taking more exercise lessons than normal; at least I looked better—even if I didn't feel very relaxed."

Monitoring Your Energy Level

Some activities may cause you to use up one type of energy while replenishing another. Travel may be tiring physically, but a change of locale can be stimulating and increase your emotional energy level. Exercise is usually physically tiring, but for most people it helps repair frayed nerves and relieves tension and stress buildup. The important thing is to recognize where your energy supply is depleted and do something about it.

"I watch my energy level very closely," explained a much-traveled consultant. "Meetings with clients are tiring, especially so when I'm working with them for the first time. It takes all my energy to learn how to work with them, to find out what they really want to achieve, and then to figure out how to help them do it. It's quite a strain, so I've set up certain rules to avoid overtaxing myself—particularly when I'm on the road. For example, I try never to go to dinner with a client. Continuing the long business day into the evening is counterproductive for me. In the evening I prefer to recharge my batteries by doing some jogging or swimming. I've found that physical activity relieves my nervous tension and helps me think more clearly."

Two women executives who travel together frequently have discovered that, when jetting great distances, both are equally taxed by changing time zones, but the younger woman recovers faster. They take this into account when they schedule their work, upon arrival at their destination. The younger woman usually takes the heavier work load at the beginning of the trip, enabling her partner to catch her breath and perform later, when she's at her peak.

Study your own energy pattern. What kind of energy do you have the most of? Is it intellectual, physical, emotional, or nervous —and how much of each do you have? Are you physically strong, or are you the sort of person who seems to run mostly on nervous energy? What causes you to deplete your energy in any of these areas? What happens to your total energy reserve if you are particularly upset about something? How long does it take you to recover if you overtax yourself in any of these areas? What do you have to do in order to recover?

A very slim dynamo of a woman accomplished what appeared to her friends to be limitless quantities of work. She had physical stamina beyond the resources of most people. She worked long hours and produced outstanding results. While doing this over a period of years, she found herself sleeping less and rarely eating much. Eventually she could sleep only with the aid of sleeping pills and she began to suffer from recurrent stomach pain. Finally, when sleeping pills no longer helped her, she sought medical help and found that she was on the verge of an ulcer. Her sleeplessness was also a symptom of overdrawing on her energy supply and of prolonged stress. She went for counseling to find out why she forced herself to work so hard in a sustained manner, why she couldn't let herself relax. She got some interesting insights into the fact that she was, to some extent, searching for the approval of her father.

But she was not satisfied that this was more than a small factor in her stress symptoms. She had another physical exam, and this time the doctor discovered that she had a significant loss of hearing from childhood illnesses. Straining to hear what was going on around her drained her nervous system and made her very tense. Fortunately, her hearing loss was treatable, and this hidden stressor was removed. She also learned to take life more easy and relax more through her counseling sessions. She has avoided the ulcer and now sleeps without pills. She probably doesn't accomplish quite so much at work, but she doesn't feel she needs to.

USING STRESS AND ENERGY

An understanding of your optimal stress level and the ability to keep it high enough to be able to accomplish a lot, yet avoid the ill effects of too much stress, is essential to professional success. Maintaining your energy at a highly productive level is equally important and closely related, since excess stress drains you of energy.

A goodly supply of energy and sufficient stress for a high level of motivation can help you to utilize effectively the executive resources we've looked at in this section. It will help you to:

1. Invest your time where it will do you the most good
2. Be decisive and take risks
3. Accept change and encourage the constructive aspects of conflict
4. Influence other people

5. Communicate clearly and understand what is being communicated to you

It will also help you to make the professional moves that are required if you are targeting the top. We'll look at the moving further in Part IV—"Making Your Moves."

PART IV

MAKING YOUR MOVES

20

MOVING OUT AND AROUND

To move up, you have to move. You may have to make your moves within your organization, or it may be necessary to move to another company.

ROUTES TO THE TOP

When considering your career moves, it is best to take a very good look at what is required to move through the organization where you are now working. How do people progress up the ladder? Who makes it to the top? Does the company promote only from within, or does it bring in outside talent to manage at senior levels? Does there seem to be any sort of formal or informal career development plan in the organization? How do you get on the upward track? Does this path fit with your values and your abilities? Will your personal obstacles get in the way?

Almost 70 per cent of the senior executives in a 1979 study made by Korn/Ferry International started in a functional discipline—that is, in finance/accounting, or a professional/technical capacity, such as law or engineering. About 20 per cent started in the marketing or sales areas. Almost half of them hold graduate degrees. Most of them feel that the way that they started still remains the fast-track way to the top and that marketing is no longer one of the best entry spots. One third of these senior executives feel that finance/accounting is currently the "fast route to the top" and they believe it will remain so.

Regardless of what route you take, remember that specialists don't usually become senior executives, generalists do. Find out what kinds of experience you need to be a generalist in your company and go after it—even if it means accepting lateral moves and relocation. Nobody promised you a rose garden around your career path, in fact, many experienced women might warn you that at times it will seem more like a forest of thorns.

Sometimes, the information about what is expected of rapidly moving middle managers is not easy to unearth. Karen, a manager in an industrial company, was very clear on the fact that it would take her ten years and three moves to get solidly into middle management. But, once there, she says, "It gets very fuzzy. I'm not sure what's best to do when you're established fully as a middle manager in order to get selected to become part of senior management. As soon as someone is selected to move on up, a specific series of jobs is spelled out, all at headquarters. But I still have to find out how to make sure that I'm one of the ones to get tapped."

Karen saw the first part and the final part of the path clearly, but she needed help in making the right moves in the middle section of her career.

And the routes to the top don't always stay the same. Very often, they reflect the way the current chief executive officer and the senior executives around him have risen to head the corporation. If the senior people who have come up the financial route are replaced with people who rose through marketing, it's a pretty good bet that a strong marketing background will now be especially useful. Keep observing what's really going on in your company.

VIEWING YOUR CAREER FROM TWO PERSPECTIVES

Edgar Schein, professor of organizational behavior at M.I.T.'s Sloan School, says that career development in organizations has to be viewed from two separate but interrelated perspectives; the first is the career from the point of view of the person who moves through the organization and the second is the career as seen by the organization—the company's expectations about who will move into what positions and how quickly.

You have probably been doing a good deal of thinking about your career from your own point of view. You've probably been considering the questions raised in this book. What fits your life stage? What are your constraints? What are your goals and how soon do you hope to achieve them? How can you prepare yourself to achieve them? But to decide whether you can realistically pursue your career in the company where you now work, you must also view your career, on a continuing basis, from the perspective of the company and its overall personnel needs as well as its prejudices. It's fine to identify your personal goals clearly, but if you want to achieve them, you must assess your work situation. In Chapter 23 we will look at organizational assessment in greater detail, including an evaluation of the corporate attitude toward professional women.

GIVE YOURSELF TIME TO MOVE

You may be starting to feel that in order to get requisite experience or to move up, it will be necessary for you to look at opportunities outside your company. If this is the case, give yourself lots of time to look, and keep an open mind about your own company in the process.

When Myra, an experienced business woman, was about to complete her M.B.A. after five years of studying at night, she felt that it was time for her to look at other job opportunities. The company where she had been working during this time had a bad record for moving women up. There were very few women in the ranks above the level of first-line supervisor. Although it was a large corporation, Myra found few women in middle management and none above. The field was traditionally one for men, with women only recently making any inroads at lower levels. So she thought she'd best look at other options.

Myra was quite clear about what she wanted to do. She wanted a middle-management job in marketing in a company where women had been successful and where she could use both her experiences and her education. She was willing and able to relocate. Her résumé was impeccable. It was an almost perfect product, and she had refined it to the point where she had it professionally typeset and printed.

Myra asked her friends to look for any negative image she might be projecting. They pointed out that she had a nasal voice and a fairly pronounced regional accent. She enrolled in a speech clinic to modify these characteristics. Her interview wardrobe passed muster on all counts. She got many leads from the placement office of her graduate school. However, despite having covered all her bases thoroughly before embarking on a job search, she found that her job search was a long one—a year—with many interviews and many disappointments. She was fortunate in being in the position of continuing to receive a weekly paycheck.

While Myra looked, she kept telling everyone where she worked that she really would like a better job with the company. It was obvious to them that she couldn't be expected to remain in her dead-end position once she had received her graduate degree. A happy ending to this story is that her employer did manage to find her a better job in corporate headquarters in their marketing department—where she was the first woman.

"Give yourself plenty of time to make a career move," counsels Myra. "Even with a first-class résumé, ability to relocate, a clear idea of what I wanted, and a shiny M.B.A., it took me a year to make the right move."

MOVE AROUND PRODUCTIVELY

Before World War II it was almost unheard of to move from company to company if you wanted to succeed. In the sixties, it became more acceptable—even desirable—in many fields to have worked for several companies and to have a variety of experience. But it's interesting to note that even though the senior managers in the Korn/Ferry study say they believe in executive mobility, and that an executive's chances for advancement are greater if he does not remain with one company for his entire career, the people surveyed have been with their present employers for almost twenty years.

Length of service with the same company is underscored in a survey of 470 chief executive officers of banks done in 1974 by Heidrich and Struggles, which showed that typically these men had had only one or two employers and been with their current employers for at least eleven years.

When considering a job move, make sure every move counts. Then, though it has become more acceptable in recent years to be a mobile manager, you still want to make sure you don't make too many moves. Three or four jobs is considered by many people to be the ideal maximum if different companies are involved, before you settle into an upward track in the company where you plan to make your mark.

COPING WITH PREJUDICE

There is currently a pervasive attitude that women are more likely to leave a company than men holding equivalent positions. Part of this is a holdover of the attitude that men have about women's seriousness of purpose in pursuing their careers. In the fifties, a serious-minded career woman applied for a management training program and was accepted. She asked if the salary she was offered was the same as the starting salary for men with an equivalent education—she held a degree with honors from an Ivy League college. The answer was "No, you are much more likely to leave the company because of marriage or children than a man we would hire." She didn't take the job. She went to another company that was more open-minded, and she achieved senior management status in the next seven years.

Theoretically, this type of discrimination has been removed by national laws since then, but an article on the front page of the *Wall Street Journal* in July 1979 about a survey done by Youngs, Walker & Co. of 280 male executives (mostly senior executives in banks) reports that 75 per cent believe that women don't take their careers as seriously as men. When discussing the problems of helping women to become managers, one third specifically mentioned the risk of pregnancy or "male attachment." The same prejudices seem to be holding ambitious women back today as they did twenty-five years ago.

Facts refute this antiquated attitude. In 1979 *Business Week* did a study of women executives in forty companies. Only two companies reported a higher rate of turnover for women than for men and these two companies were in the technical/engineering areas, where women are in short supply. Despite the fact that women still marry and have babies, it doesn't appear to make them any less stable as employees in middle and upper management than their male counterparts, who, after all, also marry and sometimes become parents as well.

RELOCATION

Your professional moves, either to broaden your experience or to get a promotion, very often mean that you have to relocate. Be prepared for this eventuality.

Karen, whom we mentioned at the beginning of this chapter, worked for her company for eight years. The path to the top in her organization involves three or four different jobs before employees achieve a lower-middle-management position. Each of these steps involves a relocation. Management employees typically spend two or three years at each of several widely flung locations. It's an international company, and this makes the moving still more complex because of the different cultures involved and the logistics of overseas moves. Karen has moved from the West Coast to the East Coast to Europe and to the Midwest. One of these assignments lasted only a few months. This is not a life-style that will appeal to everyone.

To further complicate her life, at one of these locations, Karen met a man whom she liked very much. "We said good-bye when I was transferred to the other coast, but our relationship endured despite the distance. We conducted a jetting romance for some months and then decided that we really were right for each other. Our decision to marry took some very heavy planning. My fiancé had to find a way to continue his career near where I was working because I didn't expect another transfer for at least two years. Fortunately he was able to join a consulting company where he is on the road from Monday morning until Friday evening. This way it doesn't matter too much where I live. To succeed in the company I'm working for, I have to follow the traditional route—especially because I'm one of the first women who has a chance of making it. I never said much about my marriage at work; it would only make them nervous. And not everyone would agree with the choices we've made."

The kind of weekend marriage relationship that Karen shares with her husband is not for everyone. But they are both happy with it and actively pursuing their careers full speed ahead.

An even more dramatic story of the need for relocation is found in Doris's job requirements. She is training to become a manager in an international company. Her intensive training period consists of five years of living around the world at the various headquarter locations, usually staying only about six months at any one place. She is in her early thirties and had worked for the company for seven years while she was married. When her marriage ended, she asked to be considered for the middle-management training program, something which would have been virtually impossible for her to undertake before her divorce. She was chosen for the program and was willing—perhaps even eager—to keep moving about so rapidly for several years. "It certainly does help you avoid any kind of deep personal commitment," she commented. "It's funny to watch men's reactions when they meet you. At first they think it's glamorous, all this flying around the world. Often, for example, I go to Rio just for the weekend, since it's my favorite city. Then the men stop and think that tomorrow I'll be gone, and they'll just be my man in that city. It's a real role switch from the days when the sailors had a girl in every port. I don't think men like it, but I'm enjoying my freedom—and I'm really on the way up in my company."

Choose Your Time to Relocate

It's often better to consider the problem of relocation separately from a specific career move. Try to seek out your career moves when other life events are under control. But be prepared if your company should ask you to move when it's inconvenient for you personally. And be prepared if another company offers you a job that requires a move; you'll be able to bargain better.

When Marty was called to interview for a job located in the suburbs of a major city, she scouted the area on a quick one-day trip to see what the living situation would be there for herself and her son. She was appalled to find out that the living costs were at least 50 per cent higher than where she was now located. This information helped her to determine whether she would want to consider the new position at all. She decided to go ahead with the interview, since she knew the position was probably a good career move for her. But she decided not to move unless she could at least maintain her present living conditions. Marty was very clear on her personal values versus her desire for professional progress, "When you are in middle management, there is no reason why relocation should work personal hardships on you. I sacrificed a lot when I was at lower levels to get where I am now. A good neighborhood and a good school for my son are very high on my list of necessities. I think companies respect you only if you know what you want and ask for it."

Relocation is difficult enough without its causing serious financial hardships. Moving yourself and a family, if you have one, is very disruptive. It's hard on women, and it's hard on men as well. Karen, mentioned before, is using her position as the token fast-track woman to point this out gradually to the senior people in her company who are in a position to change its policies. She feels that the company's standard procedure of forcing upwardly mobile young executives to make four major moves in ten years is causing them to lose many good men, as well as making it extremely hard on their talented woman managers. "Many companies who used to follow the same pattern are not moving people around so much anymore," Karen believes. "IBM used to stand for 'I've Been Moved.' Now the best people sometimes refuse to go. They have some other options due to more and more dual-career marriages like mine. On the one hand, it's hard for us to plan our careers so that they mesh comfortably; but on the other, it keeps us from having to go along with decisions that are strictly for the good of the company.

"My company is large and changes very slowly. I think I can help them change in this area by discussing the problem informally with the right people. It will be too late for it to do me any good; but in the long run, it will help the company, because the employees can live more balanced lives."

If you are asked to relocate by the company for which you work, you might ask yourself and the important people in the company if the move is really necessary. In a study done in 1979 by Korn/Ferry, of 1,700 senior managers who held the next to top job in their companies, few reported the need to relocate often during their careers. Many had never moved at all, and, at most, these senior people had made only two or three moves before settling at headquarters. Most of them had been with their present companies for twenty years or more. There may be a suggestion in the results of this study that the people who get moved around too much are not the ones who are scheduled for the best upward moves.

Each company is different, and you have to know what your company expects and how it arranges the route to the top. One thing you can be reasonably sure of though is that, if you are successful, you'll end up at corporate headquarters. Keep this in mind if you are joining a new company—be sure that you'll be content in the headquarters location.

In the next chapter we'll consider some of the ways of locating opportunities if you decide you want to and need to move around.

21

FINDING THE OPPORTUNITIES

Many, if not most, fast-track positions are in high-risk situations. In order to succeed, you must risk failure—and sometimes you will fail. You may even find yourself out of work. Sometimes you lose your job even though you have been doing excellent work. The company may have to cut back. It may change its direction and no longer need your talents. Some industries, such as the advertising business, are by their very nature "revolving doors." You must protect yourself by preparing for the eventuality of losing your job.

You must keep your options open at all times and you must know how to use the four major sources for locating another position.

KEEPING YOUR OPTIONS OPEN

There are some straightforward measures you can take to ease the difficulties inherent in finding yourself unemployed. Keep current in four key areas: (1) your contacts, (2) your résumé, (3) your marketable skills, and (4) your savings account.

The broader your professional contacts are, the more quickly you will have access to information you need to find a job. Build relationships with people who can help you and keep these contacts ongoing. Keep a careful record of your professional contacts and be sure to be helpful to them whenever you can. Be especially careful to keep in contact from time to time with people whom you plan to use for references. Let them know what you are doing. You'll get a more comprehensive reference from them than if they hadn't heard from you in years.

Keep your résumé up-to-date; make sure to include increased responsibilities as you get them. It's much easier to allow your résumé to evolve than to start from scratch when you are under pressure to find a job.

Build your skills in areas where there seem to be a lot of job openings. Try to broaden your skill base and try to avoid becoming too highly specialized in areas that do not readily transfer outside your job or your company. Be alert to fields that are growing and consider what abilities are required to succeed in these fields. Gain as much experience in these areas as you can.

When you get your paycheck, pay yourself first. Put away 10 per cent of your check until you have three to six months' salary in a savings account. This will tide you over when you are looking for a job. There is nothing more discouraging and detrimental to your career than having to take a job because you can't afford to keep looking for exactly the right position.

LOOK WHILE YOU ARE WORKING

If you are financially secure, you are in a better position to take the risk of leaving the company where you are now working if it looks as though you can better move up elsewhere. But the single most important piece of advice about looking for a new job—advice that is constantly reiterated by women who've been through it —is to look for a job while you've got one. If you can hold onto the job you have now, while you look for another one, you'll be under less pressure to make a choice, because you'll have a regular income. In fact, if you don't find what you want, you have the option of staying where you are. You can resume your search again at a later time when conditions are more favorable, or after you've gained some essential skills you needed to make the right upward move. Potential employers are generally much more receptive to job seekers who are currently employed. There is a very strong psychological advantage in your favor: they, too, know that you have the option of staying right where you are.

Being Discreet

The major problem in looking elsewhere while you are presently employed is how you will handle yourself if your current employer discovers it. This is something you should work out beforehand so you are not caught unawares. Most employers are not pleased by this; they tend to think you are being disloyal. If you are looking in an area where there are few opportunities and few candidates, it is very difficult to keep your search confidential. Sometimes you will just be unlucky. Plan ahead—and don't be caught unprepared if your employer confronts you. Know precisely what you will say.

When the group leader of a seminar on developing your career suggested that the seminar members bring in an up-to-date résumé, she found that the participants were very nervous about preparing them. When she asked them why, they all mentioned that they felt their jobs would be in jeopardy if their employers happened to see that they were working on a résumé. She told them, "In the first place, make sure you don't do it at work; but, more importantly, give a lot of consideration to the amount of risk you are willing to take to move up. If you are either unwilling or unable to take any risk, you probably will stay right where you are. The decision is up to you."

Don't Wait to Be Chosen

This seminar leader continued, "And, what if your employer should think that you might be looking elsewhere? Couldn't you use this as a chance to discuss your job opportunities where you're now located? It's almost always better to stay with your present company if you can get an opportunity for advancement. This can be your cue to tell the company you really want to stay with them, but you also want a chance to move up.

"Women have too often waited to be chosen for the better job. Their feeling is that if they do an excellent job, their performance will be rewarded. All too often it's rewarded by allowing them to continue to do an excellent job in that spot. If you want a chance for advance, you've got to take the risk of letting it be known at some point."

Fortunately, most people manage to conduct a discreet job search without word getting back to their employers if they don't want it known. One of the ways you do this is by asking anyone with whom you interview to keep your search confidential. Be extra sure to make this point when discussing a possible job change with friends and acquaintances. They may not realize that your current employer is unaware of your plans, and how complicated it might become for you if they were indiscreet.

Occasionally, it can be advantageous to you to have this information reach your present company. More than one executive has been given a promotion when his company found they were about to lose him. Some people even threaten to resign in an attempt to achieve what they want where they are working. This is a dangerous game and is something you shouldn't do unless you are willing and able to carry out the threat. It's usually far better to attempt to persuade the right people in your company that you are eager and able to move up than to bring it about as the result of a threat.

You've got to know your company and what behavior is rewarded with promotions. "Until recently, my company almost always eliminated people from the upward track if it was learned that they were looking elsewhere," reported one executive. "But, in the past couple of years, the company has lost a lot of its best people. They've changed their minds now. Since the salaries in this company have recently been made very competitive, they now almost encourage us to look elsewhere so we know what a good deal we have here. And they encourage us to tell them if we want to move up. At long last we seem to have some sort of a career-development system, even if it's still rather informal. At least we're now free to look around if we want to without fear of losing our in-house momentum."

Once you've made sure that you're carrying out your search in a discreet manner, if this is necessary, and have planned how you'll use possible discovery as an attempt to move up in-house if you want to, the next step is to start looking.

HOW TO FIND THE OPPORTUNITIES: Your Four Major Sources

If you are fortunate enough to be searching for another job while you are working, or if you are unemployed and under pressure to find something, the sources of new opportunities are the same: (1) personal contacts, (2) advertisements, (3) mailings, and (4) placement agencies. Different specialists in the art of job hunting place different weights on the effectiveness of each of these four sources. However, if you are seriously looking for a job, you should explore fully all sources and leads so that you can choose from as wide a range of job opportunities as possible.

Personal Contacts

Bearing in mind the need for discretion, tell everyone you know who may have useful contacts that you are looking for a job. Richard Bolles, who is one of the foremost counselors of people seeking career positions, estimates that 80 per cent of all executive jobs are found in this manner. Other job counselors rate this method as high as 90 per cent. Whatever the percentage, it is undoubtedly your best single way of finding a career move.

However, there are two caveats with regard to this method. Don't take the time of busy people unless you are really sincere about your job search, and don't use this method as a ploy. Some job-hunting manuals suggest that you approach all the professional people who might possibly be relevant to your job search under the *guise* of looking for information. Then, if they don't happen to have something for you, these manuals suggest you ask each person to send you on to three more people "for information." Business people are quite sophisticated in interpreting motives and will usually realize that you are really hoping they might think of a job for you and that you are not just seeking information. Don't go to your contacts—or to the people with whom they are kind enough to put you in touch—under false pretenses.

Ask for help in finding a job and for information when you truly need it and ask for what you really need.

When Miriam redid her résumé, she wanted an outsider's view of its effectiveness. She asked a friend, who was the president of a corporation, to review it for her and give her a frank opinion. She chose him as her editor because she knew that because of their friendship he would not feel obliged to try to find something for her in his company; they both knew she had neither experience nor interest in his business. His comments on her résumé proved to be very valuable because he was able to be totally objective. A side benefit of their get-together was the fact that an associate of his had just taken on the presidency of a company for which Miriam was ideally suited. Miriam's friend offered to send him her revised résumé and his personal letter of recommendation.

The possibility of just such an outcome is the reason for letting your contacts know that you are available. If you are seriously looking for another job, tell everyone who could possibly be of help. But don't use your contacts lightly or too often, or you will lose your credibility.

And don't forget that when people go out of their way to assist you, the least you should do is to let them know the results of their efforts. Brenda asked a former employer to help her locate a job in San Francisco, where her fiancé was working. Her former boss counseled Brenda extensively in an effort to help her and made many calls and wrote many letters. She went out of her way to help Brenda and used her own contacts to do so.

Brenda then moved to San Francisco, and her boss never heard from her. As it turned out, Brenda interviewed with several of the people to whom she had been recommended, but decided not to take a position until after she was married. She communicated this decision neither to the prospective employers, nor to her former boss who had been so helpful, thereby failing on two counts. This lack of consideration impressed both of them badly. Because of it, Brenda has used up her credits with her former employer for some time to come and perhaps forever. Be scrupulous about following through on any personal contacts and then letting the person who helped you know what happened. It's only common courtesy, and you'll be able to call on this person again in the future, should you need to.

In a similar situation, Faye helped a former employee to find a number of opportunities by contacting her associates. Moira kept Faye informed on the progress of her interviews and her final job choice. "I've always heard that no good deed goes unpunished," Faye commented, "but I've never found that to be so. I guess I'm just not cynical, because I've always been rewarded for my efforts on someone else's behalf. Right after I sent my former associate out after a number of good possibilities, my husband was fired, and I needed to find a higher-paying job myself. I called Moira and got a full rundown on the status of each organization and that made my job search much easier. I actually did go to work for one of the places where she, in effect, had done some useful scouting for me."

Who Are Your Contacts?

Think of people you know and who know you, whose work brings them in touch with many other professionals in your area. These people are usually your most valuable contacts in a job search. They include advertising agency executives, space salesmen, editors of trade publications. People in such jobs are excellent sources of information on what's available and whom to contact. They usually have a wealth of inside information as well, which you wouldn't normally be given during an interview.

In one town, the editor of a leading trade publication knows virtually every job opening in the field he covers and most of the jobs that are going to open up. He shares this information with people he knows well and whom he would like to help. Although he does not do this on a quid pro quo basis, needless to say, he has many friends in his industry.

Do you have close contacts with people like this editor? If not, begin to develop them. Invite them to lunch, for a drink after work. Offer to write an article for their publication. If a friend of yours has a useful contact, take them both to lunch to get to know the third party. And perhaps most important, always be ready and willing to help the people who are potentially of help to you.

ADVERTISEMENTS, AND HOW TO RESPOND

Job counselors will tell you that your chances of getting a job through an advertisement can be as low as 5 per cent. Yet, if companies did not want to hire someone, why would they run an advertisement that often costs them several hundred dollars? Of course, there are occasionally reasons other than the fact that they actually are looking for someone to fill the advertised job, and we'll look at these later in this section. But, for the most part, the jobs advertised are legitimate, and someone will be hired to fill the position.

If you are a manager, the *Wall Street Journal* and the financial section of the New York *Times* contain many job listings that are probably of interest to you, and they have advertisements from companies to whom your background would be useful. Scanning these publications regularly is a good habit to acquire in order to keep informed about what's available. Read the trade publications in your field as well. It will help you to know what you are worth and to what you can realistically aspire. Many companies lack the contacts to be able to fill their open positions informally through friends of friends. Others have had good luck with newspaper and magazine advertising. Some companies would like to use executive search consultants but are not big enough.

When you are looking for a job, answer any advertisements that seem to fit your requirements, but keep two things in mind: other methods of job seeking are less likely to jeopardize your present position, and, for the most part, you won't receive an answer to your letter and résumé.

If the ad is a blind ad with a box number in care of the publication to which you must reply, there is no way you can prevent it from going to your own company, if it is the one placing the ad. Companies who list their openings without identifying themselves do not usually reply to you if they do not feel your qualifications are suitable. You'll reply to lots of blind ads and never hear a thing. You'll also not hear from many companies who have identified themselves. This is hard on the ego, but don't worry about it. There are many explanations that have nothing to do with your application.

Often companies don't acknowledge responses because an ad for a good job in a desirable location may bring in hundreds of replies. This is something to keep in mind if the ad appears to be for a position for which you are truly qualified and in which you are really interested, as opposed to those where you may just be testing the water. Often a secretary prescreens the responses, and they tend to come in very heavily during the week following the ad. It's worth sending a copy of your original letter and résumé with a short cover note about two weeks later. This way, your résumé is sometimes reviewed twice, after the company has a clearer idea of what kind of people are available and what they are really looking for.

Sometimes companies place ads because they are trying to prove that no qualified minority candidates are available or because they are trying to see what kinds of people might be possible alternatives to an in-house employee they are considering moving up. Companies occasionally advertise to cover themselves, because they're afraid a crucial job may open up—and it never does.

One woman who was conducting a full-scale job search answered a blind ad for a job in New York City. Although she received no response, a few weeks later she got a call from a company on the West Coast that had heard she was available and wanted her to come out for an interview. While she was interviewing, she asked them how they had heard of her. It turned out that they were in close contact with the New York company whose blind ad she had answered. She took the job on the West Coast, so her answer to the ad was actually what helped her to get placed—though indirectly. Many other women report getting favorable responses to their replies both to blind ads and ads in which the companies identified themselves.

A woman had been told of a company in her city for which she might be especially suited. She did not know anyone in this company and hesitated to make a cold contact. In her continuing perusal of "Help Wanted" ads, she saw a blind ad that she felt might have been placed by this particular company. She believed that her answering the ad would be an effective first contact for her, since she could tailor her reply specifically to the advertisement. In truth, she was not actively looking for a new job, but, on the other hand, she was open to a move if there was a good fit between her qualifications and the needs of the company. For several months she did not receive a reply, and she put it out of her mind. Then one day she received a call from the company, which indeed was the one she had wanted to reach. They told her that they had several job openings that they thought would suit her even better than the advertised job, and they wanted to talk to her. As it turned out, one of the positions seemed the right upward move for her, and she took it. A very minor gamble on her part eventually paid off very handsomely.

"It takes a lot of time and energy to reply to any advertisement, since at the very least you must draft a cover letter that replies directly to the ad. You may have to redo your résumé as well. I always plan to set aside a half a day on the weekend or a full evening during the week in order to respond properly. But I've found it's worth it," reports a mobile woman manager. "It's worth the time to reply to twenty, thirty, or fifty ads even if I get only two or three responses out of it. After all, I'm only looking for one job. I don't have to win them all. And every letter I write helps me further to refine my material."

If you are prepared for the limitations and risks inherent in job seeking through advertisements, the effort expended can turn out to be most worthwhile. In the next chapter, "Presenting Yourself," we'll offer some specific advice on résumés and cover letters.

DIRECT-MAIL CAMPAIGNS

For a period of time, direct-mail campaigns were very much in vogue as a means of locating a higher-level job. As with the ploy of appearing to seek information, this method of searching for a job seems to be less used today than a decade ago. But, for certain people, in special situations, it can still be an effective means of locating the right position. The direct-mail method probably also proves more effective today for women than for men, since the demand for skilled women administrators is still somewhat greater than the supply. Domestic circumstances may dictate a particular city or area of the country as the one where you must work. This is one reason to research the firms in that area who might need your expertise, and to contact them directly. Or, if you want to work for a certain type of company that is easily identifiable, direct mail could be useful.

After Liz took the time to answer an ad in which the company was identified, it occurred to her that she might as well send her résumé to key people in other divisions of the company, as well as to the division advertised. The company was high on her list of possible places for a career move, and she wanted to get the maximum benefit from the time she spent carefully writing a résumé and cover letter especially for it. She felt sure that the résumé sent in response to the ad would not go any further within the company than to the personnel people who screen replies to the ad. She identified the division managers by name in the other areas, rather than addressing the résumé to their personnel departments and contacted them all by mail.

When you write to someone in a company where you have no personal contacts and without knowing whether there is an opening, you are sending what is referred to in the direct-mail business as a "cold" letter. This kind of letter must be designed to have a strong impact and must be directed to a specific person—preferably either to the head of the department where you would like to work or to the president of the company, if the job you are seeking is in the upper echelons. Each letter must be individually typed, and you are probably wasting your time and money if you have not correctly identified the person and spelled his or her name correctly. (There are machines that will type these letters automatically, if you are sending a lot of them.)

In the direct-mail business, a 2 per cent response to cold letters is considered good, and a 5 per cent response is excellent. If you prepare an appropriate letter for the job you are after and address it correctly, you may get a response rate as high as 50 or 60 per cent, although most of the replies will turn you down politely. Usually the answers you receive, in which you are asked for more information or invited for an interview, will be in the range of 2 per cent to 5 per cent, but you will have the names of specific people in the personnel departments in all of the companies from whom you received a reply. In a month or two, if you are still looking for a job, you can write back to each of the people who said they'd put your résumé on file, or even call them. Some of your follow-up letters or phone calls may result in more interviews as job needs and requirements change with the passage of time.

In his book, *The Three Boxes of Life,* career counselor Richard Bolles says that companies on the average grant only one interview for every 245 résumés they screen and usually make only one job offer for every three people interviewed. Even though it appears that the odds of finding a job by sending a cold letter and résumé are quite slim, you only need to find one right job move at a time. Yours may be the résumé that the company reacts to and you may be the one who gets the offer. So it's worth a try.

PLACEMENT FIRMS

When seeking positions in business in the salary range under $20,000 or $25,000, sometimes you have to go to an employment agency and pay the agency a fee for the job if you obtain it. At entry or low-management levels, the employers sometimes pay the fee—usually when they are searching for a talent that is in short supply. But if you have a job and can hold out for your terms, you can frequently get the company hiring you to pay the fee as one of the terms of your employment, even if the usual procedure is for the employee to pay. It is worth being in a strong bargaining position because employment agency fees are expensive.

If you must go to an employment agency, get recommendations from friends. Many agencies are excellent and can be a great help to you; others are "body shops" that are merely interested in placing someone in a position and collecting their fees. These firms have little interest or skill in finding a fit between the candidate and the needs of the position.

In the last chapters we mentioned that there are two points of view about a job: the company's and yours. Beware of the agency that doesn't inquire into your needs. You should find a job that is a good fit between both what the company is seeking and *your* personal situation. Poor employment agencies ask only about your experience to see if you are remotely possible as a body to send on to the employer, in the hope that you might fit *their* needs. Little or no information is requested about your needs.

Universities frequently have their own placement departments and help their graduates to find jobs. Often large corporations come to campuses to recruit candidates, particularly in schools that have graduate management programs. M.B.A. candidates generally go through a grueling series of interviews both on campus and at various corporate headquarters, as they near graduation. Although the graduates-to-be may find these tough going, the extensive interviewing experience will be useful to them throughout their careers. By the time they get through all the interviews, they will have experienced virtually every type of interview, including the particularly difficult ones that are hostile or nondirective. In the next chapter, we'll look more closely at interviewing. Even if you are not a recent graduate, there is nothing to be lost by contacting your college placement office to see what prospects they might have for you.

As you move into the ranks of middle management, you are very likely to become involved with executive-search consultants, sometimes referred to as "headhunters."

EXECUTIVE-SEARCH CONSULTANTS

When companies need to find someone outside the organization to fill certain management positions, they frequently use the services of an executive-search consulting firm. Executive-search consultants are not to be confused with employment agencies or organizations that purport to help you find a better job—career counselors whom you pay a substantial amount of money for guidance in your job hunt. Headhunters are paid by the employer, usually on a retainer basis. They are interested in executives who are currently employed, who are doing well in their present positions, and who are on a fast track where they are currently working.

Searchers gather information on this kind of person by asking others in the industry. Your first contact with a headhunter may well be in the form of a phone call or letter, possibly directed to you at your office, enclosing a description of a job and asking you if you know anyone qualified to fill the position. Disregard a phone contact only if you are not interested in moving up; throw the letter away only if you expect to be totally content where you are until retirement—but it's a rare person whose job isn't in jeopardy sooner or later. It's good to keep all your options open.

If you prefer not to deal with the inquiry during business hours, you can reply to the letter on your own time, or you can ask the consultant to call you at home after work. If you are interested in the job, tell the searcher so. If you are not, pass on some names of possible candidates. Cultivate the executive-search consultant. You can help each other.

There is no need to feel guilty about responding, or to do what one woman did and show the letter to your employer. This woman's boss became irate and asked the searcher to refrain from contacting his people. Your employer can legitimately complain about your spending work hours in helping a consultant find someone for a job in another company, so it is best to act with discretion. But don't make an issue of it, because you will show yourself as extremely naïve—both to the consultant and to your employer.

Instead, use the contact to find out more about the position. You can ask about the salary, the location, the industry. They will generally tell you a good deal about the job, virtually everything except who the company is. If you are not interested, say so. But take the opportunity to inform the consultant fully of your experience, abilities, and career interests.

Contacting the Headhunters

Consider contacting some recruiters on your own if they don't come to you and you feel you are poised to move into a position with a salary range of $30,000 or more. This figure is considered the point at which executive-search consultants start to handle positions. It is far better to let them know of your background and abilities when you are successfully employed. Searchers generally subscribe to the theory that truly good candidates are happily employed and on the move where they are now working. But experienced women are in short supply and can be difficult for companies and recruiters to locate, so make yourself known as a candidate who's available to move on to bigger and better things.

An organization called Management Woman is happy to receive résumés from women who fit the general outline of people they place. "We have more than 18,000 women currently on file who have advanced degrees—usually M.B.A.s—and whose present or next salary will be more than $35,000," says Anne Hyde, president of the search firm, "and we expect that number to double or triple in the next few years.

"Even with this base, we do not have nearly enough women with the right credentials. Women must get line and field experience. This is just beginning to happen. Women are just beginning to learn how the corporate game must be played."

Executive-search consultants provide a great deal of help and guidance to both the corporations for whom they work and the people who are being considered for key positions. Recruiters are frequently paid as much as 25 per cent to 30 per cent of the annual salary for the jobs that they are helping to fill, regardless of whether, in fact, they actually locate the candidate who is hired. This allows them to be objective and thorough in attempting to match the person's needs with those of the company. Search consultants can and will provide you with a great deal of background information on both the position and the company for which they are considering your qualifications.

Recruiters generally keep a low profile, but don't let this stop you from contacting them directly if you feel you are well qualified. Headhunters tend to specialize. It's best to make an effort to find those who place people in your field and limit your contacts to these firms. You can usually find out who they are by telephoning them. You can get a list of the approximately fifty-nine member firms of the Association of Executive Recruiting Consultants at no charge by writing to them at 30 Rockefeller Plaza, New York, New York 10112. A list containing about 2,300 recruiters is available for $12 prepaid from *Consultant News,* Templeton Road, Fitzwilliam, New Hampshire 03447. Management Woman is located at 115 East 57th Street, New York, New York 10022.

22

PRESENTING YOURSELF IN PRINT AND IN PERSON

There are two major ways in which you present yourself as a candidate for a job: the first is in writing, through your résumé and the covering letter; the second is in personal interviews. Are you able to present yourself in a totally polished and professional manner, both in writing and in person? If not, start working on perfecting both approaches.

Before you can get an interview, you have to sell yourself through your résumé. You will usually be asked to send a résumé if you are being considered as a possible candidate for a position for which an executive-search firm is recruiting. Do you have a current résumé? Honestly, is it something that you are completely proud of, and that you feel shows your professional skills and experience to the greatest advantage? Or does it need some revision and improvement?

PROFESSIONALIZING YOUR RÉSUMÉ

If you were to look at one hundred résumés, you would probably find something to reject in about ninety-five of them. It is amazing how many résumés contain misspellings, are badly typed, are badly reproduced, or have a combination of these three easily avoidable errors.

The Quality

Your résumé is a graphic representation of your professional abilities; it constitutes a vital first impression for you. Have someone who has never seen your material proofread it for you before you have it printed. Pay to have the résumé typed on an electric typewriter with a carbon ribbon. This is the only way you can ensure clean, clear reproduction. Your old portable with its fabric ribbon won't do. Your résumé should be a first-class product, well reproduced, without errors. You won't win any awards for seeing that it is this way, but you probably won't get the interview you're after if it isn't. Take the time and spend the money to do it right. *The function of a résumé is to get you a personal interview.* Keep that in mind when you come to determine the quality, the style, and the content of your résumé.

The Look

There is no set way to write a résumé. Résumé styles vary from year to year and from industry to industry. In academia, for example, they even have a different name: they are referred to as Curriculum Vitae, or C.V., for short. (This is also how business résumés in many European countries are referred to.)

Look at as many different styles of résumés as you can. It's not a bad idea to keep a file for future reference of résumés that you like. Find out what style is currently most popular in your industry. Ask business associates to let you look at their résumés; ask friends in personnel departments to let you look at some of the résumés they have on file. Ask them what they think is a good type of résumé, and get them to show you some they particularly like.

You'll find that you have a lot of choices to make. Will you or won't you include a job objective on your résumé? Should you limit your résumé to one page? Should you use white paper in the standard size or should you show a little flair and use an off-white paper, or stationery in the smaller, executive size? Make choices like these according to the industry you're entering, the type of job you are seeking, and how much experience you have.

Show that you have a feeling for the industry in which you are seeking work. If you are looking for a position in the advertising business, it is useful to show a certain amount of creativity in order to get attention. If you are looking for a position in the financial field, a straightforward, no-nonsense résumé would be more appropriate and better received. This leads to an interesting problem. Suppose you were looking for a position, such as the director of human resources, and were applying both to an ad agency and a bank. It might be advisable to have two different résumés. Or, perhaps the content could remain the same, but you could have the résumé printed on paper that shows a bit of distinctiveness for the agency, and on good-quality white bond for the bank.

The Focus: Prepare Several Different Résumés

Another common misconception is that a résumé is a résumé is a résumé—that there is no room for variation or manipulation of the facts presented in this sacrosanct document. Wrong. You should be aware of this and take advantage of it.

A recent M.B.A. graduate with some business experience got many more interview opportunities and ultimately a wider range of job offers than many of her classmates, some of whom had broader experience and better grades. When asked about her secret of success, she admitted that she had many different résumés, despite the rigid formula that her school suggested and, in fact, required of its graduates. Certainly she had one that conformed to what was expected, but she had nine other versions that she felt were better suited to certain industries to which she was applying. The facts on her résumés were the same, but their presentation was different, and not all the information was given on all the résumés. In each case, she selected what was directly relevant to the job for which she was trying to get an interview.

For example, she had both marketing and management consulting experience, but when she was applying for a product-management job she stressed the marketing. She also had a background in management development. For those positions where this was a major factor she listed this experience first; for the other positions, she listed her business experience first.

Remember: the function of a résumé is to get you a personal interview. You can always keep a chronological list of your past experience on hand for filling out corporate personnel forms that require every detail of your past. In fact, you should always have such a list with you to assist you in filling out personnel forms rapidly and accurately. But—your résumé need not fulfill that purpose.

An experienced woman manager in her forties was seeking a job and knew that her background qualified her for several different fields and some different positions in those fields. Having been schooled in the attitude that there must be only one résumé, she wasn't having much luck job hunting. When a friend suggested that she create a different résumé for each type of job in which she was interested, she decided to try it. She emphasized different talents in each résumé and even used different styles and approaches. As a result, she got more responses to her résumés and many more interviews. Her former, comprehensive résumé was too long, too detailed, and lacked focus.

What to Leave Out

Study your résumé to make sure that the information you present is appropriate to your experience. Nothing shows a lack of business judgment more clearly than a résumé that includes the college activities of someone who has been out of college for a decade or more. Stick to the facts that are directly relevant to the abilities needed to perform the job you are seeking. Laws have changed a lot in recent years with regard to employment. You should not include a photo. You need not mention your age, your marital status, and whether you have children. In fact, many professional mothers would caution against any mention of children at all on résumés.

What to Include

Business people want to see what responsibility you have had. Stress active verbs that point this up. Also, quantify the responsibility whenever you can. Use very specific phrases such as: "supervised six executives and a total staff of 42"; "increased net sales 50 per cent in the first year, 25 per cent in the subsequent two years"; "responsible for an annual budget of $14 million in advertising."

If you are doing a chronological résumé, list all your relevant jobs, along with a description of the responsibility involved in each. Describe your educational background. Include professional memberships, publications, and awards. The material should be complete, yet brief. After all, it is a résumé. You should be prepared to fill in this outline during the personal interview.

Get an Editor

Nowhere is the need for an editor greater than when you are writing your résumé. Preparing this document can be even harder than writing an autobiography, because you must be very concise and selective about what you include. You are too close to your own experience and too subjective about it to be able to write a good résumé on your own.

Gather all the information together and all your old résumés, plus samples of some styles of résumés that you like and feel are suitable for you. Then, get yourself some expert help, such as friends in personnel. Get some rough drafts done with their help, or the help of other experienced business people whose judgment you value. Next, have the final draft reviewed by at least one acquaintance who holds a position at the same level as the people who will be interviewing you. Listen to their comments and make final revisions on your résumé.

The higher the position you are seeking, the more likely you are to be interviewed and selected by senior people in the firm. While they may not be doing the original screening of your résumé, they will probably look at it before or during a talk with you. Don't make the mistake made by a college professor who wanted to switch to private industry. The personnel department of the company she approached was fairly used to reviewing academic-style C.V.s and could make some translations from them. But when this applicant was passed on to the executive for whom she might possibly be going to work, the potential boss read through the C.V. and told the candidate, "After reading through your entire résumé, I really have no idea of any skills that you have which could apply to this business." Happily, this interviewee was face-to-face with the woman for whom she wanted to work, and she had a chance to explain her experience in detail. But she would never have gotten the interview if her résumé had gone directly to her future boss.

Revising and Updating

Does your résumé work? Does it get you interviews? If your rate of success is low, do a major overhaul on it. Otherwise, keep it up-to-date, both in information and in style. If you have a good résumé ready, you'll be much more inclined to answer an ad, or to respond quickly to an executive-search consultant's request. While you're on the job, improve your résumé every time you see something that could be phrased better, or discover an important idea that should be included. A résumé is never in final form for an active, upwardly mobile person.

AT THE INTERVIEW

During job interviews, there are two primary assets that will get you the position: the relevant *experience* you have had; and your *potential,* based on your education and your personal history. On the other hand, there are two handicaps that will prevent you from getting the job: lack of experience and specific negative factors. Therefore, you want to do all you can to stress the experience you have that relates to the job and, at the same time, avoid calling attention to negative factors.

Almost everyone has negative factors. The trick is to discover what the company considers a negative and then keep the discussion of these factors to a minimum or try not to discuss them at all. Is the company youth-oriented? Then don't keep referring to the good old days—especially if you spent a fair amount of time there. Stress what you have been doing recently, what you have been learning, and what you plan to do professionally in the future. Is the company uncomfortable about hiring woman executives? Downplay overtly feminine dress and keep any discussion about home and family to the barest possible minimum. Were you planning to take courses in market research but haven't gotten to them yet? If the job requires this know-how, don't say you have the background if you haven't—but don't raise the issue if it doesn't come up. If you get the job, take the courses very quickly. Take every opportunity to accentuate the positives and minimize the negatives.

Here are some interview guidelines that will help you to do this:

1. Prepare thoroughly for the interview.

Read all the background information you can find on the company. You won't become an instant expert on the company, but it will prevent you from asking uninformed questions. Ask people about the company and get impressions and opinions. If issues come to mind that you want clarified, write them out in a notebook. It's much easier to refer to this list than to try to recall them during the pressure of an interview.

One woman did her research in great depth because she wanted to work for the company with which she was going to interview. She was able to discuss many of the positive factors that she had unearthed about its consulting reputation and performance. The company was impressed both by the extent of her research and the breadth of her contacts. She got the job.

2. Analyze the needs of the job for which you are interviewing, based on the information you can get ahead of time.

3. Prepare an oral presentation of yourself and your experience that emphasizes the positive aspects of your background in relation to the needs of the job.

4. Arrive early for the interview.

Many interviewers prefer to review your qualifications from their standard corporate form. They are more comfortable interviewing this way than having to seek information on résumés with various layouts. An early arrival enables you not only to catch your breath and gather your thoughts, but also to fill out company forms, if required.

5. Be confident about your appearance.

Wear a well-tested outfit in which you feel comfortable. Dress in something that you know looks good on you. Ascertain that your style of dress is suitable to the company for which you are interviewing. If you have any doubt about the appropriateness of your outfit, test your interview clothes with people who know what's acceptable. Different industries or fields of employment react positively to different styles of dressing. What you are after is a good first impression; it's a lasting impression.

Keeping a variety of dress in mind, the woman we discussed earlier chose two different outfits to interview for the job as director of human resources. She wore a tailored denim suit with a designer label when she went to interview with an advertising agency. She was well aware of how sensitive ad agencies are to the image of their employees. She also knew that the designer was one of the agency clients. When she went for the bank interview, she wore a tailored suit in an unobtrusive color so that she would come across simply as a well-groomed person.

6. Now, forget completely about what you are wearing and concentrate at the start of the interview on your physical demeanor.

Do you appear relaxed? What are you saying with your body language? Folded arms indicate you are closed to information from the interviewer. Nervous gestures reveal a lack of poise and are distracting. Try to maintain an open position toward the interviewer. Look directly at the person to whom you are talking. If you haven't read *Body Language* by Julius Fast and *How to Read a Person Like a Book* by Gerard Nierenberg, read both paperback books before your next interview. Review the tips on public speaking in this book in Chapter 17. Many of the techniques for discharging nervous energy when in front of an audience will work for you in an interview, such as unobtrusively pressing your feet into the floor or pulling up under the arm of the chair. A few deep breaths will help steady a quavering voice.

7. It's important to appear relaxed, but you also want to seem alert.

Learn how to give this impression; better still, learn how to be both alert and relaxed in an interview. Don't hesitate to take notes. This will enable you to concentrate on what is being said and on your reply. After the interview, these notes will help you remember to send something the interviewer asked for. You won't find yourself repeating your questions at a subsequent interview because you'll have a record of the reply. Even very experienced people find interviews a stressful situation, but they have learned to use the stress as an energizer and to keep any signs of nerves well under control.

8. Let the interviewer open the interview.

There are three common types of interview openings: (1) some pleasant small talk, (2) a direct question, and (3) a fairly lengthy pause that becomes slightly uncomfortable. With the social opening, interviewers attempt to put you at ease, using the opportunity to size up your poise and appearance. Reply pleasantly and wait for them to get down to business. If they don't, you can turn the conversation to the job at hand by asking something about the nature of the position. If you are given a direct question, answer it and wait for another. If none is forthcoming, it's better to pick up the ball yourself and show some initiative. A comfortable way to proceed is to ask the interviewer how he would like to learn more about you—whether he would like a brief history starting from your college days or, rather, information about the experience you have gained on your present job. Not all interviewers are skilled in their jobs, and the interview goes better when you can make it easy for them and make *them* comfortable.

When there is a long silence, often a special technique is being used: a nondirective technique. Pick up the ball again with a question about the job, or about how they would like you to begin discussing your background.

There is another interview technique that is not used too often, but is quite disconcerting when it happens. This is the hostile interview. Some companies think it's a good way to get an impression of your reactions under pressure. Watch out for this, relax, and stay in control. Then ask yourself if you want to work for a company that plays these psychological games.

One woman was called in for a weekend of heavy interviewing and felt it all went very well, but by Sunday night she was very tired. She was rather surprised to find someone from the company

on the plane with her when she traveled home. This man sat next
to her and encouraged her to have a few drinks. Then he put on
the pressure, and she revealed far more about her negative side
than she had intended. She mentioned her ex-husband with a degree of bitterness that she didn't usually allow herself to show in a
professional situation. She was off guard because of her fatigue
and the drinks. She didn't realize until the next day that this was
the last stage of the interview and was apparently part of the normal procedure for this company. She didn't get the job.

9. Listen.

The interviewer will do some talking about the company and
the job. Listen and encourage him or her to provide this information. You don't learn anything while you're talking. Ask direct
questions to elicit this information. The more information you can
get, the less likely you are to make a blunder.

A recruiter for a large company telephoned a woman to say
that she had been highly recommended for a position they had
open. His next question was whether she preferred a staff or a line
position. Knowing the firm, she assumed that the job would be a
staff one, and that is what she replied. As it happened, the opening
was a line job, and she knew she had excluded herself from strong
consideration. She would have been perfectly happy to take a line
job, but found it hard to recover from her initial blunder.

If you are asked the sort of question to which you don't know
the right answer, try to hedge until you know more about the job.
This woman could have answered the question by saying that she
had both line and staff experience and was open to either. That's
what she'll do the next time.

10. Sell yourself as the person to fill the job.

Point out those qualifications you have that the company needs.

11. After you have done this and have found out all you can about the nature of the job and the company, you can go on to some of the other details you need to know to make an informed decision.

Often this opportunity does not arise until a second interview.
What you are after in the first interview is to have the company realize that you are the person to fill the job.

12. Try to get a firm idea of what the next step will be before the interview ends.

For example, ask when you can expect to hear from them or when they would like to have you come in to talk to some other people. It is especially important for you to try to get this information if you are interviewing for several possible jobs at the same time.

13. If you are sure that the job is not for you because of a factor such as location, salary, or chance for advancement, it is often best to say so directly during the interview.

Your frankness will save the interviewer's time, and he or she will appreciate it. Tell them why you don't feel there is a good fit between you and the job and what it is you are looking for. Interviewers, in turn, usually do this if they feel you are either overqualified or underqualified for the position.

14. Write a note to the interviewer after the interview.

This is a courteous as well as useful step. In this letter, you can thank him or her for his or her time and the information provided. The letter also gives you an opportunity to reiterate briefly any points you made that you would like to emphasize or to add any information that you may have omitted. Use the letter to confirm or suggest follow-up plans. Write this letter even if you have decided not to take the job, or if you mutually agreed during the interview that the position was not right for you. You might want another job in that company, or someone might ask that interviewer to recommend a candidate for a job that you do want. Your letter will serve as a reminder.

What Questions to Expect

Questions in job interviews tend to fall into certain categories. You should consider these categories in depth and think about your answers ahead of time. The areas in which you will be questioned are:

1. Your experience and qualifications for the job.
Why are you suited to do the job? Why should you be hired?

2. *Your availability.*

Why are you willing to leave the job you now have or why are you unemployed? Be prepared for this question regarding all previous jobs you have held. Avoid showing dissatisfaction with former employers and put the emphasis on your desire for growth opportunities as the reason for leaving former positions.

3. *Your career plans.*

Prospective employers want to know where you are heading and how you plan to get there.

4. *Your life situation.*

You'll be asked or expected to volunteer a certain amount of personal information. Employers are looking for evidence of stability and a well-balanced life-style. They are also interested in your ability and willingness to relocate.

5. *Your motivations.*

You'll be asked what is important to you in a job. Often you are asked this about former jobs. Your description about what motivates you gives an interviewer some good insights about how well you and the job are suited to each other.

6. *Your weaknesses—or what interests you least in your work.*

This question can be a difficult one. You should be prepared with at least one modest failing. No one's perfect. Sometimes you can choose a weakness that is a strength in disguise. For example, you might answer that you don't like to do a lot of detail work yourself and that you usually delegate it. (That's what a manager is supposed to do.) You can also hedge and ask for time to think about it because you concentrate on your strengths and use other people to complement them.

7. *Salary.*

Try to turn this question back to the interviewer by asking what the salary range is for the job you are discussing. Salary varies from industry to industry and from area to area. Salary is such a complex issue, and women have been underpaid for so long that we've devoted a whole chapter to salary in this book and another one to perquisites, which are really just another form of salary.

Try to avoid a discussion of salary, perquisites, and benefits until you know you are the candidate chosen for the job. If you can't avoid it and have been able to obtain information about the salary range, concentrate your continuing discussing on a figure toward the top of the range. If you have no idea of the range, try suggesting that you need more information about the job before you can name a figure.

Sometimes you have to come up with a figure. If you do, try to keep it general, such as "in the low thirties," or, "a minimum of forty, plus the perks I now have, such as a company car." In order not to commit interview-suicide at this point, you must have done your homework and be well informed as to what is reasonable. It's just as damaging to set your sights too low as to have them unreasonably high.

How to Fail the Interview

Herbert Mines, president of the executive-search firm Business Careers, cites seven major reasons why candidates do not get the high-level jobs for which they interview:

1. Inability to "project a special competence" in interviews, to point out why they are the best person for the position.
2. Frequent job moves without marked advancement in salary or responsibility.
3. Failure to "project objectivity," or appearing to be emotional or subjective.
4. Aggressiveness or verbosity.
5. Lack of clarity in expressing views.
6. Overcriticism of previous employers.
7. Poor dress or grooming.

Janet Jones, chairman of Management Woman, mentions three more reasons for not getting the job:

1. Failure to listen, understand the problems, and project the ability to do the job.
2. Unclear reasons for seeking the new position.
3. Lack of knowledge about the company, its product lines, and its current financial picture.

Prepare properly and succeed by being considered as a serious candidate for the position.

Stumbling Blocks for Women

Herbert Mines also has some very specific suggestions to help women who are on the move. "The central issue of an interview for a job is that you be able to show a prospective employer why your qualifications fit the needs of the position that is open, and that you are a mature and thoughtful individual. Women are not as good at this as men are for a variety of reasons. They are not as used to top-level interviews as are men. This is purely a matter of experience and seasoning, so women should get all the interviewing experience possible. At issue in being successful in an interview is not whether you carry a briefcase or a pocketbook or both, or whether your skirt is short or long. Women in business are distracted by these fads and gimmicks. My feeling is that a woman must be sophisticated enough to dress in a businesslike fashion and then forget it. You can't phony up this part of the presentation, nor should you. And, although your appearance may lose the job for you, it is not what gets you the job. Your experience, your overall impression, and your ability to sell yourself in a low-key but convincing manner are what count.

"Women must develop the sense of self-confidence that comes from a combination of the right experience and proven competence. Then they must top this off with being able to communicate their backgrounds in the context of the companies with which they are interviewing. More men than women come prepared for the interview. They've done their homework. They have read the annual reports and therefore know about the company. Women must become more thorough in this regard.

"Some women seem to feel that they are owed a job simply because they've decided to commit to a full-time, vigorous career effort. It doesn't work that way. More men still have the right track record and have indicated high levels of flexibility. Women also seem to raise different kinds of objections that have more to do with environment than with the job content and its value in their total career progress. I've had women tell me they didn't want the job because the person to whom they would report didn't speak English correctly. More women than men turn down jobs because of personality considerations, too.

"Perhaps even more importantly, I've found many women who were truly ambivalent about the job they were theoretically seeking. They *seemed* to be pursuing a particular job opening but, in fact, if they did indeed get the job, they would be really shocked. They were not personally committed to the sacrifices that accepting the job would entail, and this was apparent during the interview.

"Another stumbling block for women in high-level interviews is their self-righteous posture when difficult or illegal questions are posed. If a woman has family responsibilities, that area will be a focus of concern until the question comes out in the open. It's far better for the interviewee to plan ahead with a very professional answer and, perhaps, even to give the answer before the question is raised. Be prepared to deal with the home question. It's always there and it will usually come up in one way or another. Frankly, it makes me uncomfortable if a woman's attitude is, 'You wouldn't ask this question of a man, would you?' The fact of the matter is that in our society it is still the woman who is expected to discharge most of the home responsibilities and who has primary charge of the children, rightly or wrongly. I'm just as concerned about this issue when I'm talking with a man who is divorced or a widower with children. I make sure to find out what arrangement he has for his home situation. Expect to provide information in this area and be relaxed about it."

Anne Hyde concurs with the fact that you must explain how you handle your home, and she suggests that you can mention that you "handle your commitments at home as efficiently and effectively as your business responsibilities."

23

ASSESSING THE SITUATION

You've sold your ability to do the job, and the company is interested in hiring you. Now it's your turn to find out about the details that can spell success or failure for you in a new undertaking.

There are many questions to which you need the answers. You will already have gleaned a great deal of information from your research prior to interviewing, and as a result of the interviews themselves. Now, go to as many other sources as you can to gain additional background. Then weigh the advantages and disadvantages of each position with respect to any other opportunities you may have and the position that you are now in. In this chapter we'll give you ideas about the kinds of things you should know about a prospective job, and we'll suggest a method of evaluating the information.

Keep in mind that the answers you get from the company are often one-sided. Try to talk to people working for the company, particularly someone at the level for which you are being considered. Ask them about their jobs, the company, and their problems. If you can, talk to several people. It's reasonable to ask to do this. Talk to people outside the company who deal with it on a regular basis, such as suppliers, customers, editors of trade publications, and advertising agencies. Ask them about the company.

What you can't find out from employees and from outside sources you'll have to ask directly of the company. Ask it before you accept the job. Issues that are not satisfactory can often be negotiated at this point to suit your needs better.

One woman who was taking a job in another state had to commute temporarily until she was able to make a permanent move. The corporate policy was to pay for her commutation and lodging in a motel for one month. She needed more than one month to organize her move. There were four months left in the school year, and she felt the move would be far easier on her children if they could stay where they were during this period. The company wanted her to start work immediately, as is often the case once the hiring decision is made. She asked for five months' commuting time at the company's expense, and management agreed. But she wouldn't have gotten it if she hadn't asked. More often than not, this kind of policy is a starting point for negotiations with new employees who are expected to express their own reasonable needs. But adjustments will rarely be volunteered; you've got to ask.

NOTING THE NEGATIVES

Before you start evaluating the merits of any particular job, one of the most useful exercises you can do is to make a list of all your negatives with regard to any job. This will help you make a decision that is more objective and less emotional.

You will want to distinguish between absolute negatives and factors that you do not like but would be willing to put up with under certain circumstances. Reviewing your negatives also helps you identify important positive features that you want in a job.

Katherine listed as an absolute negative the greater Los Angeles area and New York City. She is among the estimated 20 per cent of the population who are seriously affected by smog and pollution, so she does not want to move to these areas where she frequently does not feel well and rarely can operate at peak efficiency. To compensate for this, she researched the country thoroughly and selected certain places that are still relatively pollution-free. She is making an aggressive attempt to find appropriate employment in one of these locations, where the environment will be a positive feature.

Here is a list of some questions that may help you to identify negative factors with regard to your own situation:

The Field:

- Are there industries in which you choose not to work?
- What size company does not seem to suit you?
- What stages of a company's development may be wrong for your career? (See Chapter 8)

The Location:

- Are you unwilling or unable to relocate?
- If you can consider relocation, what locations are unacceptable or less preferable?

The Job Content:

- Do you dislike working exclusively with numbers and things or working with people?
- Do you find a fast-paced job with a lot of pressure stressful?
- Are jobs with very long-term results and feedback uncomfortable for you?
- Do you dislike a lot of structure?
- Would you prefer to avoid jobs requiring a lot of selling? A lot of customer contact? Heavy writing? Detail work?
- Are you unwilling or unable to devote many more hours to the job than the normal forty?

The People:

- What kind of people do you not like to work for? To have as peers? To have working for you?
- Do you dislike strong competition? Or does the lack of competition cause you to lose motivation?

Opportunities for Advancement:

- Are you willing to break new ground never tread by women?

· Are you uneasy about taking on a lot of responsibility?
· Are you unwilling to move up or laterally if relocation is required?

The Financial Considerations:

· Is there a salary level below which you will not consider a job?
· Are there certain perquisites you must have before you will take the job?
· Are you unable or unwilling to accept a position that seems insecure?

The Personal Considerations:

· Can you take a position that will not give you enough chance for self-realization and development?
· Will you take a job that you expect will adversely affect your personal life?

As you go through these questions, you will think of more negatives. Write them down along with all the positive ideas that come to mind. You are trying to determine what you do not want in a job, and what you do want and need in a situation in order to succeed and to enjoy your work.

Some of Katherine's other negatives are that she would rather not work for a small organization where the job may be in jeopardy. She wants both the job security and the greater employee benefits that are usually available in large organizations in stable industries. But she knows she is uncomfortable in the slow-paced environment that is often found in large companies. She'll look carefully for a situation that offers competition, some pressure, and a chance for advancement based on performance.

REVIEWING A POSSIBLE POSITION

The negative questions we've posed have probably raised some unanswered questions in your mind about jobs you may be considering. We're going to give you some more questions to think about with regard to any career move you may be considering.

The Industry and the Company:

- Is the industry growing? Does the company appear to be a growing company within the industry?
- Does the industry or company have any characteristics that may affect you—i.e., is it seasonal? cyclical?
- What stage of growth is the company in? Is it at the beginning, middle, or end of this stage? What are the implications of this for your career?

The Location:

- Is relocation required? Will the move be paid for by the company?
- Is the company located in a place where you'd like to live?
- Are you likely to be moved again? Where? When?
- Where is corporate headquarters located? Would you like to live there?

The Job:

- Do you think you will really like the work?
- Do you feel qualified to do the work?
- If you don't feel fully qualified, do you see some means by which you can become sufficiently knowledgeable?
- What—exactly—will you be doing on the job? What responsibilities will you have? Will you have the authority to go along with the responsibility?
- How many people will be working for you? What do they do?
- How many people work for them? What do they do?
- How will your performance be evaluated? How will you receive this evaluation?
- Does a formal, written job description exist? Can you read it?
- Will you be able to enlarge the scope of the job?

The People:

- What do you think of the person for whom you will be working?

Generally, it is unwise to take a job without at least one interview with your potential boss. Try to find out as much about this person as you can. How long has he or she been in the job? How long with the company? A manager who moves up fairly quickly leaves open spots behind. Is the person considered good at developing and moving subordinates? How fast have subordinates been moved to other positions? What positions?

- Why is the job open? Where is the person who formerly occupied that spot?
- How many hours a week did this person typically spend on the job? How many hours a week do people in similar jobs generally work?
- What kind of people will you be working with? What kind will be working for you?

Opportunities for Advancement:

- What jobs are two or three levels above the one you are considering? What is required to move up?
  Get some case histories if you can of people who have moved up, along with an idea of the amount of time it has taken them.

- What opportunities are available for experience in areas other than the one in which you will be working?
- Does the company help its employees with career development plans? Offer on-the-job training programs? Pay for courses or degree education?

The Attitude Toward Professional Women:

- How many women does the company employ at your level?
- How many women at levels above that one?
- Are women mainly located in highly visible positions?
- Are women occupying power positions? Line jobs?
- What cultural stereotypes have you seen evidence of while visiting the company and interviewing there?
- What do you think of the chances of a woman's making it up the ladder in this company? What do you think of the chances of your doing so?

Financial:

- Is the starting salary satisfactory? What about salary increases?
- How secure is the job?
- What benefits are there? What perquisites? How much are they worth? (A benefit is something available to every employee of the company. A perquisite is a special advantage available only to certain executives. See Chapter 25.)
- What is the top salary you can earn with this company?
- If relocation is necessary, will it be paid by the company?

Personal:

- How does this job appear to fit with your other life needs and choices?
- Do you think taking this job is the right move for you?

These questions are merely starting points for you and will trigger many more questions that you will want to ask and find the answers to. Write them down as they occur and get the answers.

ASSESSING THE FIT

Once you've collected the information you feel you need to make a reasonably objective, informed decision, you may find it is difficult to assess one job against another, or against the job you currently hold, because certain considerations are much more important to you than others.

One useful method to compare unequal factors is a weighted assessment. To prepare a weighted assessment, first write out the factors that are important to you. Then assign a numerical weight to each factor, using a scale of 1 to 10. Assign a number that reflects the relative importance of each factor in your career and life planning. Low numbers indicate a relatively unimportant consideration and high numbers indicate important factors.

Here are some of the factors for you to assign a relative weight
to:

_____ Industry
_____ Company
_____ Location
_____ Job content
_____ Amount of responsibility
_____ Method of performance evaluation
_____ Chance to enlarge scope of the job
_____ Opportunity for visibility in company
_____ Opportunity for visibility outside the company
_____ Opportunity for advancement
_____ Opportunity for development
_____ Who the boss is
_____ Who my peers are
_____ Who my subordinates are
_____ Starting salary
_____ Salary potential
_____ Benefits (Specify any you need, such as a vested retire-
           ment plan, major medical, etc.)
_____ Perquisites (Again, specify any which you need, such
           as a car, paid education, etc.)
_____ Suitability to career plan
_____ Desire to take the job
_____ Opportunity to use full range of talents

You will probably think of more considerations to add to this
list. Once you have weighted each factor, then give each company
a rating for that factor, and then multiply the numerical weighting
by the rating to get a total. For example, if you feel salary is of
vital importance to you, you may give it a weighting of 9. If one
company meets the salary you want, you would then give that
company a 10 when you rate it for salary, which will give a total
of 90 (9 × 10) to this company for salary. If another company
you are considering is offering $2,000 less than the salary you
want, you might only rate that company 5 in the area of salary,
for a total of 45 points (9 × 5). Once you have calculated the
amount for each consideration by multiplying the weighting times

the ranking, add up the figures and see which company gets a higher score.

Let's look at an assessment chart filled out for Dolores, who is about to make a major career move. This is a vital mid-career step for her. She has heavy home responsibilities: she supports two children. She feels that she could relocate right now, since her children are about to enter new schools. She wants to be particularly careful of a misalliance because she doesn't want to move her children and then have to move again because she chose badly. In her assessment, she is comparing two very different job opportunities. One is a marketing job with a very large electronic corporation seeking to broaden its staff in her specialty and also looking to hire more women to meet affirmative-action guidelines. The other job is with a fairly small firm that does consulting in her field and appears to be growing quite rapidly.

Dolores doesn't have any strong feelings about the industry in which she works nor the company for which she works, so she weights these factors at a medium level of 5 each. Since her field is marketing, she is comfortable with a variety of services or products. She rates the large company high for both these factors, as it is well established and well thought of in a stable industry. Moving into the consulting business may ultimately spoil the upward momentum of her career. The company she is talking to is well regarded in the industry, though it is not one of the major names in the business, hence her rating of 7. Her calculations would look like this:

The Field:

Factor	Weight	LG ELECTRONIC CO X Rating = Total	SM CONSULT CO X Rating = Total
The Industry	5	X 8 = 40	X 6 = 30
The Company	5	X 9 = 45	X 7 = 35

It's vital for Dolores to work at a job she really likes, and it really affects the rest of her life negatively when she doesn't. This is why she gives this item a very heavy weighting. She doesn't care a lot about being able to enlarge the job—she plans to get a promotion and has ideas of the next step up in each case. She's had enough experience to be able to adjust to either a fast-paced or slower-paced environment, but she knows that she does her best work in a reasonably fast-paced environment. Her assessment of these factors looks like this:

The Job:

Factor	Weight	LG ELECTRONIC CO			SM CONSULT CO		
		X	Rating	= Total	X	Rating	= Total
Job Content	10	X 6		= 60	X 8		= 80
Opportunity to Enlarge	4	X 2		= 8	X 9		= 18
Pace	6	X 5		= 30	X 8		= 48

Dolores is pretty independent and has a lot of friends outside work, so it's not vital to her to have a support group or a social life at work. But she enjoys working with challenging people, so she gives this a middle rating. She finds the people that she'd be working with in the large company about average, and above average in the smaller firm, hence her ratings of 5 and 7. From experience, she knows that the person she works for has enormous control over her success or failure in the organization, so she gives the factor of her reaction to the boss a high rating of 8. Her impression of the man she would work for in the large company was not too good, but her boss in the consulting company is the outstanding person in the company. He has a lot of power and is committed to the growth of the organization. She felt this would give her a chance to move up quite rapidly. She evaluated these factors as follows:

The People:

Factor	Weight	LG ELECTRONIC CO		SM CONSULT CO	
		X Rating = Total		X Rating = Total	
Peers	5	X 5 = 25		X 7 = 35	
Boss	8	X 4 = 32		X 8 = 64	

Dolores went through each of the factors in this manner. Her totals thus far are as follows:

FACTOR	LG ELECTRONIC CO	SM CONSULT CO
The Industry	40	30
The Company	45	35
Job Content	60	80
Opportunity to Enlarge Job	8	18
Pace	30	48
Peers	25	35
Boss	32	64
TOTAL	240	310

By the time she is finished, the weighting will probably move still further apart, thereby causing her to consider one more favorably than the other.

Weighted assessments can be a useful tool in helping you make many complex decisions where a variety of identifiable factors are involved. It's a way to give a quantitative assessment to qualitative factors. Naturally, you won't make your decision solely based on the totals, but it's helpful to have this type of indication. Frequently, the results of weighted assessments turn out very differently from what you expect. They can help you avoid a career misstep.

THE BOTTOM LINE

If you are looking for a move up, keep in mind that a genuine promotion gives you:

- more authority
- more responsibility
- more pay

Be sure to give heavy consideration to these factors. In the next two chapters we'll look in much greater detail at pay and perquisites—which are another form of remuneration for which you become increasingly eligible, as you move higher in the corporate structure.

24

MONEY: OR THINGS YOUR FATHER NEVER TAUGHT YOU

Women have been trained to see their worth in terms of other people—whom they're married to, whose daughter they are—and they have been discouraged from understanding and exploring the subject of money. Quite possibly your father did not expect you to be actively striving for a position that could ultimately be senior to anything that he achieved, or even to which he aspired. It is also likely that your mother did not work outside your home; or, if she did, she probably did not work at a thoroughly planned career.

Men, on the other hand, have been raised to realize that they will spend most of their lives working at a career and that much of their worth in the community is measured in terms of salary and related income. For this reason, men are likely to have spent more time investigating and becoming knowledgeable in the area of financial compensation. Women must now become equally knowledgeable, or even more so.

It is part of our culture not to discuss money matters, and information concerning job compensation is not readily available. Professional people are usually loath to discuss salaries, and they are even more taciturn about the perks that go along with high-level positions. One leader of executive seminars states that executives are more willing to discuss their sex lives than their salary ranges and other benefits. And, lest you think that men know all the answers, a study reported in *Working Woman* in 1979 showed that fewer than 10 per cent of the managers surveyed could accurately guess the salaries of the people just above or below them, or on the same rung of the corporate ladder.

In this chapter we'll take a look at how salaries are determined and how you can secure the salary you are worth—either where you are now employed or in a new company. We'll also consider two other related sources of compensation: bonuses and commissions. Then, in the following chapter, we'll examine benefits and perquisites.

For most people, a salary represents not only their largest single and regular source of income, but also a gauge of their value to the organization for which they work. Salary is important in itself, and also as an indicator of a person's status in the power structure of the company. Specific amounts can help you define your rank not only to the company but to the world at large. In June 1978, *Business Week* stated that people with jobs in the $30,000 to $50,000 range were clearly in middle management, and it is not until the salary for a position exceeds $50,000 that the paycheck reflects top management status, and starts to reward the responsibility and accountability that goes with it. The *Wall Street Journal* also used the figure of $30,000 as the one to define the lower limits of middle management.

It's encouraging to know that more and more middle-management positions are becoming available for women. However, there still aren't many women in the middle ranks, and women in senior positions are very few and far between, despite the publicity and visibility given to some women who have made it.

In 1978 *Business Week* made a survey of forty-three corporations; only seven companies identified women in what they termed "top management" positions. Many of these women had titles such as advertising director or research manager and salaries from $20,000 to $50,000; yet both title and salary indicate middle-management status. In *Forbes*'s annual survey of the highest-paid executives in America, there were no women on the list in 1978 and only one in 1979.

And at the lower end of the scale, the salary figures are still bleak for women. The government information released for 1977 showed that the median income for women college graduates was only 60 per cent that of men with the same education ($10,861 vs. $17,861). Furthermore, only 8 per cent of female full-time wage earners earned salaries of more than $12,000 per year, compared to 42 per cent of the men in the labor force.

As a group, women have been underpaid for decades, and it's difficult to catch up. To get paid what you are worth and to set about helping to remove sex distinctions in salaries requires an understanding of why salaries are what they are, and how they are arrived at. Once you begin to have a feeling for this, you can evaluate how you are being paid, both in your company and in your industry. In this chapter, we'll give you some background on how compensation is calculated.

COMPENSATION PROGRAMS

In the past, a title was often given to a woman employee as a panacea. Sometimes this title came with some additional power, but most often not—because power is usually rewarded with money. With equal opportunity legislation it has become more difficult for companies to give a title instead of a raise, particularly as women are becoming more knowledgeable about pay.

Titles are important. But what counts the most is what your company thinks your job is worth and what the company thinks *you* are worth. Not all companies are large enough or organized enough to have formal salary programs. Usually a company doesn't begin to establish formal guidelines until it has about one hundred or so employees. Even when you are working for a company that does not have an explicit compensation program, an understanding of how such programs work will help you position yourself more accurately with regard to salary. It will help you understand: (1) how a company decides what a job is worth, (2) why people in the same job get different salaries, and (3) how salary increases are decided upon.

Salary Grades and Ranges

"When a woman is promoted into a job previously held by a man, the job is often redefined and classified into a lower pay range," explains Elaine Wegener, President of PACT, a Los Angeles-based consulting firm specializing in compensation and human resource management. "In order to prevent this from happening, a woman must understand the salary system in her company and how it applies to her job."

The monetary worth of a job is based on an evaluation of the requirements of the position relative to the requirements of other positions in that company. Each job is closely examined with regard to its complexity and the knowledge required to perform the job well. The position is looked at in terms of the authority it carries and the number of people who are supervised, as well as the required decision-making responsibility. Each job is studied from a negative point of view as well—what would be the effect or cost of a mistake made in this position? All this information is put together, sometimes formally, by assigning points to the various requirements and arriving at a total point value for each job. Whether formally or informally evaluated, jobs are classified into salary grades based on their relative worth to the company.

Jobs may have different duties, but have similar value to the company. For example, an engineer and an accountant may be classified in the same grade. Each grade is assigned a dollar value, often on the basis of what other companies are paying for similar jobs in that business community. This dollar value becomes the midpoint in the salary range for all jobs in that grade. Generally speaking, line jobs—those that directly contribute to and affect profitability—have higher grades and pay higher salaries than staff or advisory positions.

Once the salary valuation is placed on a job grade, a salary range for that grade is developed. The minimum of the range represents the salary a company will pay to someone who is starting the job and needs to be trained. When these employees are fully trained and productive, they will be paid the midpoint of the range —what the company believes the job is worth. An employee goes from midpoint to the maximum of the range usually for outstanding performance. The maximum of the range is also used to reward long-service employees in situations where a promotion to a higher salary level is unlikely.

To cite one concrete example of a salary range, in 1978 *Business Week* quoted a salary range for a Grade 8 job at Lockheed as

$19,864 to $33,384. The midpoint—the value of the job—would therefore be $26,624. The percentage spread from top to bottom of a range for middle- and senior-management positions is typically from 65 per cent to 130 per cent, with the senior jobs usually embracing the larger spreads. The Lockheed range quoted illustrates a 68 per cent spread. That is calculated by the fact that the maximum of the range is 168 per cent of the mimimum, or a spread of 68 per cent.

The midpoint of a salary grade is often about 10 to 12 per cent higher than the next lower grade midpoint. We might expect, for example, that Lockheed's Grade 7 would have a midpoint or value of about $23,962, if Lockheed separates its grades by about 10 per cent. For this reason, the top of one range usually overlaps the bottom of the next highest range.

"A sophistication in the area of salaries was very useful to me when I took my last job," reported a woman middle manager. "Once I decided that I really wanted one of the positions open in a major company, I asked everyone I knew who worked there what they knew about salary grades and ranges. I found out that I probably could go in at midpoint of a certain grade or rather low in the grade above it. Since I didn't have to take the job, I decided that it was to be the higher grade level or nothing. This had a couple of advantages for me. First of all, I didn't have to compete with a lot of people for a promotion to that next higher level. And since I came at the lower end of my range, I'll get some raises sooner than I might have otherwise. My starting salary would have been the same in either event, but I'm much further ahead because of the research I did before taking this job."

Elaine Wegener says, "Many women have had the experience of being promoted to their male boss's job, as a result of his leaving the company or being promoted himself. Often the woman is earning so little that even a 20 per cent promotion increase will not bring her salary to the minimum of the range for the new job. When that happens, some companies will downgrade the job, lowering the grade level and salary range to fit the woman's salary. Typically, the job description is rewritten to justify reclassifying the position. But if a woman understands the compensation system and how grades and salary ranges are determined, based on job value, she is in a better position to prevent this from happening to her," she adds.

"Most people are somewhat aware of the grades of various jobs and can find out if they don't know them, but the specific ranges for management jobs are rarely made public. However, when an employee is being considered for a new position, she is entitled to know the previous incumbent's salary range, as well as the present range if different. If the range has been changed, she is entitled to know why—in specific terms. To get this information, you have to ask for it. After all, you wouldn't buy a car without asking the price, so why should you accept a job without knowing the salary opportunity that is represented by the job's salary range."

If the direct approach does not work, make a few friends in the personnel department. One successful woman who works in a very large corporate environment even recommends serving time in the personnel department, for perhaps a year or so, on your way up. She says, "You will then really understand the salary grading system and how it works. Even though companies try to be objective, all these areas are subjectively influenced. It is good to know how decisions are made in order to make sure you and the people who work for you come out on top."

If all else fails, there is always the technique of the "roving eye." "I always make sure to learn what people around me are making," admits one upward-striving woman. "Most people are careless with their salary checks or other information that is relevant to what I want to know. The big picture is not hard to put together once you have enough of the pieces. If I didn't have this background, I wouldn't know what salary was realistic for me to aim for."

Raises, Not Roses

Even when you have found out the information you seek with regard to salary ranges, you will still want to keep abreast of what is going on in your company, your community, and in your industry nationwide. While increases depend upon the company profits and industry practice, and to a certain extent each company is a different case, there are still some helpful general indicators with regard to raises.

According to Ms. Wegener, "On a nationwide average, job values are currently rising about 8 per cent per year. Thus, if a company keeps its ranges current, it will increase the minimum, midpoint, and maximum of its ranges by about 8 per cent for the year. If an employee has performed satisfactorily during the year, she should get a corresponding percentage increase, or 8 per cent. If the performance is below average, it should be less. If an employee is doing an outstanding job, she should look for raises in the nature of 10 per cent to 12 per cent or more, to reflect the fact that she is contributing more than is expected from her, on average."

These indicators were confirmed in an article that appeared in *Business Week* in September 1978 in which it reported that a consulting-firm survey showing an average white-collar increase of 8.16 per cent for 1978 and 8.35 per cent for 1979. *Business Week*'s own survey reported in the article showed an even higher average increase, of more than 10 per cent. Although in 1978, President Carter set wage guidelines that limit raises in pay and fringe benefits to 7 per cent, this figure need only be an *average* for a particular management group. In this way, some people in the group can still get a 10 per cent or 15 per cent increase and others, 5 per cent or nothing at all—and the 7 per cent guidelines can still be met.

Men have frequently sought salary increases aggressively while women have *waited* to be recognized. It is not easy to encourage your employer to part with substantial salary increases, even when they are fully justified. Being forearmed with accurate facts is one giant step toward getting your share of the raises in your company.

Where to Look for Information

"Keep up with your industry as a whole by studying the surveys," suggests Elaine Wegener. "These surveys can be difficult to interpret, but you can learn the skill. One way to do it is to take a course in salary administration, frequently offered at local colleges. An understanding of this area is of value to all managers who have performance responsibility."

There are eight major national salary surveys that are used as

guides by senior executives, but most middle managers are unaware that they exist. Most personnel departments of larger companies subscribe to one or more of the national surveys plus some
local ones as well. Business libraries often have some of them.
One of the most useful is the AMS Guide to Management Compensation, which compiles middle-management salaries and is sold
by the Administrative Management Society. This guide gives average salaries for jobs in different types of businesses and in
different geographic areas. The address is: Maryland Road, Wil-
low Grove, PA 19090, and in 1980 the cost of the guide, called
AMS Management Compensation, is $75.

The American Management Associations publishes not only a
guide to middle-management salaries, called *Middle Management,*
but also specialized guides for sales personnel, called *Sales Personnel Report,* and for specialists, called the *Professional and
Scientific Report.* These and other specialized salary guides published by the AMA ranged in price in 1980 from $70 to $405,
depending upon whether the company placing the order participated in the survey. The AMA sells these guides to individuals
for the higher, nonparticipant rates. To keep your expenses down,
split the cost with some friends or order the guide on the corporate
stationery of a participating company if you can—or visit personnel departments and your local library to do your research.

Take your personnel friends to lunch—it could be a good investment. Remember: you're not asking for confidential information,
just published data on other companies and the industry as a
whole. When you do get to look at these surveys, keep in mind
that the information is always a little out-of-date—it took time to
do the survey, and to compile, print, and distribute it. But it will
still show you trends. What has been happening in your industry
over the past few years? What is happening in related industries?
How does your company compare to the industry as a whole? Be
sure you know the answers to these questions.

Another way to keep informed about your company is to obtain
a copy of the proxy statement, which is published annually by all
publicly held companies. The proxy reports compensation for top
officers, including perquisites, and is available to the public. If you
want to remain anonymous, have a friend call your company and
request a copy of the annual report *and* the proxy statement.

These are usually available through the corporate secretary's office.

Watch the Trends

The salaries of the chief executive officer and other senior executives are generally estimated on the same *basis* as middle-rank executives. But pay opportunity is significantly higher, reflecting top management's greater responsibility and the impact their actions have on profit results. Senior management is often defined as the top jobs in a company—chairman of the board and president plus one or two levels below, depending upon the size and the structure of the company.

Watch what annual increase these people are getting, both in base salaries and bonuses. If business is bad or profits are down, and their compensation is not being increased, it would be unrealistic to expect a major increase yourself. However, even in a bad year when top management receives no increase, companies will often provide some salary increase in the budget for lower-level employees, in order to maintain competitive salaries. The higher your job, the more likely your salary will be affected by company profits, good or bad. But, as often happens, if the profit picture is less than rosy and the salaries of senior management are going up substantially anyway, there is no reason for you to have to accept "business is bad" as a rationale for skipping or lowering your increase.

Look at the Location

"The area where your company is located is an important factor in salaries and raises," advises Elaine Wegener. "High-cost-of-living areas tend, quite naturally, to have higher salaries. But area-pay differences disappear as you climb the executive ladder. What vice-presidents or senior vice-presidents earn is more likely to relate directly to the job and the industry in which they work than to the location of the company."

Anomalies exist, too, in pay scale versus cost of living. Boston is considered one of the most expensive cities in the continental

United States. However, salaries are low because so many people want to live in Boston and jobs are scarce.

It's wise to research the cost of living and industry salaries for the areas in which you are interested before embarking on a job search. To give you an idea of salaries for a job by area, this is what the AMS Guide to Management Compensation showed in their 1978 edition for a bank branch manager:

	U.S. AVERAGE	EAST	EAST CENTRAL	WEST
Annual salary	$18,900	$17,300	$19,800	$21,000

If you want to be a branch manager in banking, it might pay you to "Go West, young woman," with salaries averaging more than 20 per cent higher than the east.

Sexist Attitudes

It is also vitally important to be aware of attitudes about salaries and raises for working women. Be prepared with appropriate counterarguments. One old saw: "You are married and don't need the money. Good old Jim here is supporting several children and is in dire financial straits." This reasoning is fallacious because salaries are paid according to what the job is worth to the company, and on how well that job is being done by the employee.

Companies are not charitable institutions. They exist to make a profit—or to achieve their goals, if they are nonprofit organizations. This success, in turn, enables the organization to continue to exist. Be aware that such reasoning is illegal: by definition, it constitutes sex discrimination.

A variation of this fallacious reasoning is the idea that it is more difficult to get a raise when you are in a higher-level job than when you are at a lower level. For example, you may be told that it is easier to get a $1,200 raise on a $15,000 annual salary than a $3,200 raise on a $40,000 annual salary. (Particularly if you are a woman and don't need the money anyway!) Again, the company is using a convenient escape route to avoid bringing you up to an appropriate salary level. Earlier, Ms. Wegener stated that an 8 per cent annual increase in today's market is what it takes, on average, to keep salaries on a par with their job value. This is a matter of *percentage,* not of *dollars.* Thus the entire company payroll would have to increase by 8 per cent overall to keep up with increased pay levels. The grade level of your job should have no bearing on the percentage increase available. The company's increased budget, as a per cent of *all* salaries—and your performance—should be the only real influences on the size of your increases.

Melissa was asked to return to a company where she formerly had an outstanding record. All items seemed to be in basic agreement between her and the owner until they started discussing her salary. She asked for a salary based on what she was presently earning and what she—and the owner—knew she was worth to the company. His response to her salary request was that the senior men in the organization would never be comfortable with a woman earning as much or more than they did. Melissa's decision was an easy one. Because her salary was going to be based more on the fact she was a woman among men than on her performance, she didn't return to her former company.

SETTING YOUR SIGHTS

Women have often put themselves at a disadvantage with regard to salary increases by setting their sights lower than a man would. A study of Stanford University M.B.A. graduates (reported by Gordon and Strober in the *Sloan Management Review* in 1978) showed that the average maximum salary expectations of the women surveyed was 30 per cent below that of the men—$42,000 vs. $60,000. These women, graduates of one of the top business schools in the country, who had the same education as their male competitors, were not even aiming at an annual salary that is generally considered to be in the *low* range for senior management!

Women must increase their salary expectations and aspirations if they're ever to close the 40 per cent gap that exists between salaries for well-educated men and women—and if they are to succeed in the business world.

Raises are given where you work by proving your performance

and your responsibility, and by producing the quality of work that indicates to the company that you are promotable and someone that they can't afford to lose. Document your value to the company and then seek the raise at an appropriate time. But remember that companies are pyramidal in fashion, and that these pyramids are getting tighter and tighter at the top as our economy's growth rate is slowing down. Not everyone can continue to move up and get increases. Sometimes you have to look elsewhere to get paid what you are worth.

MOVING FOR MONEY

Until relatively recently, the only way to make it to the top as a woman was to build your entire career within the confines of one company. Margaret Hennig, in her doctoral thesis at Harvard, written in the late sixties, studied 25 senior women managers. All were one-company women. These 25 women were virtually the only senior women executives Dr. Hennig could identify just a little over a decade ago. Her study is reported at length in her book, *The Managerial Woman,* written with Anne Jardim.

This single-company orientation has persisted for both men and women holding top positions today. As we've already pointed out, studies continue to show that senior people typically have spent at least twenty years with their company. Nonetheless, the practice of gaining experience in more than one company seems to be becoming more widespread today. Moving to another company to acquire a variety of experiences, or because your present situation lacks upward mobility, or in order to get paid what you are worth, can be beneficial. But, since there is always a great deal of risk involved in changing companies, you should have a good grasp of the payoff you can obtain by changing jobs before you decide whether to take the risk.

In order to avoid being a victim of low expectations, and to be able to negotiate from a position of strength, know what salary improvement you can reasonably expect if you are making the change to improve your income. Sometimes when you change jobs you can improve your salary—for other reasons as well.

According to Elaine Wegener, "Companies often have a fixed idea of what increase they are willing to give in order to get you to come and work for them. They generally aim for a 10 per cent increase over your current salary, with a maximum of 15 per cent. Once again, women are disadvantaged, since their current salaries are often substantially below that of a man with the equivalent experience and education. But companies also aim to hire a person who is fully experienced in the job at about the midpoint of the job's salary range, which can be one way around this pitfall."

Many people have increased their salaries very substantially when making a move from one company to another by being fully aware of their leverage with the potential new employer. For example, there may be an amount of money below which it is not worth it to you to move and you really are not particularly interested in moving. If so, it doesn't hurt to deal on those terms.

Heidi, a bright young woman on the rise, was living in ideal circumstances with regard to her life values. She was approached by a company 3,000 miles away, whose plant was located in a fairly small town. Even though it had more status than her present one, the job was less challenging than her current job and had less national visibility. Yet, on the positive side, it was a chance to broaden herself by living and learning in a totally new environment, and it was the type of field experience she needed in order to make the move to the next higher position. Since she really didn't want to move, she decided upon a minimum salary figure that was 35 per cent higher than her present salary. She felt that at least that much money would be necessary for her to be willing to put up with the job's disadvantages. When Heidi established her position firmly in her own mind, she stated the amount she wanted. The company didn't even hesitate in offering her that salary! There was another leverage factor acting to her advantage, as well. The company had *no* women at her level or above. They needed a woman for an affirmative-action move, and there are very few women with experience in her particular field.

These last two reasons are other leverage points that you can use when appropriate—and they occur with a certain degree of frequency. Companies located in remote or otherwise undesirable areas often will reach further in terms of money than companies located in the more desirable areas. What many people resist may be just what suits you. If you recognize that a company does have a difficult time finding people, you may want to increase your salary requests. You have the best leverage when you have a choice among several desirable openings, or when you are not totally convinced you want the job.

Making a job change entails considering a very complex set of variables, many of which we discussed in the last chapter. Being fully informed of grades and salary ranges helps to reduce some of these variables to concrete and manageable considerations. A recent article on the front page of the *Wall Street Journal* stated that it was often perfectly reasonable to try for a salary increase of 35 per cent, as Heidi did, when making an upward move—if you have the right experience and if you know what you are doing. There are four points you should know about when considering a move:

1. The salary range for your position.

Specifically, you want to know the midpoint of the range—the price put on the value of the job. You will want to know the top of the range because that's all the money you can earn if you stay in that spot. It is also useful to find out the salary *range* for any job you may be considering, so you can see how that compares to the salary you are being offered. Get this information for the grade above that position, so you know what's ahead for you. Most companies will give you this information if you ask directly. Few will volunteer it.

2. Timing of salary reviews.

Ask when and how often are salaries reviewed. You will probably be told that salaries are reviewed on an annual basis. Some companies, however, still use an old-fashioned review system of eighteen or even twenty-four months. There may be no point in changing jobs if, once you change, your next possible raise will not take place for two years—and particularly if the size of the increase is no greater than you would get in one year at your present job. Also, find out if increases are retroactive when salary reviews are delayed. More than one company saves substantial amounts of money by being chronically slow in doing appraisals and then not making the increase retroactive. Remember: it's money out of your pocket.

3. The mechanics of performance appraisals.

Ask about performance appraisals. How are appraisals made? Are they formal or informal? Are they oral or written? Find out how appraisals relate to salary increases.

Some companies have unusual methods of performance appraisal that can work for or against you. One company requires that its employees write out what amounts to an annual contract, listing what they expect to accomplish in the coming year. The appraisal is then based on this double-edged sword: the employee may possibly place herself in the position of setting her sights too high, and then not being able to achieve her own goals, or of setting her sights too low and not being able to justify a raise. Some employees may see this kind of avant-garde management by your own objectives as an advantage. Others will find it difficult, if not impossible, because they don't feel adequately informed about the company's long-range goals and the place of their job in this future planning. It's a good thing to know ahead of time about unusual management practices that may affect your opportunity for salary increases or job advancement.

4. The company's policy on salary levels.

Ask directly how a company positions its salary structure. It is usually preferable to work for a company that has a stated policy of paying salaries that are equal to or higher than those in its industry and business community. It will help your income level if you work for a company that is concerned with keeping its salaries competitive. It is also useful to know how frequently the company reviews its salary levels. If it is less than once a year, salary opportunities will probably fall below competitive levels.

BONUSES

Companies often reward employees with bonuses. A bonus plan provides a pool of funds to reward management employees for exceptional performance. The size of the bonus pool is often related to a predetermined level of achievement; for example, annual earnings, return on investment, or other measures of company success. Sometimes the pool is a discretionary amount established by the board. An individual participant's performance may be measured against previously stated objectives, although sometimes bonuses are awarded for performance in areas that are not measurable.

Bonus plans are more typical in certain industries, but there is no set pattern. Usually bonuses are not available in positions with salaries less than $25,000 or $30,000, although bonus practices vary by industry. Senior-level executives are often eligible to receive bonuses that are 40 to 50 per cent of their annual salary. In a year where corporate and individual performance results are outstanding, they can receive bonuses of 100 per cent or higher, thus more than doubling their gross income. Most middle-rank executives are eligible for bonuses that range from 10 to 30 per cent of their annual salaries. At the middle-management levels, employees who are eligible for bonuses are usually people in line management, whose work has a direct impact on profit.

Do you know any people in your field who receive bonuses for performance? This once-a-year lump sum can do a great deal to ease the financial pressures of life. Don't hesitate to ask if a company has a bonus plan and if the position for which you are being considered is eligible to participate. If the answers are yes, you can then ask how the bonus pool is established, what the basis is for bonus distribution, and what percentage of your salary you can expect if you reach your performance targets.

COMMISSIONS

Theoretically, commissions are the fairest form of remuneration, since the amount you earn is in direct proportion to the amount you produce. However, commissions are usually available only in jobs involving direct sales. Until recently, companies rarely considered hiring women for high-paying, direct-selling jobs. This attitude is changing, but slowly. The sales manager of a large pharmaceutical company mentioned proudly that they had recently integrated the firm's work force. "We have a girl working for us now as a salesman." In fact, this "girl" was one woman among several hundred men—hardly an integrated sales staff!

Women have also hesitated to take the risks involved in gambling on income from commission. "When offered the choice between higher base pay and lower commission, versus higher commission and lower base pay, women almost always opt for the steady, dependable, higher guaranteed pay rather than gamble for higher rewards." This comment was from a sales manager who supervises both men and women who sell advertising space.

Paula Hughes, one of the outstanding salespeople of our time, frequently advises women who are seriously considering going out to sell on commission. She says, "Many women just aren't able to take the risk. They are unwilling and unable to give up the security of a salary. Women have got to develop a 'can do' attitude, because they *can* do it." Ms. Hughes is a customer's representative (a stockbroker) and a senior vice-president at Thomson & McKinnon Auchincloss & Kohlmeyer, Inc. She entered the brokerage field in the late sixties and today manages more than $30 million in her customers' money and earns a six-figure income. She's an excellent example of what a woman can earn when she's willing to work hard and to gamble on her own ability.

RISK TAKING

Striving for more money involves taking risks. These risks may include forgoing a secure salary for a potentially more rewarding but less sure commission arrangement. It may mean taking the risk of asking for the salary that you should rightfully be earning, or negotiating to get the raise you rightfully deserve. Occasionally it means taking the risk of accepting a lower salary to acquire new skills or to change fields to get where you want to go.

In calculating your risk, timing is of crucial importance. At certain times in your life, you are much better able to take risks than at others. You've had a close look at some of the things that affect your ability to take risks in Chapter 4. Now might be a good time to go back and review those factors. Find out when would be the best time for you to take a risk. Then think about your risk/reward ratio.

The Risk/Reward Ratio

Risk/reward ratio is a standard measure applied to all forms of opportunity; the higher the risk, the greater the potential reward. The risk/reward ratio is used by corporations to establish bonus and commission-opportunity levels, and this ratio applies to speculative investments and all other forms of potential gain. Learn to evaluate your monetary decisions using the risk/reward ratio as a measure, and you will have a better foundation for your decision making in this area. This is especially true if you are considering taking the risk of asking for a raise, or the even greater risk of taking a new job. What are the rewards to be gained, and are they worth the amount of risk?

Louis Pasteur put forth the idea: "Chance favors the prepared mind." In this chapter, we've helped you prepare your mind with the information you need to increase the chances of earning your rightful income, while reducing the risk of going after it.

In the next chapter, we'll discuss some other ways to increase your chances of getting and using all the compensations for which you may be eligible: perquisites.

25

PERKING UP
YOUR NET INCOME

A significant portion of the compensation for today's executive is in nonmonetary form. Regular employee benefits frequently add as much as 30 per cent to the value of an employee's salary, and they are given out equally to all employees. Benefits include such things as health insurance, life insurance, and retirement plans.

In this chapter, we'll first look briefly at the benefits that a company offers all its employees, so that you'll have a basis for comparing one company against another. Then we'll consider the perquisites that become increasingly available to executives as they move up the corporate ladder. These "perks" are available only to certain classes of employees, and then often only by individual negotiation. In order to secure perks for which you may be eligible, you've got to have a realistic understanding of what's available.

BENEFITS

Social Security contributions and contributions to unemployment insurance, workman's compensation, and state disability are required of your employer by law so that you are covered in the event of a layoff or injury. Employers also pay for vacations, a certain number of holidays, and usually for sick days at the executive level. Most companies provide basic insurance, which includes health and life and retirement, but the amounts of these benefits vary widely from employer to employer. Generally, larger companies offer more generous insurance benefits because they can spread the risk more broadly; hence, it costs less per employee.

If you are in the fortunate position of being able to compare a new job with your present one, get the details on their employee benefits, *after* you've been offered the job, and study the comparative benefits in detail. When you can, try to assign a dollar value to the benefits to help you in your comparison. If you have more than one job offer, do the same thing with each. Compare the benefits of each company, and then see how the total compensation packages stack up.

Some companies offer major medical health insurance in addition to hospitalization. Some have quite extensive retirement plans that become vested after a number of years. You can receive income from them even if you leave the company before you retire, or their plans can be transferred from one company to another. The buzz word is "pension portability," and it's a very valuable company benefit.

Other employee benefits that are sometimes available are savings and investment plans, where the company may match part of your savings. Usually you can't collect the matching portion of the savings or investment in company stock until you have been with the company a required length of time. Some firms have credit unions, where you can obtain low-interest loans if you are a depositor.

"Although I would have preferred to work for the smaller of two companies that offered me jobs," a woman executive related, "I felt I had to choose the larger firm because of their outstanding benefit package and because I could get a company car. The smaller company had only poor hospitalization coverage and no major medical. With three rambunctious children to care for, this is a very big consideration for me. The small company offered profit sharing by way of their contribution to a retirement plan. But the amount of profit generated each year, and the way it was split among the employees, was largely determined by the whim of the owner. So it didn't seem a good way for me to build up a sound retirement program. I'm going to have to supplement Social Security, and there is no time like the present to start on a good retirement plan. I would never take a job with a company that didn't offer the health and retirement benefits that I know I need. This kind of economic security is very important to me."

Some companies offer an extremely valuable benefit: a tuition-reimbursement plan. With M.B.A. degrees costing around $8,000, it could be worth your while to seek a company that provides this benefit. As of January 1, 1979, payments by your company for education and training are no longer considered taxable income to the student. Thus the actual value of the money you receive is increased by the amount of your taxes, which is usually in the area of 40 to 50 per cent, if you take into consideration federal, state, local, and Social Security taxes. You'd have to earn around $15,000 before taxes to pay for your M.B.A. out of your own pocket. Some companies offer educational benefits to all employees; others make them available only as a perquisite at certain levels of jobs.

PERQUISITES

A perquisite can be thought of as a supplementary benefit given at the discretion of the employer. The government has been looking closely at perks, which are now tax-free, and from time to time there is a movement afoot to place many more of them in the taxable category. But the Revenue Act of 1978 affected only two areas. Tax deductions for maintaining boats and lodges for entertainment purposes were eliminated. Since not many of us have access to corporate yachts, we probably won't feel the effects of this change too keenly. The other change might be something that does affect you at some point, and this provision has to do with special health coverage for executives. We'll discuss that in detail later in the chapter.

First let's look at some of the things that fall into the category of executive perquisites, and who has a chance at securing them. According to an article in the *Wall Street Journal* in April 1977, the starting point for the availability of perks used to be in the vicinity of $75,000 annual salary. This figure has now been lowered to around $50,000. In order to attract good managers, many companies are offering a variety of fringe benefits at even lower salary levels, starting with items like prestige office space, keys to the executive washrooms, and the use of the executive dining room. While this type of benefit may enhance your ego and assist you in establishing your place within the power structure of an organization, the perks of real value are the ones that add significantly to your net income. Some of the perks that favorably affect your pocketbook include a company car, parking privileges, expense accounts and an entertainment allowance, WATS line, education, moving expenses, and an executive medical plan. The federal government is looking at executive fringe benefits with ever-closer scrutiny and many perquisites may ultimately lose their tax-free status. When a benefit becomes taxable, it is usually better for an employee to take its equivalent in additional salary. But even a taxed perquisite—or its cash equivalent—is better than no perk at all.

How and When to Ask for Perks

Women have been shortchanged on perquisites since few women held positions high enough in the executive scheme of things to be eligible for them. But, in this era of a shortage of experienced and able women managers, the time is ripe for women to get their fair share of the cream of the perks. After reading this chapter, you will have a better idea of the range of possible fringe benefits available to you. Many of them are available to employees with salaries well below the $50,000 mark, particularly if you are a woman. The two elements in the skill of securing perks are knowing *what* to ask for, and knowing *when* to ask for it.

Perks are rarely given to an employee while she is holding a job. They must be negotiated for before you accept a position. One excellent time to ask about perks is after you have been offered a job, but before you have accepted it. You can simply ask if the salary includes certain perks that you have decided you want. Sometimes it is helpful to phrase the perk you are after as a foregone conclusion. Whatever method you use, be sure you get the discussion out in the open before you accept a job, but move carefully. This area can be one that needs great delicacy and diplomacy. *Don't assume* that you will receive perks because others in the company in equivalent positions are receiving them. There is nothing democratic about the awarding of special enticements—*you must actively seek them.*

One woman was asked to return to a company she had formerly worked for. This gave her an advantage because she knew what benefits the senior executives had. Although her salary was just over $25,000, she nonetheless asked for and received all the perks that the senior male executives enjoyed, including club memberships, tuition payments, entertainment allowance, credit cards, and free parking. The only perk she did not get was a company car because she did not feel it was realistic to request one at her present level. But she fully intends to ask for one when she comes up for promotion.

This executive is aware of the fact that, when it comes to perks, what you don't ask for you won't receive. She also understands that it is easiest to seek benefits that the company is used to providing. Don't be discouraged from asking for perks because your salary is in the low range for a middle manager. Middle managers are continually becoming eligible for a variety of interesting fringe benefits, which are proving very valuable to them. Let's take a close look at some of these.

The Company Car

Probably the single most valuable perquisite is the use of a company car. According to a study by the Executive Compensation Service of the American Management Association, a car is by far the most popular perk. Of the 907 companies surveyed, 83.8 per cent provided a car for senior corporate executives. Executives who receive this perk have full use of a car—either completely free, or with a small payment for personal use. Notice whether men in jobs similar to the one you have been offered have company cars. If so, ask for one before you accept the position. With car costs skyrocketing, a company car adds substantially to your net income.

One woman vice-president asked for a company car as part of

her compensation package when she accepted a transfer, and her request was granted. She then specified that the car be air-conditioned and have power brakes and power steering. The personnel manager told her that this was against company policy and that all company cars were economy models. She didn't take this as the final answer, and she wrote to the president outlining what she wanted and why. She got the car she wanted.

Direct your requests to someone who is empowered to grant them. Don't take your first no as an answer if it is something you really want, and if you have reason to believe the company wants you for the job.

If you are turned down in your request for a car, make sure you will get adequate mileage payment if your job requires use of a car for business purposes. While the U.S. government now allows a cost of 18½¢ a mile, a number of businesses still pay only 10¢ or 12¢ a mile. Taking depreciation into consideration, actual operating costs on new models are 30¢ a mile or higher. At this rate, it's easy to see why you should try to get a company car.

If you don't get reimbursed for mileage at a reasonable level, be sure to claim the expense on your income tax return.

Parking Privileges

If it is necessary for you to drive to work, access to free parking can save you money as well as aggravation. Parking fees quickly mount up, particularly if you work in a city. You pay these fees with after-tax dollars; but if you receive the parking space free from your company, it is not included as income to you. Don't forget to ask about parking privileges.

Executive Medical Plan

A select group of executives, usually defined by salary grade, is sometimes eligible for an executive medical plan. This plan reimburses executives for medical expenses not covered by the company group insurance plan. Generally, these plans specify a maximum amount an executive can receive, and this may be defined as a flat dollar amount or as a percentage of the executive's salary.

Under these plans, reimbursements of from $2,000 to $5,000 are not uncommon, but in some cases they can be as low as $500.

Reimbursements under these special health coverage plans for executives have been subject to tax as of January 1, 1980. The coverage becomes a taxable benefit as of the time the medical bill is paid. Even though this formerly tax-free perk is now taxable, many companies and many executives will probably elect to retain it.

Financial Counseling

Because of the increasing complexity of the income-tax laws, many companies offer professional financial counseling to their managers. This can prove to be an invaluable perk to you if it is available. Even though these services may be considered taxable as income, a large company can purchase services at less than the cost to an individual, and often the fee is deductible to the individual because it is tax advice.

Stock Options

Prior to recent tax-reform legislation, stock options were a valuable perquisite available to some executives. They are less financially interesting since the enactment of new legislation and will probably become even less valuable as the tax laws continue to be rewritten. Simply stated, stock options give you the option to buy a certain number of shares of stock in your company, at an agreed-upon price and at a specified later date. If the price goes up, you exercise your option at the agreed-upon price and the resulting profit is yours. However, you must hold the stock for three years in order to qualify for capital gains tax treatment. Today it is usually smaller companies that still use stock options as an important enticement for senior executives.

Should you be eligible for a stock option plan, you will want to get a good tax accountant who can help you interpret both the law and the tax implications for your specific case. In terms of power, there are some advantages in being part of the elite group that qualifies for stock options. But the advice given in the *Wall Street Journal* on November 14, 1977, on this topic is "next year get

your company to create some other benefit that avoids the pitfalls
of stock options: old-fashioned cash money, for example."

Credit Cards

Find out how many company credit cards you can have and get
them. Credit cards save time in making out expense reports, and
they save you from having to use your own money. Your own
funds are better off in a savings account, rather than financing the
company you work for. Occasionally, cash advances can be secured from a company, but credit cards are safer than carrying
cash. If the company does not provide credit cards, secure your
own, but see if the company will reimburse you for the annual fee.

A telephone credit card is particularly useful in saving you time
and in getting calls through when needed. Many areas of the country have installed phones that will take only credit-card calls.

Carry several car-rental credit cards. It speeds reservations and
time spent in checking cars in and out. There's usually a discount
on car-rental cards held in a corporate name.

Be sure you have an American Express, Visa, or other credit
card. It makes paying for business entertaining a lot easier.

Business Entertaining

Ask if you will have an entertainment budget and find out what it
involves. Try to ascertain if the allowance is adequate for the level
of entertaining and negotiation on which you will be dealing. If
you want to be considered a peer and respected as a professional,
you must pay for your share of business entertaining on exactly
the same terms as your male counterparts.

Entertaining at home is sometimes part of the expected company duties. If it is part of your job, be sure that you can hire a
caterer and are reimbursed for all the food and beverages. Companies have had use of free social hostesses in the past in the form
of executives' wives. This situation is becoming less frequent because women are pursuing careers of their own, and business must
realize it. You don't need to go home and cook a gourmet dinner
for a client after a hard day at work. Let the caterer do it. You
might add a special dessert, if you'd like to demonstrate your

prowess in the kitchen, as well as at the conference table. But don't take on the whole meal.

Business entertaining for women raises some new questions because new situations present themselves. After arranging one of the larger financial packages in her field, Florence found that all the members of the group would be convening in her city to sign the final papers. They would be arriving from all parts of the globe on Sunday evening in order to be ready for a Monday morning meeting. All the partners were men, except Florence, and most of them had never met. "Should I get the group together for dinner Sunday night?" Florence wondered. "It certainly will smooth the flow of the meeting on Monday if I do. Should I have a dinner at my home, or should we go to a restaurant? Would it be better for me to include my husband, or should I manage this alone?"

Florence reviewed these questions with another woman executive. They decided that she should indeed get the group together on Sunday evening, and that a restaurant would be more appropriate than her home, since they were a group of strangers. The women further determined that Florence should appear on her own and not as the wife of someone, since it was a purely professional get-together. These decisions were based on the fact that the dinner was simply a group of business people convening in order to meet each other so that they could continue their professional association as rapidly and effectively as possible. Florence further arranged to pay for the dinner by credit card before the other guests arrived.

Paying the bill, even with a credit card, is not always easy for a professional woman. As the first woman sales manager of a flourishing company, Chris wanted to entertain her largest client in order to get to know him better. He balked, as he had "been around for a long time, and no woman has ever taken me out." Chris made it a point to discover his favorite restaurant and invited him there to lunch. He succumbed, and Chris arranged with the maître d' ahead of time to have the bill taken care of without its being brought to the table. Over lunch, she put the client at his ease first by discussing his family and making the kind of small talk he expected of women, but then she moved as quickly as possible to their business discussions. "It was essential to my doing my job that I get him over this feeling of 'a woman's role' and get him to consider me an able business person and valuable resource. I had to get him over his stereotypes and started the process at the lunch table. It wasn't easy, but it was worth the effort."

These new and not-so-new situations crop up in the field of business entertaining when women move into positions that they have not held before, and where almost all of their associates are male. Make sure that you will have an adequate entertaining and expense allowance to carry out your job effectively. Call on your professional woman friends for advice and ask your male associates as well. The counsel you receive will often differ radically. Do what you think suits your style best and will achieve your desired results, but do your share of the entertaining.

Clubs and Associations

Business entertaining is often most comfortably done in a private club. This eliminates any problem about paying—you can simply sign for the expenses. It is somewhat akin to a home situation, since you are part of a group and, in all likelihood, known to the persons who are serving you.

Many of the formerly all-male clubs now accept women as members. Find out which club or clubs would be useful to you and to which clubs the men in your position are given memberships. Often these are business, luncheon, or athletic clubs, and sometimes country clubs are included as well. Get your own memberships and make use of the club facilities just as your peers do.

Most professional people need to belong to several professional organizations, as well as social clubs, in order to keep up with the advances in their fields and to develop and maintain useful contacts. Ask your company to pay for these memberships.

Education

Many companies will pay for additional education, particularly if it has a direct bearing on your job. Some companies will even pay for schooling that doesn't relate directly to what you do, on the theory that an educated person is a more valuable employee.

Find out if you will be eligible for educational benefits. This is an idea that you might suggest if it is not now being done in your company. Assisting women to become further educated for professional opportunities can help a company fulfill some of its affirmative-action obligations. At the same time, you can save yourself tuition payments, which are considerable outlays when you pay for them with after-tax dollars. Additional education usually repays you with a larger paycheck and increased opportunity for promotion.

Even when you do not undertake formal education, you still need to keep up with rapid changes that are likely to be going on in your field. Get your company to pay for subscriptions to a variety of publications that will keep you informed. Get an allowance for books, home-study aids, and attendance at seminars to keep you abreast of the state of the art in your field.

Work Schedules and Vacations

Professional women can sometimes do a better job with a slight variation in their scheduled work day. You may want to begin your day earlier and end it earlier, or start later and end later. Some employers are willing to adjust working hours slightly. Know your own needs and discuss them with your employer. Most executives work far more hours than the normal forty, in any case, so you might as well make it as easy on yourself as possible with a schedule that meshes comfortably with your other obligations.

Two weeks' annual vacation—the norm in the United States—is very little time to regain mental and physical balance after the rigors of a work year. One enterprising mother negotiated an additional three weeks to be taken at another time of the year from her regular vacation, as a leave of absence. This allowed her time for a summer vacation with her family and another break to go off by herself.

Another woman asked for six weeks' leave, unpaid, in the summer in order to work full-time on her M.B.A. degree—this in addition to the two weeks' paid vacation that she took in the winter.

The easiest time to negotiate for added vacation time is before you accept the job. It's hard to secure after you are on the job.

Executive search consultant Janet Jones advises leaving the subject of hours alone if you really want a job. She says, "It's likely you won't get the job if you bring up hours." This same

holds true for vacation time. Many employers will react very negatively if you suggest any variation in the normal vacation allow-
ances. It's really up to you what your needs are in terms of adjustment of hours and vacations. If it is worth the gamble to you of
not getting the job, that is a decision only you can make. And potential employees sometimes succeed in getting their needs met,
and the job as well, resulting in a better life-style for them and a
happier employee for the company.

The Commuting Couple

A perk that men have sometimes enjoyed is the ability to take
their wives along on business trips, with the ticket and the expenses paid for by the employer. If this is the case in your company, request the same privileges for your husband. Mini-vaca-
tions here and there do a lot to refresh you, and it's more
enjoyable if you can bring your husband along free.

As more and more couples find it necessary to live apart at least
during the work week, some other perks are becoming necessary
to entice and hold onto good employees. These include the use of
a WATS line and plane tickets to home base.

Some companies see that their employees get round-trip airline
tickets home every weekend or every other weekend as part of an
employment package. Some companies will see that you get home
for the weekend at their expense anytime your job requires you to
be away for more than a week. Decide what your transportation
needs will be and negotiate for them.

One woman took an excellent position as head of a division of
her company with the understanding that the division would be located in Dallas, where her husband had just taken a job. The company decided to move the division to corporate headquarters, but
this woman had already purchased a house in Dallas and fully intended to make it her primary residence. She discussed the matter
with the company, which agreed to pay a round-trip ticket to
Dallas for her every other weekend, or to see that she got there
from wherever her corporate travels took her. "It works out so
that I only get there about once every three weeks," she explained.
"Because of my job requirements I can't make it every other
weekend on a regular basis. But the knowledge that the company

will pay for it whenever I can get there helps, and also I work such long hours that I take a three- or four-day weekend when I do make it. This can't go on forever, but I want this job and the company needs me in this position. It's worked well enough for the past two years to continue for a while longer."

One of the major management consulting firms pays first-class air fare for its employees to come home every weekend. It feels this is an absolute necessity, since its employees are usually on the road at least four days a week, and the travel may be international as well as national. "I've been in South America three weeks out of four for the past six months," lamented one mother of two young children. "But the children seem to manage all right with their father. I'm the one who suffers. It's a tough travel schedule, and I miss my family. I have to see them every weekend, or my life would really be unhappy."

Telephone Perks. The WATS line is a convenient way of keeping in touch without being bankrupted by telephone bills. See if your company has a Wide Area Telephone Service line that covers the places you need to call, and get access to it. "A daily telephone call to my husband is the way I keep in close touch with him," one highly placed woman executive explains. "It allows us to share all the trivial parts of our lives and keeps our relationship comfortable and ongoing." Living apart from your spouse is not easy, and hard-working business people rarely have time to write personal letters. Telephone calls paid for by your company can help smooth the path of communication for commuting couples.

New Perks for New Life-styles. An interesting perk has surfaced for couples with children where both parents travel on business. The company pays for a housekeeper for the days the employee is out of town (whether the employee is a man or a woman) if the spouse has to be out of town on business at the same time.

New life-styles and newly defined roles require new ways of acting and reacting. It is advantageous to your pocketbook to have as many of them as possible underwritten by your company.

Living Accommodations. In this age of commuting partners, it is not impossible to get your apartment paid for if you must move from your home base, but your partner must remain. One woman not only got her apartment paid for, but her garage rent as well.

Clothing

Some women receive a clothing allowance or have their clothing paid for by the company. This happens most often in the fashion-related industries, where you must appear professionally in certain designer clothes. This is one of the tricky perks that may be taxable, and the kind you should check with your tax accountant.

In one company, where all customer contact staff were women, a man was hired. His wardrobe was inappropriate for the clientele, and the women discussed with management the possibility of an annual clothing allowance for all of them, allowing the man to purchase a suitable wardrobe. They succeeded—and the women came out with a tidy bonus, amounting, in effect, to a raise in pay.

Unless clothing is a uniform allowance, it is usually taxable to the recipient. Many people would probably prefer to have a raise. But this is often not an either/or decision. The clothing allowance is given for a particular reason and to cover certain fixed expenses.

If your income bracket for income-tax purposes is 40 per cent, and you are expected to appear at certain times in designer dresses that cost $3,000, then you can reasonably ask for a clothing allowance of $5,000, which gives you $3,000 net income.

Moving Expenses

One of the most costly ventures you may undertake for the sake of your career is moving. Formerly it fell to the wife to look after all the details, and, in fact, the company had the unpaid services of a moving manager. If you take a job in another city, or if your company relocates you, you should expect not only to have your moving expenses paid by the company, but also all other indirect expenses that moving can entail. This is particularly important for a professional woman, since you are not likely to have someone available full-time to take care of the myriad aspects of the move.

Be sure you have a clear understanding of *all* the expenses that can be incurred during a move. Most people overlook many of these expenses, so the move costs them a great deal of their own money. Things you might include in moving expenses are:

· Visits to the new location to select housing in advance of the move. Several visits may be required and you may want to bring your spouse or other family members with you.

· Living expenses in the new location until you are ready to move into the new permanent house.

· Expenses connected with selling your present residence.

· Losses entailed in selling your present home.

· A "bridge loan" to cover the down payment on your new home before you have recovered the money from the sale of your present home. Often a company will lend this money to you at no interest or at a modest interest charge. But you must ask for it.

· Expenses such as security lost in breaking a lease, or the amount needed to buy out a lease.

· Differential in the rate of interest on your new mortgage from the old one. Mortgage rates have gone up steeply in the past decade. Trading a new mortgage for an old one can cost you a great deal of money. Some companies will reimburse you for this amount or part of it.

· Closing costs on the new home.

· Items that you may have to purchase in the new location. For example, in some states you are expected to leave the refrigerator; in other states, you must provide your own. Draperies and rugs are always necessary when you move. Some companies will give you a lump-sum allowance for such purchases.

· Expenses incurred in cleaning and removing refuse from both the old and the new homes. Neither of these jobs is recommended for the busy career woman in the midst of a major move, yet it is amazing how rarely one remembers to budget this as a very real problem and cost of the move.

· Upgrading of present car or purchase of second car. With the trend toward corporate headquarters moving from large cities, it is often a necessity to have a totally dependable car or a second car. Companies moving employees from city center to suburbs often make a cash contribution toward this expense.

· Payment of storage charges if storage is necessary.

· The move itself, including packing and unpacking of all items.

· Transportation of the family and possibly a housekeeper, if you are fortunate enough to have one, and who is willing to move with you.

· *Most important of all,* an allowance for taxes for the additional income you incur in the form of payment of your moving expenses. It is not at all unusual for a move to cost $10,000—and even more. April 15 can be a horrifying time if you have not arranged for your company to meet the tax payments on moving-expense reimbursements, since this is taxable income to you.

This list of moving expenses is not exhaustive, but it is intended to give you an idea of some of the unforeseen and burdensome expenses of moving. Talk to everyone you know who has recently moved and learn about as many problems as you can. Get your company to handle all the expenses and to give you a tax allowance as well.

Remember that you don't have a wife to take care of the details of moving for you while you carry on with your job. Make the entire process of moving as easy on yourself as you can, both physically and financially.

Other Perquisites

The range of perks that senior male executives have managed to secure is truly impressive. As yet, few women have moved into this territory, but they are on their way. For this reason, some of the more elegant and imaginative corporate contributions to a pleasant life are included here for your consideration:

· A condominium apartment fully furnished to your specifications.

· Large low-cost or no-cost loans.

· A chauffeured limousine.

· A second-home hideaway of your choosing.

· College tuition for your children.

· All-expense-paid vacation for you and your family.

These benefits are usually added on to salaries that are already in the six figures, and they are often considered taxable income. They are real perquisites that have been enjoyed by male executives—and their relatives!

You may want to discuss the income-tax implications of perks with your tax accountant before negotiating for them because in some cases certain perquisites are taxable and other times they are not. An apartment is an example of a perk that is sometimes taxable and sometimes not, depending upon circumstances.

In this chapter, we have suggested a wide variety of possible perks that have been obtained by many different people in many different circumstances. You must look over the range, try to get an idea of what is reasonable at the company where you are negotiating, and decide which ones you want to try for. Again, it must be stressed that negotiations for perquisites must be handled very skillfully and at the appropriate time.

What you can secure for yourself will be a matter of what is worthwhile to you in terms of net income—and of what your company will allow, and what you are successful in bargaining for. As women move into senior positions, it is time for them to share fully in the corporate largess.

26

GET SET TO JET

Moving up professionally usually means an increasing amount of business travel. This can present some special problems for women. For one thing, families and friends do not like being left behind. Also, you may be concerned about coping on your own in strange places and, often, at strange hours of the day or night. Eating alone may not be a pleasant prospect. There are many aspects of travel that can be disconcerting. But despite the penalties of travel, the benefits can be substantial. The pleasure you derive from professional travel will increase as your skill and experience on the road broaden.

Many women on the rise still find the prospect of business travel disquieting, even though there is no shortage of advice on the subject. Since this book is intended as a resource book addressing all aspects of professional life which must be understood and mastered in order to be successful in the business world, it seems appropriate to include some recommendations from experienced women travelers. If you feel competent in this area, you may want to move on to the final chapter. Still, it is the rare traveler who doesn't enjoy picking up an additional tip or two from someone who has learned how to make business travel a little easier and a little more pleasant.

The first lesson is: *expect* travel to be a part of your job. An extended career program will almost always mean that you will have to go out of town. Visibility at conferences and availability as a lecturer can be a significant step forward on your success program. Firsthand knowledge of your company's various plants can be a vital ingredient in becoming a generalist with a broad knowledge. Professional training programs are often held around the world.

One senior woman manager, responsible for hiring women executives in four western states, includes the question on her application: "Are you willing to travel?" The answer to this question is the first one she looks at when she reviews applications. If the answer is negative, she automatically disqualifies the applicant. As she explains, "About 75 per cent of the applicants answer no to this question. When I ask why, there are three basic responses: 'My husband doesn't like it'; 'It ruins my social life'; or 'I don't have adequate child-care to remain away overnight.'" This manager has also found she has travel-related problems with those women who respond that they *are* willing to travel. So, during personal interviews, she tells applicants that half of their job time may be spent traveling, when, in fact, it is rarely more than 30 per cent. She pushes the issue because she has found that, in fact, many women who *think* they are willing to travel actually find business travel difficult.

How to answer the travel question? To get ahead, answer not only affirmatively, but eagerly. Being able to travel easily means finding a way to arrange your life so that you can be away for several days—or several weeks—at a time. This can be especially difficult for women with children, or other relatives for whom they care, but your chances of solving this problem are enhanced if you look for a solution well in advance of the need. Take steps to implement your program, and test it while you are still at home. Don't wait until you're about to get on the plane for Acapulco, or trying to write the keynote speech for a sales meeting, to begin worrying about whether your housekeeper can cope in your absence.

The most important element in comfortable relationships is knowing what your friends, your husband, and your family expect. If their expectations don't fit your business travel requirements, gradually work on changing the psychological contracts and minimizing the strain on everyone involved—especially yourself.

TIPS ON KEEPING A HAPPY FAMILY

Constant contact with your spouse and children is essential when you are away from home; both to reassure them that you are thinking about them, and to comfort yourself that they are getting along fine without you. They almost always get along better than you think they will, but plan to phone and write often.

You can prepare your family for your business travel. Teach each member of the family to cook simple dishes—or elaborate ones, if they are so inclined. Most husbands and children find they enjoy cooking and are pleased to do all or part of family meals when you travel. No professional woman needs the added pressure of having to make casseroles before she leaves so that her family will have something to eat while she is away. Knowing how to use the washing machine is another essential for every family member. Washing, sorting, and putting clean clothes away is a never-ending task. Unless you are blessed with a full-time housekeeper, you probably find laundry a bête noire. Coming home to a pile of dirty laundry after a taxing trip can be pretty discouraging.

But remember that the training or retraining process usually is best if it is gradual. Too many demands too quickly can result in unnecessary antagonism, particularly if your family is already uneasy about your traveling.

When the Man Gets Left Behind

Your husband's needs and attitudes about your travel can be particularly complex. Most marriages involve psychological contracts between the two parties, which may be implicit rather than explicit, but few of these contracts entailed, in the husband's mind, the fact that his wife would travel extensively on business, or even occasionally. More than likely, it was the expectation of most couples that any traveling would be done by the husband. The wife would be waiting at home. Bear this in mind when you begin traveling or when your business travel increases in frequency or duration. It can sometimes be very difficult for a man to be left behind.

Lisa, an international consultant, travels abroad on extended trips. She arranges for her husband to join her at the end of her work at a destination of his choice, and they take a few days' vacation together to get reacquainted in a relaxing atmosphere. Another traveling executive looks for clients for her husband in places where she visits regularly. Then her husband can moonlight and accompany her from time to time, yet still hold his full-time position at their home base.

A Few Solutions to the Child-Care Problem

LeAnne has been bringing her children with her on business trips abroad, one at a time, since they were six years old. She places them with friends abroad while she is working and, in turn, hosts her friends' children when she is at home. This way a new generation of international business executives is being raised, and LeAnne is not missing out on the childhood years of her offspring.

Another woman, a college professor who is determined to become nationally known, has purchased a two-family house and has live-in help in one half of the house. Her son has a room of his own in each half, so that he can comfortably move to the baby-sitter's half of the house when his mother makes one of her many trips. Having household help nearby also enables this woman to spend maximum time with her husband and child when she is home.

KEEPING YOUR SOCIAL LIFE GOING

Close friends are often discontented if you travel a lot, and they need extra attention when you are at home.

When Rita's work took her to Europe each summer, for most of the summer, she would find herself bereft of friends when she returned in the autumn. Her method of combating this problem was to keep up a very active correspondence with the people she wanted to see upon her return. When possible, she invited friends to join her in Europe. Immediately upon return, she gave a big reunion party, to remind everyone that she was back and that she valued knowing them.

PAMPER YOURSELF AND THOSE WHO HELP YOU

Once you have arranged to take care of others in your life while you are away on business, make plans to take care of yourself. Travel can be taxing. Jetting off on business may seem glamorous to those who have not done it, but to the regular traveler, it just means a more complicated commute to get to where the work is to be done. It is easier and more efficient to do the same work in your own home base, so make every effort to conserve your energy when you are on a business trip.

The *Wall Street Journal* reported that an estimated 10 per cent of hotel rooms are now used by women travelers. There has been some practical recognition of women's problems when traveling alone. For example, Chicago's famous Drake Hotel has a policy of protecting lone women guests from male harassment in the hotel's bars. The management of the Drake also plans to retain the elevator operators, rather than automating the elevators, so women will not be traveling alone to their rooms.

The New York Hilton provides an overnight kit for women executives if they must unexpectedly remain in town. The kit contains nightgown, toothbrush, toothpaste, comb, and mirror.

Western International Hotels has some rooms with a bed that will fold out of sight for women who need to conduct business meetings in their rooms. "A bed is rather suggestive," a spokesman says.

Francine, a specialist in real estate financing, reports that she finds more and more hotels providing pleasant accessories for women travelers, like skirt hangers, shower caps, sewing kits, and perfumed soap. She particularly commended the Hyatt hotels in this regard. "Not only do they have the small things that make me feel welcome, but I feel that the employees in the restaurants go out of their way to make me feel comfortable when I eat alone."

Ask for the amenities you need in hotels you visit regularly, and perhaps this trend will spread more quickly. Don't forget to men-

tion how much you like the extras and the special service you get
as a way to let the management know you are aware of it and that
it is worth their expense.

Use Airline Clubs

If you have been successful in securing a membership in an airline
club as one of the perks for your position, you have already
significantly eased the wear and tear of business travel. These
clubs, located in major airports, offer many time and energy
savers.

First, they offer a convenient place to hold meetings, which
might save you the necessity of traveling into the nearby city.
Often meetings at an airport can enable you to return home the
same day, instead of having to stay away overnight.

As a club member, you are also saved the annoying necessity of
standing in line to check in and make your seat selection. This is
usually done for you while you are comfortably seated in the
clubroom. Help can be secured, too, in changing flights, making
hotel reservations, and arranging for rental cars. If there is a
weather emergency, waiting in the club facilities is much more desirable than sitting in the public areas at the airport. Also, in a private club you can take out a portable dictating machine, or papers
to read, and work.

Most successful business travelers train themselves to do a great
deal of work on the road, where they are away from interruptions.
The airlines club is a well-equipped spot to work while you are
waiting for your plane. If you do not have a membership paid for
by your company, consider paying for at least one membership
yourself.

Aim for First Class

Almost without exception, people who do a lot of business traveling recommend securing first-class accommodations. Regular in-
tercontinental travelers need to be able to sleep comfortably, as
well as to work, on their flights in order to combat jet lag.

Sleep is essential for all travelers. Select a hotel in a quiet area, and ask for a room on a floor high enough to enable you to get a good night's sleep, without being disturbed by traffic noise.

Well-prepared food in good restaurants will be kinder to your stomach; coffee-shop fare may save you time, but eventually you may pay a digestive penalty. Cab it when you can; standing on buses or subways does not add to your composure when you reach your destination.

One fast-moving California-based vice-president strongly recommends first-class travel. She says it is especially essential when she is working all day and traveling all evening to arrive at a new destination in time to work the next day. It is her policy to fly first class on any flight that lasts more than two hours. "The benefits of this policy are twofold," she explains. "It's more comfortable, and, since I'm usually working, I need all the space I can get, plus room to take a nap. In first class, your seatmate is more likely to be a fellow business traveler, and less likely to disturb you with chatter."

Don't overlook train travel. Amtrak has brought first class back to trains. A train trip that brings you into midtown of your destination can give you an ideal opportunity to do some uninterrupted reading, writing, or that all-important future planning.

Tipping

Show your appreciation for service, too, with good tips. Women have the reputation for being light tippers. You will often find that frequent business travelers tip well and often. You need all the service you can get when you are on the road. This is even more true in places that you frequent.

"The bell captain held my favorite scarf for me until my next trip, on the chance that it was mine," LeAnne said. "What a pleasant surprise it was."

Another fast-moving executive left her briefcase in a cab. "Because of the generous tip I gave the driver, I found it waiting for me at the hotel reception desk." It pays to be considerate of those who smooth your way.

But it is not necessary to overtip. Some women err on the lavish side because they are not accustomed to handling money and paying bills in restaurants, taxis, and hotels. General guidelines may be helpful. Tips usually run from 10 per cent of the bill to 20 per cent; the former is on the light side and the latter is somewhat generous. Fifteen per cent is a good rule-of-thumb to follow in most situations, unless the service was extremely good or very poor.

Learn quick and easy ways to figure tips. For example, in New York City, people simply double the 8 per cent restaurant tax for a normal tip. This avoids adding a tip on the tax as well as being a very simple means of calculating a normal tip.

Give a larger percentage of tip if the bill is small—50 cents is proper for a $2.00 charge. For porters and bellhops, 50 cents a bag is usual, so that most often you will be giving them $1.00 or $2.00. It's handy to have lots of single bills and quarters when you are traveling.

Read travel guides for tipping customs in other countries, and then ask people in the country to verify your information. In many foreign countries, a 15 per cent service charge is automatically added to most bills, so only very minor additional tipping is necessary.

FOR YOUR HEALTH

Business travel can be hazardous to your health. Your sleep pattern may be disrupted, you'll eat at unlikely times, and often eat food that is less than totally compatible with your digestion. Jet lag is a fact of life, and it can impair your ability to make important decisions. Your normal body rhythm determines the level of gamma globulin in your blood, the substance that helps ward off infections. When your sleep pattern is disturbed by jet travel or too many nights without enough rest, you may find yourself with more than your share of colds and other illnesses. Sleep patterns are less disturbed when you travel by train or boat, so consider these alternatives when time permits.

Veterans of frequent jet trips make these suggestions that you might find helpful. First, arrive early for your flight. A last-minute panic and a rush to catch a plane puts an unnecessary assault on your body and gets you off to a poor start for any trip. Drink lots of fluids on board, but go very lightly on the alcohol. Eat lightly, too, and get up and move around often. This movement minimizes swelling in feet and ankles.

More is being discovered all the time about how to minimize the effect of jet travel. Keep up with the new information.

There is a travel health hazard unique to women. Too much time spent in pressurized cabins causes a buildup in the lining of the uterus over a period of time, and menstrual periods of constant travelers can become heavier and heavier. This could be rather frightening unless you are on the watch for it. If you notice you are developing this symptom, be sure to mention to your doctor the amount of time you spend in jet travel; it can be an important cause of menstrual difficulties for many women.

An in-depth session with your doctor is often helpful to the frequent traveler. Get some good pain pills. Your road show must go on despite headache, hangover, or cramps. Sleeping pills can be prescribed if you have trouble sleeping the first night in a strange bed—a most common occurrence. Tranquilizers help some people whose sleeplessness is caused by stage fright before tomorrow's performance in front of a large gathering.

However, most professionals suggest avoiding calming drugs immediately before you have to be at peak performance level. It is far better to harness that nervous energy in constructive ways—by using some of the tips pointed out in this book on presentation techniques.

Many travel problems can be overcome by allowing yourself time to get enough rest, during the trip and upon your return. A dark eyeshade is great for napping on a plane, or trying to get maximum sleep on a long night flight. Even better is taking a day flight, but unfortunately this is not always possible. Many regular travelers develop the art of sleeping through most of a flight regardless of whether it is day or night.

Research reported in *Fortune* magazine has found that you do not recover your normal body rhythm until one day has passed for each hour of time zone you have crossed. That means that you will not be at peak performance on a Washington-to-Paris trip for the first five days of your stay. Recovery time seems to increase with the age of the traveler. It is better to add a little extra recovery time to your schedule when possible—you and your organization will both be further ahead.

ON THE ROAD, SOLO

Arlene, who spends about half of her work time on the road, does not like eating in restaurants alone. Also, she finds that, with her heavy travel schedule, she needs to use all her time in her hotel room to rest and to prepare for meetings. Therefore, she orders as many meals as possible from room service, preserving both her time and her energy; this also eliminates the discomfort she feels when eating out by herself.

Arlene is not alone in her dislike of dining out alone. Womenpoll, a survey service dealing specifically with women, discovered that 53 per cent of the women questioned said that they felt uncomfortable eating dinner alone in a restaurant.

On the other hand, Dorothy, a lover of gourmet food, uses her travels to try new restaurants; it's a hobby that goes well with expense accounts! "I used to feel uncomfortable dining by myself. I don't know whether I've adapted, or whether social custom has changed, but I no longer feel any qualms about this. I always call ahead to make a reservation. This ensures that the maître d'hôtel knows that I will be dining alone and helps me obtain a table that is not in too obvious a location. I often have more attentive service because of the advance notice and because I'm alone. A paperback book can be an excellent companion—at home I never have enough time to read."

An international traveler, Alexandra elects to relax with friends while traveling. Over the years, she has built up a group of friends in the areas where she travels, and she keeps in touch with them; she can have a home-cooked meal almost everywhere she goes.

Dining in, out, alone, or with friends—for a woman business traveler today, all options are open. Plan ahead and do what makes the trip most enjoyable for you.

EXPLORE THE WORLD

If there is an event going on in town that you want to see, go by
all means. Use your business travel as an inexpensive means of exploring the world. Ask the hotel bell captain if you will have any
trouble returning to the hotel from your intended location. Call on
him to get any tickets you may need.

One frequent traveler and opera buff was on a business trip and
noticed that the local opera company was having a spectacular
debut that evening. She found the opera house was located in a
dangerous area of the city, where she might have trouble finding a
cab. She asked the bell captain to find out whether any other
guests were going and whether he would arrange for her to return
with them. "He called a couple who were only too happy to give
me their seat numbers so we could meet after the performance.
I've done that a number of times now and met some very nice
people that way."

TRAVEL SAFETY

Nobody can assure you that you will not have occasional frightening moments when you are traveling alone. But no one can give
you that assurance when you are in your home town either. Follow
the same sensible precautions on the road that you do at home.

Should you make casual acquaintances on your business travel?
That is really up to you. Most chance encounters tend to be like
those of ships passing in the night: no further contact will be
made by either party. Some passing encounters turn out to be very
beneficial. One public relations specialist says, "During a long
flight from Paris to New York, I sat next to a senior editor I'd
been trying to reach unsuccessfully for months. We got well acquainted, and I've been placing stories with his magazine ever
since. Not only that, I now hire him to write some tough technical
stories for me. Our meeting was mutually rewarding." Valuable

business contacts can occasionally be made this way, and, at the least, you may miss some entertaining moments if you remain totally self-contained on your travels.

There is also an unexpected penalty for isolating yourself during jet travel. Dr. Art Ulene reported on the "Today Show" that studies show that people who travel in groups suffer less jet lag than solo travelers. No one yet knows why this is so, but it gives another rationale for striking up an acquaintance with a group of travelers on your next long plane trip.

Not all unplanned meetings turn out well, however. Erika, a successful salesperson covering a six-state area, was surprised one evening when dining with her sales manager to receive a call in the restaurant. The caller turned out to be a sales manager for another company. This man had often seen Erika on planes and had gotten her name from the tag on her luggage. He had seen her at the hotel that evening and asked the desk clerk where he could find her. The clerk had overheard her dinner plans and passed on the information under the impression that the inquirer was with the same company. "The caller's inventiveness so intrigued me I asked him to join us, since I was safely in the company of my employer. However, it turned out to be an awkward evening—it rapidly became clear that he was really looking to spend time in my hotel room."

To avoid just such unwanted attention, Joy, who always dresses meticulously for business, prefers to travel in casual and unobtrusive attire. "I've found that most men don't bother to try and start a conversation with me if I look like a plain Jane. Also, I do not look like a professional woman when I travel, so they don't try to find out what I do or where I'm going. Since my job on arrival consists of talking to people almost constantly, I need to conserve my energy. I've also learned not to tag my luggage with my name—just my business address and phone number. It's safer, since potential burglars often locate their victims that way. When you just arrive in Seattle, you obviously won't be at home in your apartment in Los Angeles. A potential burglar knows he can get there first."

You may end up in a compromising situation from the most unexpected quarter. One woman attended an international conference with hundreds of men and only one other woman. Each day in her room she found a large bouquet of flowers, with no card. On the third evening, she rode up to her room in the elevator with her boss and another man whom she had known for several years through a professional organization in her home town. He was also a client of her company. As she stepped off the elevator, the client followed her, making references to the flowers. He accompanied her to her door and made a very clear pass. She took him by his elbow, turned him around in the hall, and walked him back to the bank of elevators, telling him she was not available. She thanked him for the flowers, pushed the elevator button, and waited with him. In the elevator was her boss, returning from one of the top floors. To this day, she does not know whether he was coming back to rescue her or to check up on her.

Be prepared for both the civilized request and the uncivilized encounter. One executive, alone in a compartment of a train in Europe, found herself joined by a very drunk and insistent male. She managed to maneuver her way out of the compartment door as she mentally reviewed the word for "help" in the language of the country through which she was passing.

Planning and good judgment are the keys to safety.

WHEN IN TOKYO

Inger McCabe Elliott, who makes several three-week trips to the Orient each year, has two rules for international travelers: learn the customs and learn the language. "If you expect to be traveling to a foreign country regularly, take the time to learn the language. Although your foreign business associates may speak English, your work and your travels will go much more smoothly if you are familiar with at least the basics of the native language."

Barbara Perrin says, "If you have to travel to Tokyo, you may be surprised the first time you are almost knocked down by a Japanese man who grabs the taxi as you are about to step into it; even for a seasoned New Yorker like me, this 'custom' took a bit of getting used to. It would have been a disastrous experience for me if I had not been warned that it might happen, and also that I would probably get no help with my luggage, which consisted of an entire fashion show. Luckily, I had been instructed in local customs and had arranged for shipment by commercial means."

Americans traditionally have expected people from other countries to speak English. If you truly wish to be respected in another country, show the people of that area the courtesy of learning the fundamentals of their language, starting with such indispensable words as "please" and "thank you." Cassette language lessons have become practical with the advent of tape recorders that are very lightweight and small enough to fit into your briefcase or purse. If you spend much time in a foreign country, you will find that you can rapidly increase your vocabulary by scanning newspapers and periodicals, and by watching television.

In business dealings, when you do not understand the local language, your foreign associates will often communicate among themselves. This is the case particularly when they don't want you to know what they are saying. If, on the other hand, you know some of their language, they won't do this; they will never be sure just how much you understand.

When you start dreaming in a foreign language, you know you are well on the way to mastering it. It is an excellent goal to work toward, and quite a surprise the first time it happens. You will find foreign travel less taxing and less tiring when the hum of human voices around you is totally intelligible. When you have full comprehension of another language, a third language will seem much easier to acquire.

There are not many American men who are truly international executives. Men from other countries have long outpaced Americans in this respect because most educated people from other countries are fluent in at least two languages, in addition to their native tongue. Being a capable international executive implies a certain chameleonlike ability to merge into the scenery, an ability that has been easier for male travelers than female. But times are changing. To be an international woman executive is a goal for which almost no one has yet prepared herself. Why not be one of the first in the field?

Should you set your sights on international work, start learning a second language thoroughly, and make it a major one: French, German, or Spanish. If you want to increase your chances for advancement, select and master a third language from an area with economic growth potential. Consider Japanese, Portuguese, Norwegian, Arabic, or Mandarin.

Take your vacation time to travel as far afield as possible, as often as possible. Select those areas where the language you are studying is spoken. It is amazing how much facility in spoken language you can acquire in two weeks. Your language facility and familiarity with the country of business managers who travel to the United States will repay you well. Although business managers will probably prefer to speak English, they will find it thoughtful of you, amusing, and relaxing to be able to speak a little of their own language from time to time.

You will find that your time and effort in studying a language while working and vacationing abroad are rewarded many times over. Become familiar with local customs and work at understanding local mores. Develop a group of local friends. More than anything else, the ability to be truly empathetic in many foreign settings helps you to gain the confidence and respect of foreign nationals.

TRAVEL LIGHT

Every woman who travels regularly at home or abroad emphasizes that it is essential to travel with a minimum of luggage.

The first secret to traveling light is owning the lightest sturdy luggage available. This seems to become easier and easier each year, as lighter and stronger suitcases are perfected. Be sure that you own some of them. Do not invest too heavily, though, because airlines are rough on baggage, and even the most expensive luggage can be damaged. Buy your luggage with an eye to being able to replace it relatively easily.

Extremely lightweight luggage is particularly handy if you like to pack an extra folding case. Somehow, no matter how carefully you plan, the laws of expansion seem to make it difficult to close a suitcase that is full of used clothing. It may be quicker and easier to take out the expandable case and fill it with used clothing and work materials that will no longer be needed. It also makes a handy laundry hamper during an extended trip. When you are ready to leave, you will find your packing already half finished.

Here is another aid to traveling light on the return trip. Duplicate all papers with which you will be working, and, as you finish going over the material on the trip, discard the papers. You have a duplicate at home. If you are traveling extensively, bring self-addressed envelopes with you and send back material that you acquire. This way, you return home with the material divided properly, and you haven't had to carry it around. If your briefcase is soft-sided and fits into your suitcase, you can also pack it and not have to carry it on the plane.

Several schools of thought exist concerning the style and size of the suitcase to take. This largely depends on whether you like to carry your baggage onto the plane or not. An informal survey shows women business travelers about evenly divided, but if you favor a carry-on bag, take a briefcase too, so that you won't have to open your suitcase on the plane. There's usually not enough room. If you prefer to take more clothes, a 26″ suitcase is usually adequate, particularly if it is soft-sided. Some travelers prefer a garment bag to a suitcase. On a very extended trip or where you have extreme changes of climate on a single trip, two suitcases of even weight can prove to be very convenient. They are much easier to carry than one large one. A briefcase that fits into a suitcase is a must with this combination—or one with double handles that you can sling over your shoulder.

One inveterate traveler always makes sure that her handbag, too, has two handles just long enough to fit over her shoulder, so that she can carry it that way and then carry two suitcases. You'll find that a shoulder-strap purse will slip down if you try to carry a suitcase while the single strap of the purse is on your shoulder. Double-strap handbags are also recommended for safety in large towns. When you have two straps securely over your arm or shoulder and the opening of the bag turned toward you, it is more difficult for the pickpocket and the purse snatcher to steal from you.

Another frequent traveler always keeps loose change and dollar bills or their equivalent in local currency in her coat pocket. This eliminates the necessity of opening her purse in public places. Traveler's checks are heartily recommended by experienced travelers for most of your travel money. You don't want to carry large amounts of cash with you, and it is not safe to leave money in your hotel room. Plan your travel equipment and supplies for your safety, peace of mind, and ease of travel.

Not all travelers are able to travel *without* items of value. Barbara, who travels with expensive pearls, transports them in a brown paper bag, looking like a snack picked up at the local lunch counter. If it is essential to have a fair amount of cash with you, Rosalyn recommends that you put the cash into something in your purse other than your wallet. Be sure also to keep your credit cards separate from your money. This way there is less chance of your losing both at the same time. Keep a complete list of your credit-card numbers at home, where you can call for the information should you be unfortunate enough to lose them while traveling. It is surprising how many people do not have this information readily available.

Not all travelers are able to keep their luggage light, either. Caroline Bosly travels around the world with oriental rugs for display on television shows! There is no way to lighten her load. Fine orientals are so closely hand-knotted that they are extraordinarily heavy, even if they are small. Caroline has a selection of suitcases that have wheels on them and an attached strap, so she can pull the bag along.

If you have observed stewardesses lately, you will have noticed that many of them attach their suitcases to a handy device that enables them to roll their bags along. These luggage strollers are widely available, and they are light and easily collapsible when not in use. If you have to carry your own luggage, you can do so easily.

Try out ideas on vacation travel so that your business trips will go safely and smoothly.

A TRAVEL WARDROBE

The other factor affecting the weight of your baggage is the clothing that you pack. If you select your clothing carefully, you may find yourself with a wardrobe that is almost totally hand-washable and virtually wrinkle-free. Many traveling women will simply not buy a blouse that has to be dry-cleaned or needs ironing. Synthetics and blends are almost indistinguishable from fragile silks. Who can spare the time to iron, and who wants the extra weight of a travel iron?

You do not have to be totally limited to synthetics, although they can be very convenient. Good-quality wools, velvets, and corduroys steam out in the hotel bathroom while you are showering. Pure cotton comes with drip-dry finishes. Choose your fabrics and garments wisely, and you can resemble the elegant lady of a former time who traveled with her personal maid. You can and should look as if you just stepped out of a bandbox—thanks to old reliable fibers, and to the miracles of modern technology.

Kay, a data processing consultant who travels a great deal both for pleasure and business, has planned two basic wardrobes around the colors navy and black. "I never buy any clothes that will not travel well. Dry cleaning in European and even in American hotels is a time-consuming nuisance. Dark colors make maintenance much easier.

"I travel so much that I never have time to unpack the navy wardrobe before I have to go off again, so the next time it's the black outfits that go into the suitcase. Recently, my life has become still more complicated, and I've added a third coordinated wardrobe based on camel—so I have another complete set of travel clothes. For extended trips, the camel clothes and accessories coordinate with either black or navy. The primary reason, of course, for keeping your travel wardrobes based on a single color is to keep the number of shoes and boots you need to take to an absolute minimum. Another time-saver for me is to duplicate certain items in my wardrobe. Whenever I find a basic skirt or jacket that travels well and looks attractive, I buy one in another color.

"Although many travelers have advised me to dress for travel to suit the climate of my destination, I've handled this decision another way. I dress in layers for airplane travel because I find planes range in temperature from 60 to 90 degrees—sometimes all on one trip. With enough layers on or off, I can be comfortable no matter what the interior climate is. I pack a noncrushable outfit in my briefcase to change to, one which is suitable for my destination, and I change for deplaning. This change of clothes proves invaluable on the not-infrequent times when my luggage has been diverted to a distant city."

There are several methods of deciding what to wear. If you are very clever with accessories, you may find a basic wardrobe that can be very limited. For example: an all-weather coat, a jacket, a skirt, pants, two blouses, and perhaps also what you wear on the plane. Unfortunately, most trips require more complex wardrobes than this, but you can make your selection by analyzing exactly what business, social, and sports occasions you will participate and with whom. You can always wear an outfit more than once, if you change the people you are with. Skirts and jackets that are suitable for business with one blouse and for a social occasion with another are practical travel companions.

Don't forget to consider taking along a bathing suit. It is the rare hotel now that does not have a pool, and a quick swim is an excellent refresher after a hard day's work.

People tend to fall into two types of packers: the folders and the rollers. Try both methods and decide for yourself. Folders usually pack using plastic bags or with garments folded over in the long plastic cleaners' bag. It is very luxurious to do this if you can leave the garments on your own hangers. Then unpacking is a snap. Test your weight to see if you can do this. The rollers get far more into a suitcase and usually hang their garments right up in the bathroom with the shower running, to steam out the few wrinkles the clothes may have acquired.

Anticipating your travel needs and travel style by fully planning and testing your travel wardrobe saves you precious moments later on, and a great deal of uncertainty. You can be a more relaxed and confident traveler.

WHAT ELSE TO TAKE

Keep in your suitcase a list of the items you need to take on trips as a handy reminder each time you pack. It is amazing what absolutely essential items we all can forget. Some of the things you may want to consider putting on this list are:

To take on the plane—skin moisturizer, hand cream, toothbrush and toothpaste, cologne, comfortable, flat shoes, sweater, cosmetic kit.

Airplane travel is very drying for the skin. It's nice to be able to keep your face and hands from drying out. You can then reapply your makeup freshly just before arrival.

For travel in the United States:

- Travel alarm. The new ones that work on a battery are nice. They tick softly and do not have to be wound.
- Skirt or pants hangers as needed. These are rarely provided by hotels. Safety pins to convert regular hangers can also be used.
- Hair dryer
- Rollers. If you don't possess a wash-and-wear style, try to develop one. A do-it-yourself hairdo will save you lots of time and anguish.
- Glasses
- Sunglasses
- Folding umbrella. Nothing's worse than deplaning in a downpour when you have a meeting in half an hour!
- Sewing kit
- Cosmetic kit. Keep your cosmetic kit prepacked with duplicates of all toiletry and cosmetic items you need. You'll find it lightens your load considerably if you keep sample sizes for travel or transfer everything you use in traveling into small plastic containers.
- Medicine kit containing:
  Prescription drugs
  Something for indigestion, diarrhea, and constipation
  A fever thermometer. It's easier to know whether to call a doctor if you know your temperature
  The prescription for your glasses
  Band-Aids and a small tube of Bacitracin
  Insect repellent and After-Bite
  Suntan lotion
- Dictating equipment. Take either a micro-mini cassette re-

corder or a new lightweight mini-cassette recorder. With the latter you can also pack a few of your language cassettes or other educational cassettes or some favorite musical tapes.
· Hand-held calculator. Can anyone be without one?

If you are going abroad, there are some items to add:

· Electrical currency converter and assortment of electrical plugs. Even countries that use the same voltage as the United States use different-shaped plugs. (Bloomingdale's in New York City carries an assortment.)
· A transistor radio.
· Separate change purse for each country you will be visiting. Save your change from each trip for the next one. It's very handy to have—especially coins needed for phones. Did you know that in major U.S. cities you can often buy traveler's checks in foreign currencies? If you are going just to one or two destinations, having the foreign money with you can be convenient in these days of unpredictable devaluations. It is distressing to be caught for several days without being able to change money.
· Corkscrew and bottle opener or Swiss Army knife, which includes these and a spoon and fork as well. Trains abroad often don't serve food, and you have to bring your own food and drink.
· To your cosmetic kit add:
    Soap, which is often not provided
    Small packets of Kleenex, which can double for toilet paper when needed.

One very organized traveler brings along pretyped, pressure-sensitive labels in order to speed writing of letters and postcards.

Ease, effectiveness, and enjoyment in travel, like most other things in life, depend upon careful planning, and increase with experience. Work out your own travel secrets and pass them on to others.

A SUMMARY FOR THE PROFESSIONAL TRAVELER

She:

- has arranged her life so she can get away with relative ease;
- travels first class when possible and takes optimum care of herself while traveling;
- belongs to at least one airline club;
- keeps up with the latest ways to minimize jet lag and allows enough recovery time;
- is relaxed and confident while on the road, takes advantage of new opportunities, meets new people when she wants to, is prepared to care for herself, and eats in or out, alone or in company, as she chooses;
- knows local customs and languages when abroad and is learning more languages; and
- travels light, has a coordinated travel wardrobe, and has her travel needs ready to go at all times.

27

THE JOURNEY
AND THE ARRIVAL

As you've read this book, you've been considering your values and priorities, your obstacles and your assets. You've set down some short-term and some long-range professional goals. You've given some thought to how best to manage your career consciously and to the skills you must continue to develop to achieve your objectives. In this final chapter, you'll have a chance to review some of your strategies and objectives. Then we'll consider some of the responsibilities that go along with the rewards of being a successful professional.

YOUR GOALS

Look regularly and often at your career goals. At a minimum, you'll probably want to conduct a review annually; many people will want to do this more than once a year. Now is an excellent time for your first review.

Throughout this book, you've gained additional insights into the process of career planning and you've been able to share and learn from the experiences of some of the women and men who've made

it to the top. Take another look at how you plan to get there and
how you presently feel about your plans. Ask yourself some of
these questions:

1. What is the next position you want?
2. What do you have to do to prepare yourself for that job?
3. Who can help you?
4. Is this position likely to be found in the company where you
are now working, or might you have to change employers?
5. What is the ultimate career position that you seek?
6. Do you feel that your long-range objective is:
   Sufficiently ambitious?   Yes _____ No _____
   Realistic?   Yes _____ No _____
   Just right for you?   Yes _____ No _____
7. What additional experience and education must you acquire
in order to achieve this objective?
8. Do you think you'll achieve your long-range objective?
9. In how many years?
10. Will you enjoy its pursuit even if you don't achieve it?
11. Do you still want to target the top?

Compare your answers with the answers you wrote down for
yourself while reading Part I and Part II. If your latest answers
differ very much from your earlier answers, you'll want to work
through the strategy for reaching your new goals using the questions in Chapter 23. As your goals change so must your strategy
for reaching them.

REWARDS AND RESPONSIBILITIES

The French philosopher Montaigne set forth the idea that it's not
the arrival that counts, it's the journey. The rewards of moving toward the realization of your inherent potential are enormous. Together with the satisfaction that results from using the full range of
your abilities comes independence and, increasingly as you move
up, the power to effect change, both in your own life and in areas
that affect other people. Perhaps, however, both the journey *and*

the arrival count at this time when change is so badly needed in so many areas. It's the people who finally arrive at the top who can make more of the important decisions and influence other people to carry them out.

Unfortunately, very few women have yet reached these positions of power at the top of the economic pyramid. It's still men who are making the major decisions that affect all of us. It is still men alone who are addressing or ignoring some of the pressing issues facing organizations today, which include the need to demonstrate more concern for individuals, for the environment, and for society and still have the company remain profitable.

As Dr. Jean Baker Miller points out in her book, *Toward a New Psychology of Women,* "The dominant group inevitably has the greatest influence in determining a culture's overall outlook—its philosophy, morality, social theory, and even its science, [and yet it appears that] the people in power in our society have been unable to find ways of organizing society for human ends." Harvard professor David McClelland concurs: "One could make a good case for the fact that the world is suffering from an overdose of masculine assertiveness right now and needs above all a realization of the importance of interdependence in all human affairs. Who could play a more effective part in creating this realization than women?"

Who indeed? Society has been systematically depriving itself of the full use of the abilities of half of its population and forcing the other half into a mold that may or may not suit its talents. Men and women both need to be freed to use their abilities, both where they are most suitable and to the fullest, and to work together as equals on the tasks of reordering organizations and society.

It is not only the men and women who make it to the top who can have a hand in this undertaking. Everyone can work at it during the journey. Each person can work at ensuring equality of opportunity and finding some new answers to the new questions that are being raised as women take their places beside men in the professional world. In the balance of this chapter, we'll look at some of the elements that tend to perpetuate the traditional dominant-subordinate roles often played out by men and women so that you can help to eliminate this inequality and alter some of the counterproductive effects. We'll raise some new questions that have been identified by the people who contributed so greatly to the information contained in this book. You'll have a chance to look at these questions and discover some new answers that you can then share. At the same time, you'll probably find yourself uncovering more new questions; the relationship between men and women, particularly in the workplace, is undergoing profound changes. You can make a great contribution during your career journey by identifying the problems and working out new solutions.

THE CENTRAL TASK

Dr. Miller describes as the central task to "foster the movement from unequal to equal [for] mutually enhancing interaction is not probable among unequals." Dr. Miller identifies some of the manifestations and results of inequality as follows:

1. There are myths about the subordinate group which relate to their inability to fulfill wider or more valued roles.

2. The consequences of inequality are usually kept either obscure or denied.

3. Subordinates are encouraged to develop psychological characteristics that are pleasing to the dominant group . . . qualities that are more characteristic of children than adults, such as submissiveness, passivity, docility, dependency, lack of initiative, inability to act, to decide, to think.

4. The lesser persons have great difficulty in maintaining the conception that they are of as much intrinsic worth as the superior ones.

5. The relationship of the lesser party to the dominant one is that of service.

6. The dominant group holds the power.

Let's look further at these points that Dr. Miller makes about inequality between the sexes to see how they affect us and why they must be changed.

Myths and Stereotypes

Myths about masculine and feminine behavior and innate abilities come to mind quickly and easily, such as female emotionalism and lack of ability in quantitative reasoning, and male objectivity and assertiveness. Both men and women have grown up with misconceptions about women's abilities, particularly those that are needed in the professional world. Some of our stereotypes are taken for granted and not even consciously realized. Many of them have their basis in a deeply ingrained attitude of male superiority.

Take a close look at your own concepts of male-female behavior and what stereotypes you may be perpetuating without realizing it. By your actions, you can help to educate people around you to the fact that these myths are not true.

Study after study shows that nearly all the differences between male and female behavior and abilities are caused by cultural tradition rather than inborn traits. Stanford psychologists Eleanor Maccoby and Carol Jacklin, after reviewing 2,000 books and articles on sex differences, determined that the evidence is sufficient to reject eight myths about sex differences. They concluded that sexes do not differ in sociability, suggestibility, self-esteem, motivation to achieve, facility at rote learning, analytic-mindedness, or response to auditory stimuli. From time to time, studies do turn up some possible sex-related differences, such as visual-spatial ability, which may be stronger in males, and certain kinds of small-muscle dexterity, which may be superior in females. But even here differences *within* each sex for these traits appear to be greater than the differences between sexes; rarely—if ever—do such traits relate to managerial ability.

Obscuring and Denying the Consequences of Inequality

In analyzing a major industry where more than 60 per cent of the labor force has been female for several decades and which is currently estimated to be as much as 70 per cent, less than 2 per cent of the senior managers are women. About 10 to 15 per cent of the middle-management positions in this industry are presently held by women; this is only a slim pool from which to train and select more female senior managers. Furthermore, when we analyze the senior positions that are held by women, a disproportionate number of these jobs are in the "velvet ghettos" of personnel, public relations, and research.

Yet press releases from the industry's trade association proudly proclaim that 30 per cent of the managerial jobs are held by women. When you examine the details of this figure, you find that they include many first-line supervisory positions that lead nowhere, that titles have been upgraded, and that job responsibilities have been downgraded. This industry both denies and obscures the fact that it is still very hard for women to move up to positions of power.

But the good news is that in this industry, as in most major corporations, the government is enforcing compliance with the equal employment opportunities legislation, which not only requires corporations to make opportunity equally available to men and women, but also to have a plan, updated annually, for doing so. *And* they must act on this plan.

Upward movement for women is slow, but opportunities that have not formerly been available are there. Look for them, prepare for them, and go after them.

Disillusionment and Penalties

As any woman who is targeting the top will tell you, the struggle is not an easy one. The people who are dominant tend to want to preserve the status quo. No one likes to relinquish power, particularly to people whom they consider not quite their equal. As Elizabeth Janeway observes in *Man's World, Woman's Place,* "Talented women still find themselves at cross purposes with society."

One woman rapidly on the move up, who is also a wife and mother of two children, finds her job requires her to start work at about 5:00 each morning. Her travel schedule keeps her in the air until midnight at least one or two nights a week, so she rarely gets adequate sleep. Despite a very cooperative husband, she spends weekends getting the house in order and doing the laundry. She is truly a "superwoman," successful both professionally and at home. But one wonders at what point she will no longer be able to keep up this pace.

Adding an enormously demanding professional life on top of one's traditional roles is not exactly equality. And few women are superwomen or can sustain the role, even if they manage to carry it out for a limited period of time. One of the results of taking on these traditional roles at the same time as breaking new ground professionally has been that some women find they must opt out, and they often do so in very traditional ways.

A woman in her mid-forties suddenly found herself pregnant for the first time. She decided to give up her job and stay home to care for her child. Was this pregnancy really unexpected, or was it in some measure a reaction to the fact that she had a senior position that was highly pressured? Executive responsibility is tough, and it's probably tougher if you are—as she was—the first woman at the top in your company.

Another woman in her late forties chose to leave her highly visible senior management position because her husband wanted to retire to a warmer climate. Was she unable to anticipate that this might happen, or did she seize this opportunity partly as a chance to remove herself from the day-to-day struggle that is part of every position toward the top of the organization?

The decisions made by these successful professional women have a profound effect on the women who are coming up behind them. Male senior managers look at these two examples not merely as personal decisions of individuals, but as examples of the fact that *women* are not to be counted on to hang in over the long haul—as evidence that women will opt out when the going gets really rough, despite the time and training the company has invested in them. The two women are reinforcing some very important stereotypes that are not always talked about.

Everyone has a right to her personal decisions, but each woman executive also has some measure of responsibility to all the women coming up behind her who are also trying to achieve senior status.

One of the functions of this book has been to help you look at your professional aspirations in the perspective of your total life situation. It is far better consciously to decide on a level where you want to stop because of the demands on you, or to anticipate when you may want to drop out of the race and then lower your aspirations accordingly, turning down opportunities if you don't intend to follow through.

When given a chance to be promoted to a level never before reached by women in her company, Marielle refused. She had recently decided to get married. She was in her mid-thirties and had already determined with her fiancé that they would try to have a child as soon as possible. She felt these personal plans would interfere with a full effort on her part to prove that women would successfully perform at the level she had been offered.

While her unwillingness to seize this opportunity was a step back for women, it was probably best in the long run for the other women moving up behind her. "Furthermore," as she explained, "I felt there was a whole group of women who would shortly be qualified for this job, and who didn't have the outside demands on them that I was anticipating."

Dependency and the Relinquishment of Power

Elizabeth Janeway poses the rhetorical question: "If man's world can be purged of its difficulties and cured of its ills by men alone, perhaps the old division of roles is the right one." The old division of labor is perpetuated by women being encouraged toward dependent behavior, to find their satisfaction in serving, and to allow men to retain power and the decision-making role.

Evidence would seem to indicate that the old division of labor is not working, and, in fact, male and female roles are in a dynamic process of change. In Sweden this process is referred to as "sex-role readjustment," rather than the appellation often used in the United States of "women's liberation," which is both inaccurate and has acquired a whole host of pejorative emotional connotations as well. What's liberating about being encouraged to join the stressed, overly demanding race for professional success, particularly when this role is added to women's traditional roles of wife and perhaps mother?

Instead, what must happen is major sex-role readjustment, which in the long run will benefit men and women and their children. These readjustments require finding creative answers to newly raised questions.

NEW QUESTIONS NEEDING NEW ANSWERS

What can you do to encourage women to develop their talents and to accept the responsibility that goes along with this growth?

What can you do to help restructure institutions to meet the needs of individuals?

Recently a woman in her late fifties was fired just a few months short of full vestiture in her company's retirement plan. She will not have an easy time finding another job because of her age and the number of years she spent working for one company. Single women living alone represent the poorest single segment of the United States population, and this fact doesn't seem to be changing, much as women are moving into the labor force in vast numbers, increasing rather than decreasing the spread between the median annual income of women workers and that of men. The average woman presently has to work about nine days to earn what the average man earns in five days of work.

Married women don't fare much better. There is one divorce for every two marriages taking place, and, with the advent of less punitive marriage-dissolution laws, the number of divorces is rapidly on the rise. Many newly divorced women find themselves forced into the labor market without adequate training or updated skills, since much of their married life was spent in service in the home and in support of their husbands' careers. What can you do to help these women, who are sometimes referred to as "displaced homemakers," make up for lost time and find a useful and lucrative place in the workplace?

Even in marriages that remain intact, the problems are profound. In two out of three families today, the wife goes to work along with her husband. Yet, neither the individuals nor society's institutions are prepared for the two-worker family. Study after study show that women who work full-time spend an additional twenty-five hours working in the home, while, depending on whose study you read, their partners spend between one and ten hours a week on household tasks. Why do these women continue to bear an unfair portion of the burden?

Society is simply not set up to assist the two-worker partnership and to provide services to a couple who are both out of the home during the normal working day. Farsighted businesses and professions are beginning to change this by having evening and weekend hours so that at least part of their services are provided outside the normal work day. What can you do to encourage this trend?

The problems of dual-worker marriages become further compounded when both partners are upwardly striving professionals. Who then damps down his or her ambitions when the other partner has an opportunity that requires a move? Who acts as a support to the other? Or do both go without much nurturing? Is it possible to have a rewarding partnership between two hard-working, dedicated professionals on some new terms yet to be discovered?

The problems of dual-career couples pale when parenthood enters the picture. Society still assumes that women will take major responsibility for child care or see that a satisfactory substitute is provided. There aren't many substitutes—satisfactory or otherwise—available. Must women then forgo their upward career movement during child-raising years, or will men assume half of this responsibility? Will men's careers be penalized if they do so? And how is this economically feasible, when women's paychecks typically are only 60 per cent of men's? How can men reduce their career aspirations until women are able to earn similar paychecks without imposing an undue economic burden on the family unit? Perhaps some new career paths will emerge that will enable men and women to strive for the top despite some time out spent raising children.

The fact remains that children do need care, attention, stability, and consistent and lasting relationships with people who are interested in them—profoundly enough to look after them with love and a sense of humor. Can an adequate day-care system begin to provide some of these childhood needs—perhaps in an even more balanced way than has been occurring in the nuclear family, with a mother almost entirely responsible for raising the children, occasionally assisted by a father who is rarely at home because of the excessive demands of his job?

Can our society begin to develop broader-based concerns for the needs of the family and the individuals who are part of the family? Norway has a government family council that addresses these vital matters. In the United States, federal law requires that corporations give women equal employment, but the same government has a totally laissez-faire attitude toward doing anything to assist families in taking full advantage of these opportunities. Each person and each family must find its own way through the almost impossible maze, at the end of which is the opportunity for men and women to use their skills to the fullest and, at the same time, to raise the next generation well.

In his book, *Who'll Raise the Children?*, James Levine points out that "a nontraditional family structure, by its very existence, questions the norm, and provokes strong feelings." The old norms are being questioned and strong feelings are resulting. It takes courage to break new ground and it's hard for each person and each family to do it on its own. Does your personal dream include helping to develop some more effective norms where women can go out to work at demanding jobs without feeling that they are penalizing their children? Where fathers can participate more fully in raising their children without feeling they are jeopardizing their chances for maximum career development?

SOME GLOBAL ISSUES

Both women and men, married or single, must turn their attention toward helping to ensure that there will be an environment where it's possible to continue to live.

There is evidence that, in a larger sense, the old ways are no longer working. We face vast problems, such as the fact that major industries continue to manufacture faulty products rather than change or eliminate them. The disposal of waste materials is polluting most of our major cities, and making them increasingly uninhabitable. Even in the countryside, poisons are seeping into the food and water. Energy, already recognized to be in desperately short supply, continues to be wasted at unconscionable rates.

These global problems may seem too large for most of us to tackle, and any contributions to their alleviation on our parts would be of little effect. But there are steps that each of us can and must take as we journey along our professional paths, and our power to arrest some of these profound threats to humanity increases as we move up the corporate ladder.

Everyone who makes the attempt to target the top has a right to true equality of opportunity, of choice, and of encouragement. Women and men alike have the responsibility and will ultimately reap the rewards of helping the most talented people develop and use their full range of abilities—both in the corporation and in the outside world.